CW01501685

"*The Best Version of Me* is a valual̶ 1ess of
how dimensions within mind, ̶ :t our
well-being, offering evidence-based actions ̶ ̶ ̶ ̶ ̶ ̶ ̶ ̶ ̶ ̶ ̶ ̶ ̶ ̶ ̶ h and
happiness. I especially appreciated the richness of the references used and the
innovative way that each section ends, offering additional resources in
different formats to keep the learning going."
—Karen Guggenheim, WOHASU Founder/CEO; Co-Founder, The World
    Happiness Summit; author, *Cultivating Happiness: Overcome Trauma and
    Positively Transform Your Life*

"*The Best Version of Me* offers transformative insights into how we can
enhance our physical, mental, and spiritual health. A must-read for
everyone on a wellness journey."
—Charles Meyers, CEO, Equinix

"Are you ready to reinvent [yourself] and be reinvigorated? If so, *The Best Version
of Me* is an insightful guide to self-discovery, recovery, and metamorphism.
If you are ready to change, don't wait another day, and don't miss out on
achieving your full potential!"
—Abbe Luersman, Executive Vice President and Chief People Officer,
    Otis Worldwide Corporation

"Nick van Dam has created a compelling and comprehensive framework
about the many factors that contribute to well-being and provided insights
from some of the world's leading thinkers on each of these components.
[*The Best Version of Me*] is a must-read for anyone committed to achieving
their own full potential, or [for] any leader who aspires to help those around
them become the best version of themselves."
—Tim Welsh, Vice Chair, Consumer and Business Banking, US Bank

"If we want to create a better future for us all, then we need to start with ourselves. *The Best Version of Me* guides you through the building blocks of well-being and gives you practical strategies for cultivating each, so you can be your best self and create a positive impact in your own life and in the world around you."
—Jen Fisher, Chief Well-Being Officer, Deloitte, and best-selling author

---

"A groundbreaking work! *The Best Version of Me* is a holistic, engaging, and truly inspiring read featuring insights from a litany of accomplished experts. The unique structure, which allows readers to explore topics in their own way, makes the journey towards well-being both personal and profound. A pivotal resource in the field of personal development. If you are looking for guidance on well-being—whether it's for you[rself], your team, or your organization— then this is the book for you."
—David Green, Managing Partner at Insight222; co-author of *Excellence in People Analytics: How to Use Workforce Data to Create Business Value*; host of the Digital HR Leaders podcast

---

"Our responsibility is to relish our lives and be happy. *The Best Version of Me* offers a comprehensive, startling (for example: your DNA does not define you), supportive, and challenging guide for achieving well-being and happiness. Inspiring explorers of life and happiness, [this book] provides a practical, evidence-based, and powerful range of guides for every area of our lives—body, mind, purpose, environment. [The authors] detail in accessible, engaging, and succinct ways how to ensure we make the most of our precious existence through promoting our well-being and that of all those around us. This book is a beautiful and rich source of wisdom and practical knowledge. If you want to be happier for the rest of your life, simply put the wisdom it offers into practice."
—Michael West, CBE, Professor of Organizational Psychology, Lancaster University Management School; Senior Visiting Fellow, The King's Fund; and Emeritus Professor, Aston University

"Dr. Nick van Dam and his co-authors have crafted a great holistic guide for leaders to advance human well-being. [*The Best Version of Me*] is a must-read for thriving in mind, body, and spirit in the new age of people-centric companies."
—Joerg Staff, Executive Board Member, German Association for Human Resources Management; multi-award winner; executive advisor, chief human resources officer

---

"*The Best Version of Me* is a transformative guide, offering profound insights and practical strategies for better living. This powerhouse of a book illuminates the path to self-discovery, resilience, and fulfillment. A beacon for those seeking a holistic approach to thriving, it's a must-read for anyone committed to unlocking their full potential and well-being."
—Antonio Montes, CEO, Headspring, a joint venture of *Financial Times* and IE Business School

---

"A must-read for anyone looking to enhance their well-being. *The Best Version of Me* by Dr. Nick van Dam and 20 expert co-authors is a comprehensive guide that touches every aspect of human health and happiness."
—Dr. Jordi Diaz, Dean and Director General, Eada Business School, Barcelona

---

"I really loved reading *The Best Version of Me*, and it is an excellent collaboration of some of the world's leading minds. The comprehensive framework of focusing on mind, body, purpose, and environment creates an easy reference and learning guide that is easy to digest and can be used daily. Each section has a relatable personal story and a wonderful library of resources for easy reference and invaluable toolkits from subject experts. *The Best Version of Me* brings together the world's leading minds to create a wonderfully simple-to-use and highly effective roadmap to well-being, performance, and success."
—Chris Cummings, Group CEO, Wellbeing at Work

"[*The Best Version of Me*] offers vital guidance on continuous learning and well-being. Praised for its thorough research and practical approach."
—Camiel Gielkens, CEO, Schouten & Nelissen

"Dr. Nick van Dam brings a unique human centricity to all his interactions. He cares about the people he works with, wears his considerable scholarship lightly, and always leaves the listener wiser after a conversation. For *The Best Version of Me*, Nick has assembled an accomplished team of experts who inspire us to look at performance and well-being holistically[;] the days of pigeonholing professional success as an outcome of solely mental activity are long gone. This book is for the ambitious, yet humane, manager who aspires to be of value to their family, team, and organization, and tries to make the world a better place for all, by being a better version of themselves through small, consistent everyday actions that tap into their human potential."
—Ravi Shankar, Director, Academics and Programmes, CEDEP

"This book is a beacon of hope and a roadmap to living a balanced, fulfilling life. [*The Best Version of Me*] is a comprehensive guide to well-being in all its forms. The collected insight and wisdom is a marvelous gift for yourself and everyone you care about."
—Sabine Weishaupt, Chapter Leader, Future Leadership Design,
    Deutsche Telekom AG

"[*The Best Version of Me*] is packed with insights and resources to help you to learn, explore and flourish. It is an invaluable partner in any quest for a more sustainable, generative relationship with yourself, others and the world around you."
—Megan Reitz, Associate Fellow, Saïd Business School, Oxford University.
    Adjunct Professor at Hult Business School

"From poor sleep to bad eating habits, this book hits on the major points that are com-monly felt, yet rarely talked about, in the endless quest for professional excellence [*The Best Version of Me*] combines cutting edge research on health and well-being, with rich insights from seasoned experts, to make you completely rethink your approach to "mak-ing it." Never again will I prioritize late night doom-scrolling over slumber. This book has me convinced.
—Tessa West, Professor of Psychology, New York University. Author of *Jerks at Work: Toxic coworkers and what to do about them and Job Therapy. Finding work that works for you.*

"[*The Best Version of Me*] is a really illustrative guide to understanding and applying most facets of well-being, written by a group of leading practitioners."
—Santiago Iñiguez de Onzoño, President, IE University

"In our post-pandemic world, where self-care has gained paramount importance, this book is a timely resource. It reminds us that self-care is the foundation for a healthy and focused life, a pre-requisite to taking care of others. Reading this book will undoubtedly inspire you to become the best version of yourself. Simultaneously, it serves as a how-to manual, a source of inspiration, and a science-based approach to peak human performance."
—Dr. Raghu Krishnamoorthy, Senior Fellow and Director, Chief Learning Officer Executive Doctoral Program, University of Pennsylvania

---

"*The Best Version of Me* masterfully intertwines the physical, mental, and environmental aspects of well-being, offering practical advice that resonates deeply with today's challenges."
—Koen Becking, Chairman of the Board and Rector Magnificus, Nyenrode Business University

ABOUT THE BOOK

Uncover your path to personal growth and fulfillment in *The Best Version of Me*, by Dr. Nick van Dam and co-authored by 20 global experts. This book presents a comprehensive well-being model that explores key dimensions of your life, including body, mind, purpose, and environment. You have the flexibility to choose chapters that align with your interests and needs, each offering personal stories, insights, and practical advice to enhance your well-being. Self-reflect using guided questions, access additional resources on the book's website, and embark on a transformative journey toward becoming your best self. Discover your true potential and embrace a life of flourishing and self-actualization.

BOOSTING YOUR WELL-BEING

THE BEST VERSION OF ME

NICK VAN DAM

COPYEDITED BY ALANA DUNN

CO-AUTHORS

LISA BEVILL	PATRICIA GARCIA	MARCELLA SARNO
HEBE BOONZAAIJER	DR. LUCRECIA GRANDOLINI	CARLA SZEMZO
DR. JACQUELINE BRASSEY	JUDITH GRIMBERGEN	DR. SANAE TABNAOUI
DR. KATIE COATES	DR. MARIA KOTTARI	DR. NICK VAN DAM
BARBARA DOELEMAN-VAN VELDHOVEN	DR. SHARDA NANDRAM	DR. WOUTER VAN DEN BERG
BAHIA EL ODDI	EMILY RICCI	DR. ELS VAN DER HELM
URSULA FEAR	JAN RIJKEN	BO VIALLE-DERKSEN

IMPRINT

First Lulu Edition April 2024
Copyright ©2024 by Nick van Dam

Publisher: Lulu
627 Davis Drive, Suite 300
Morrisville, NC 27560
United States of America

Design: epoqstudio.com
Website: thebestversionofmebook.com

Photocredits: Cover: iStock; p.17: Rosario Janza/Unsplash;
p.20: Charlota Blunarova/Unsplash; p.25: Mikhail Nilov/Pexels;
p.39: Megs Harrison/Unsplash; p.40: Dane Wetton/Unsplash;
p.120: Alena Shekhovtcova/Pexels; p.202: Joshua Welch/Pexels;
p.278: Travelnow or Crylater/Unsplash; p.342: Blake Cheek/Unsplash;
p.345: Mihaly Koles/Unsplash; p.353: Shot by Cerqueira/Unsplash

ISBN: 9-789464-912753
For information about special discounts for bulk purchases,
please contact: info@thebestversionofmebook.com

Manufactured in the United States of America.

To all of those who are on a
path of self-discovery and
personal growth—may this
book be a companion
in your journey toward the
best version of yourself.

DEDICATION
THE E-LEARNING FOR KIDS FOUNDATION

The necessity of providing education to children at the elementary school age is a critical issue recognized by organizations such as UNESCO. These formative years are essential in laying the foundation for a child's future learning and development. Regrettably, according to UNESCO, in 2023 approximately 244 million children did not attend school, and hundreds of millions more could have greatly benefited from improved educational opportunities.

Understanding this, the e-Learning for Kids Foundation has taken a significant step by developing and providing free digital learning resources for children ages five to twelve. These courses are made accessible globally via the Internet and local computers, ensuring that quality education reaches even the most remote and underserved areas.

Remarkably, over thirty million children have already benefited from these e-Learning resources, including many who reside in refugee camps. This accessibility is crucial in areas where traditional schooling may be disrupted due to various socioeconomic challenges. By focusing on digital platforms, the foundation ensures that learning continues unabated, regardless of a child's geographical location or personal circumstances.

In support of this noble cause, all the royalties from this book will be donated to the e-Learning for Kids Foundation. Their work aligns with the goal of universal access to education, a vision shared by UNESCO, with whom e-Learning for Kids has developed a partnership. By purchasing this book, you contribute to the education of millions of children across the globe.

To learn more about the foundation and its meaningful work, please visit ▸ *e-learningforkids.org*.

CONTENTS

Foreword   14

Acknowledgments   16

01   **Introduction: Becoming The Best Version of Me**   20
—Dr. Nick van Dam

02   **Body**   38
Introduction—*Dr. Nick van Dam*   40
Sleep—*Dr. Els van der Helm*   42
Energy—*Hebe Boonzaaijer*   56
Nutrition—*Marcella Sarno*   74
Physical Movement—*Dr. Sanae Tabnaoui*   88
DNA—*Dr. Wouter van den Berg*   104

03   **Mind**   118
Introduction—*Dr. Nick van Dam*   120
The Arts—*Judith Grimbergen*   122
Mindfulness—*Barbara Doeleman-van Veldhoven*   136
Self-Regulation—*Dr. Lucrecia Grandolini*   152
Resilience and Adaptability—*Dr. Jacqueline Brassey*   172
Learning—*Jan Rijken*   186

04   **Purpose**   200
Introduction—*Dr. Nick van Dam*   202
Financial Empowerment—*Ursula Fear*   204
Relationships—*Carla Szemzo*   220
Contribution—*Emily Ricci*   234
Spirituality—*Dr. Sharda Nandram*   250
Values, Beliefs, and Attitudes—*Lisa Bevill*   262

05   **Environment**   276
Introduction—*Dr. Nick van Dam*   278
Nature Environment—*Patricia Garcia*   280
Social Environment—*Dr. Katie Coates*   296
Work Environment—*Bahia El Oddi*   310
Climate Environment—*Dr. Maria Kottari*   326

06   **Closing Thoughts: From Caterpillar to Butterfly**   342
—Bo Vialle-Derksen

About the Authors   354

FOREWORD

Dear Reader,

It is with great enthusiasm that I introduce you to *The Best Version of Me: Boosting Your Well-Being*. Your decision to engage with this book excites us for several reasons. First, we, the authors, have crafted this book with the hope that it will inspire you to make life-changing decisions and adopt new habits that lead you toward becoming your best self. Second, we believe that your personal growth will positively influence those around you—your family, friends, colleagues, and the wider community and society. Additionally, your purchase supports a noble cause, as all royalties from this book are donated to the e-Learning for Kids Foundation (e-learningforkids.org), which provides crucial digital education to children in need.

The idea for this book was born during a transformative wellness retreat I attended in 2019 in Thailand, a period between jobs. It was a time for relaxation and reflection, where I encountered numerous professionals grappling with burnout or teetering on its edge. This experience prompted me to delve into burnout and well-being literature and research and, alongside my friend Dr. Noémie Le Pertel, co-develop an initial version of a vitality model. This was particularly timely as, in the same year, the World Health Organization recognized burnout as an official medical condition. My TED Talk, "Unlocking Job Vitality in the Digital Age: Health, Well-Being, and Happiness," addresses this issue, which, though once considered a "luxury" topic, has become more urgent in the wake of the COVID-19 pandemic's profound impact on employee well-being.

Watch the TEDTALK:
Unlocking Job Vitality in the Digital Age—
Health, Well-Being, and Happiness
▶ tinyurl.com/49cuy3my

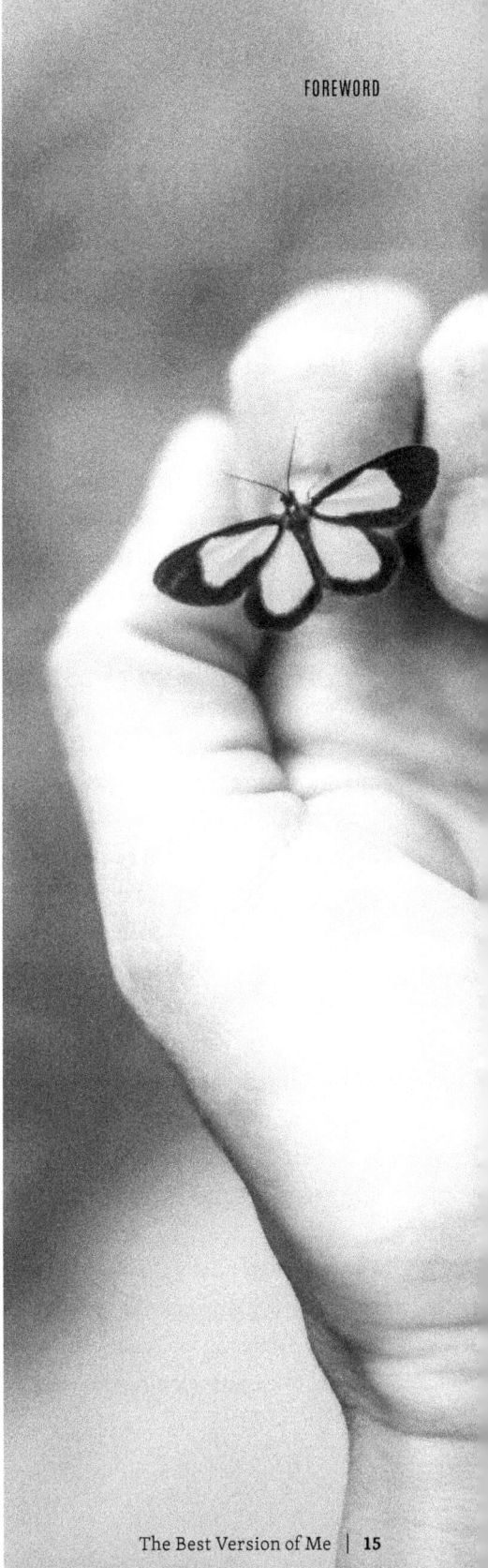

Given the heightened focus on well-being in today's challenging environment, I expanded the vitality model and collaborated with twenty experts and friends to bring you this book. We chose the butterfly as our metaphor, symbolizing the transformation we all aspire to undergo, from our potential to our most fulfilled selves.

We are hopeful that this book will serve as a valuable companion on your personal and professional journey. We encourage you to immerse yourself in each chapter, enrich your understanding through supplementary videos, podcasts, assessments, articles, and books, and visit ▶ thebestversionofmebook.com site for additional resources.

Your feedback and questions are always welcome.

With warm regards,

Dr. Nick van Dam,
On behalf of all co-authors

ACKNOWLEDGMENTS

Bringing *The Best Version of Me* to life has been a thrilling collaborative effort, involving twenty-one diverse and talented authors, a diligent copyeditor, skilled creative designer, and our website development company.

First, I extend my deepest appreciation and gratitude to all the authors. Your commitment and dedication to crafting each chapter, despite the constraints of time, has been remarkable. You met the challenges of distilling the most relevant and innovative insights into a cohesive format and sourcing key materials for our eager readers with exceptional skill and enthusiasm. A hearty congratulations to you all! Representing ten different nationalities—including Argentinean, American, Canadian, Dutch, Greek, Italian, Moroccan, Spanish, South African, and Surinamese—your global perspectives and experience have enriched this project immensely. Collaborating with you has been an absolute privilege, and our deepening friendships and mutual learning have been invaluable.

Second, a special thanks to **Alana Dunn**, whose editorial prowess brought clarity and coherence to multiple manuscript revisions. Your attention to detail and willingness to challenge different versions have significantly elevated the quality of this book. I am grateful for our connection and eagerly anticipate future collaborations and the growth of our partnership.

Third, heartfelt thanks to **Marijke Küsters** and **Monica Howe** from Epoq Studio, whose instrumental role in designing the book's layout, illustrations, and cover cannot be overstated. Your talent in bringing my initial concepts and sketches to life is truly remarkable. Stay tuned for more ideas and projects.

Fourth, I extend my thanks to **Remco van der Steen**, the founder of KlareKoek company (▶ klarekoek.nl), based in Leeuwarden, the Netherlands. As a partner of the e-Learning for Kids Foundation, Remco and his company have played a crucial role in developing the website that supports this book.

Fifth, my gratitude extends to numerous friends and colleagues for their invaluable input and endorsement quotes. Their insights have greatly contributed to the richness of this work.

Sixth, I deeply appreciate the privilege of educating students and leaders in various programs where this book will be a key resource, including in Nyenrode/ IE University's Global HR and L&D Leadership Program. Thanks to everyone for your interest, active participation, and, most importantly, your invaluable feedback.

Last, to all our partners, family members, and friends—your support has been the backbone of this journey. Your feedback, encouragement, and sacrifice, especially during evenings, weekends, and holidays, have been crucial in helping us continue writing and exploring deeper into various subjects.

The result is here:
The Best Version of Me—an extraordinary book that stands as a testament to the power of collaboration, dedication, and shared knowledge.

01
INTRO-
DUCTION

THE BEST VERSION OF ME

Written by Dr. Nick van Dam

> "I am always doing that which I cannot do,
> in order that I may learn how to do it."
> —PABLO PICASSO

HARNESSING HUMAN GREATNESS

I once attended a unique ballet performance featuring the Spanish dancer Lucía Lacarra in Madrid, in which the fusion of art forms created an extraordinary experience. The highlight of the show was the seamless integration of a background movie with the live dancers, creating a synchronized harmony between the film characters and the dancers, all set to captivating music. This innovative blend of cinema, dance, and music reinforced my belief in the extraordinary capabilities of humans to uplift civilization, showcase the beauty of life, and enrich humanity.

Scan the QR code for an impression of the ballet "Lost Letters" featuring Lucía Lacarra.
▶ tinyurl.com/5bbzw3en

In a world where the daily news often highlights humanity's darker aspects, it's important to remember the countless historical and contemporary examples of individuals' extraordinary achievements. These achievements span diverse fields, including the arts, literature, music, architecture, entertainment, technology, science, medicine, philosophy, politics, and business, among others. Such instances serve as a reminder of the positive and transformative impact humans can have across various domains.

Hereafter, I will introduce five remarkable individuals who achieved their fullest potential in various fields, each making a significant impact in their respective domains.

The Mexican artist **Frida Kahlo** is, for me, an example of an extraordinary woman who became the best version of herself, in a journey marked by unique resilience and expressive creativity. Despite enduring significant physical suffering, she transformed her pain into iconic art, particularly through her deeply personal self-portraits. Kahlo broke gender norms in a male-dominated art world by boldly portraying women's experiences and Mexican cultural themes. Her distinctive style and commitment to political and social causes further underscored her individuality and engagement with the world. Through her art and life, Kahlo demonstrated a remarkable ability to turn adversity into a source of strength and self-expression.

Nelson Mandela's journey from prisoner to president is a profound example of change and reconciliation. After enduring twenty-seven years of imprisonment for his stand against apartheid, Mandela chose a path of forgiveness and unity instead of revenge. As the first Black president of South Africa, he dedicated himself to dismantling the legacy of apartheid and promoting racial harmony, and consequently became a global icon through his moral and political leadership.

Through my e-Learning for Kids Foundation, where I strongly advocate for the education of young children, especially girls, I hold deep admiration for the work of **Malala Yousafzai**, a Pakistani activist and the youngest Nobel Prize laureate. Yousafzai has become an international symbol of resilience and advocacy for girls' education. Despite facing a life-threatening attack by the Taliban for her activism, Yousafzai continued her fight for education rights, showcasing her bravery and commitment to her cause. She exemplifies becoming the best version of oneself through her dedication to empowering others, overcoming adversity, and tirelessly working for equality and education.

As a devoted Beatles fan, I hold a special place in my life for **Paul McCartney**. His journey toward becoming his best self is a testament to his enduring adaptability and growth. Following his Beatles era, he didn't just rest on his laurels; he forged a successful solo career and formed the group Wings, showcasing his ability to constantly evolve musically. His life hasn't been without personal struggles—notably, the loss of his first wife, Linda—yet he used these hardships to foster personal resilience. Beyond music, McCartney is deeply committed to activism and philanthropy, particularly in advocating for animal rights, vegetarianism, and music education. Despite his advancing age, he continues to tour and release new music, a clear sign of his dedication to lifelong creativity and learning. Mindfulness and health are also central to McCartney's life; he practices meditation and maintains a healthy lifestyle, underscoring his belief in the importance of mental and physical well-being. Adaptable as ever, he stays abreast of the latest trends and technologies in the always-evolving music industry.

I have a tremendous appreciation for architecture. The last individual who exemplifies becoming her best self that I'd like to highlight is Iraqi-British architect and artist **Zaha Hadid**, for her groundbreaking designs and barrier-breaking achievements. As the first woman to win the prestigious Pritzker Architecture Prize, she challenged industry norms with her innovative, fluid forms and expanded her craft beyond buildings into furniture and fashion. Hadid also contributed significantly to education, teaching at renowned institutions and inspiring future architects. Despite early challenges, with some designs initially deemed unbuildable, her persistence led to a legacy of iconic structures worldwide such as the London Aquatics Centre, the Heydar Aliyev Center, and the Guangzhou Opera House. By embracing new technologies and methods, Hadid and her work were a testament to relentless innovation, resilience, and a lasting impact on the architectural world.

One of Hadid's most renowned works, the Heydar Aliyev Center (Baku, Azerbaijan).
Photo by Mikhail Nilovon on Pexels.

Each individual I highlighted made a substantial impact, yet they remain authentically human, with their share of mistakes and imperfections, just like anyone else. They demonstrate that the journey to becoming the best version of ourselves is continuous and necessitates frequent reflection and constant personal development throughout life.

PHILOSOPHIES: THE BEST VERSION OF ME

The concept of becoming the best version of ourselves has been a central theme in various schools of thought throughout history, each providing unique perspectives on its importance. I will now introduce thoughts from different schools.

Ancient Greek Philosophy and the Best Version of Me

In Ancient Greek philosophy, the concept of eudaemonia is central, especially in the works of Aristotle.[1] More than mere happiness, eudaemonia is about living a life that is fulfilling and meaningful, often translated as "flourishing" or "human flourishing." Aristotle argued that achieving eudaemonia is the goal of human existence, a state of being that goes beyond temporary pleasure or material success.

For Aristotle, the path to eudaemonia lies in the cultivation of virtues such as courage, temperance, justice, and wisdom. He posited that these virtues are not innate but are developed through practice and habit. Living virtuously, according to Aristotle, means performing the right actions for the right reasons, aligning one's life with reason and rationality. He viewed reason as the unique function of human beings; thus, living rationally is essential for achieving eudaemonia.

Moreover, Aristotle emphasized the importance of moderation, a concept known as the golden mean, where virtue is a balance between two extremes. For instance, courage is the mean between recklessness and cowardice. This balance is achieved through practical wisdom or "phronesis," the ability to make judicious decisions in various situations in life.

Aristotle also believed that though external factors such as wealth, health, and social status could influence one's ability to achieve eudaemonia, they are not its essence. True eudaemonia is found in the activity of the soul in accordance with virtue, which constitutes a life worth living. He saw human life as part of a larger social and political context, meaning that one can also achieve eudaemonia through active participation in community and public life, fulfilling one's role as a citizen.

What resonates with me about Aristotle's philosophy is his holistic approach to well-being. He moves beyond the often-overemphasized concepts of personal happiness and success, focusing instead on a life characterized by virtue, reason, and balance. This comprehensive view not only highlights the importance of individual fulfillment but also underscores the significance of contributing to society and achieving one's highest potential. This concept is further discussed in the purpose section of this book.

Stoicism and the Best Version of Me

Stoicism, practiced and taught by philosophers such as Epictetus and Marcus Aurelius, advocates for a life aligned with virtue and in harmony with nature.[2] This ancient school of thought teaches that the essence of being the best version of oneself lies in attaining tranquility and liberation from suffering. This state is not reached through external possessions or status but through the cultivation of personal virtues such as wisdom, courage, justice, and temperance.

For Stoics, the concept of virtue is more than moral righteousness; it's about living in a manner that is consistent with the natural order of the world. They believe that by understanding the nature of the universe, one can understand the role and purpose of humanity within it. This understanding leads to a life lived in accordance with reason and virtue, which is seen as the highest good.

A central tenet of Stoicism is the differentiation between what is within our control and what is not. Epictetus famously stated that our opinions, impulses, desires, and aversions are within our power, whereas our body, property, reputation, and command are not. By focusing on and accepting this distinction, Stoics maintain a sense of inner peace and resilience in the face of adversity. They emphasize the importance of self-control and the development of inner strength to manage one's reactions and emotions.

Additionally, Stoicism teaches the importance of living in the present moment and dealing with life's challenges as they come, without excessive worry about the future or regret over the past. Marcus Aurelius, in his meditations, often reflects on the impermanence of life and the importance of living a virtuous life here and now.

Moreover, Stoicism advocates for the idea of a universal brotherhood, where each person is part of a larger whole and should live in cooperation and kindness toward others. This sense of interconnectedness and community responsibility is also key to achieving personal fulfillment and becoming the best version of oneself.

I greatly value the Stoic philosophy and have integrated several of its practices into my leadership development programs. This philosophy advocates for resilience, emotional intelligence, and ethical living as essential elements for achieving genuine fulfillment and tranquility. These principles are also explored in the mind and purpose sections of this book, highlighting their relevance and applicability to various aspects of life, including leadership.

Eastern Philosophies and the Best Version of Me

Eastern philosophies illuminate pathways toward self-betterment in remarkable ways.[3] Buddhism, for instance, advocates for mindfulness to attain deeper self-understanding.[4] Embracing compassion and kindness toward every being, recognizing and releasing attachments that bring pain, and regular meditation for mental clarity are essential. Adhering to the Noble Eightfold Path, which endorses ethical and mindful living, along with shedding ego-driven perspectives, greatly contributes to self-improvement. This path highlights the significance of ethical behavior, introspection, and mental discipline.

Both Buddhism and Hinduism introduce the crucial concept of non-attachment. They teach that our struggles often arise from clinging to material possessions, relationships, or specific outcomes. Learning to relinquish these attachments paves the way for enhanced inner peace and adaptability to life's changes.

Taoism, another insightful philosophy, underscores the necessity of living in harmony with the natural world.[5] Aligning ourselves with nature's rhythms can lead to a life that is both harmonious and fulfilling.

Personally, I find these philosophies' emphasis on balance and harmony in life invaluable. Finding internal and external harmony in various aspects of life, such as balancing professional duties with rest, juggling social commitments with personal time, and regulating emotional responses, is vital for personal growth. Furthermore, cultivating compassion toward oneself and others is a fundamental aspect of many Eastern philosophies. This encompasses both empathy and forgiveness, which are indispensable for personal development and building significant relationships.

Finally, practices such as meditation and yoga, prevalent in Eastern traditions, are powerful tools for self-discovery and enhancement. They assist in calming the mind, enhancing concentration, and deepening one's connection with the self and the cosmos. These practices have been instrumental in my journey toward personal growth and inner peace and will be discussed later in this book.

Existentialism and the Best Version of Me

Existentialism, a philosophical movement epitomized by thinkers such as Jean-Paul Sartre, Simone de Beauvoir, and Friedrich Nietzsche, delves into the notion that life, at its core, is devoid of any predetermined meaning or purpose.[6] This school of thought posits that it is not within the fabric of the universe to provide us with ready-made answers or a set path; rather, it is incumbent upon all people to forge their own meaning and purpose in life. This process is what existentialists refer to as the essence of being, which follows existence, a reversal of the traditional philosophical stance that essence precedes existence.

Sartre, one of the most prominent figures in existentialist philosophy, famously declared that "existence precedes essence."[7] By this, he meant that individuals first exist, encounter themselves, and emerge in the world to define their essence or nature through their actions, decisions, and the way they shape their lives. This perspective underscores the freedom of individuals to choose and create their own paths, but with this freedom comes the immense responsibility of shaping one's own destiny.

Nietzsche challenged traditional moral and philosophical structures, advocating instead for the creation of personal values and the questioning of established norms. He suggests individuals to transcend conventional boundaries and create a life of self-overcoming and constant evolution toward one's highest potential.[8]

De Beauvoir offered a profound perspective on becoming the best version of oneself. Grounded in existentialist philosophy, she believed that one's existence is not predefined, and that it is the individual's responsibility to define their essence through choices and actions. For de Beauvoir, becoming the best version of oneself involves an authentic pursuit of freedom, where an individual consciously chooses to transcend the given aspects of their existence such as societal roles and expectations, especially those imposed on women. She emphasized the importance of personal autonomy and ethical responsibility in this pursuit. In her seminal work, *The Second Sex*, de Beauvoir explored how women have been historically "othered" and argued that becoming one's true self involves challenging and transcending these imposed limitations.[9] For de Beauvoir, the best version of oneself is realized through an active engagement in one's own life, continuously striving for personal growth, and making choices that reflect one's true desires and beliefs, free from societal constraints.

Existentialism places great emphasis on authenticity, urging individuals to live in accordance with their true selves rather than conforming to societal expectations or external pressures. This philosophy encourages embracing the absurdity of life, facing the void, and finding personal meaning despite the inherent meaninglessness of the universe. Moreover, existentialism recognizes the anxiety and despair that can arise when confronting the freedom and responsibility of creating one's life narrative. Despite these challenges, existentialism advocates for a courageous approach to life, where individuals actively engage in defining their purpose, values, and beliefs and, in doing so, realize their true potential and authenticity.

I find that certain principles of existentialism are incredibly valuable, particularly those that stress the importance of crafting one's own meaningful existence through personal choices, living authentically, and continually redefining oneself. However, adhering to these principles can be challenging. This difficulty is echoed in the insights of Bronnie Ware, an Australian nurse who worked with terminally ill patients. In her interactions, she discovered that the most common regret among the dying was: "I wish I'd had the courage to live a life true to myself, not the life others expected of me."[10] This finding shows a fundamental human conflict: our desire to belong to various social groups often brings with it the pressure to conform to societal norms, which can lead us away from living a life that truly reflects our individual essence and desires.

Positive Psychology and the Best Version of Me

Positive psychology, developed and popularized by Martin Seligman and others, represents a shift in the focus of psychology on pathology and mental illness to the factors that contribute to a fulfilling and meaningful life.[11] This approach posits that becoming the best version of oneself is not merely about alleviating suffering but actively building positive qualities. It involves cultivating positive emotions such as joy, gratitude, and hope, which Seligman and others have found to be key to enhancing one's overall life satisfaction and resilience.

In addition to emotional well-being, positive psychology emphasizes the importance of engagement in activities that absorb and fulfill us, often referred to as "flow" activities.[12] These are tasks that challenge and engage us deeply, aligning with our personal strengths and passions. The idea is that the best version of ourselves emerges when we are deeply immersed in and fulfilled by what we do.

Building and maintaining healthy relationships is another crucial component of this approach. Positive psychology research suggests that strong, supportive social connections are a cornerstone of happiness and well-being. The quality of our relationships greatly influences our mental and emotional health.

Finding meaning in life is also a key aspect of positive psychology.[13] This could involve being part of something bigger than oneself such as contributing to social causes, pursuing spiritual or religious beliefs, or engaging in work that aligns with one's values. This search for meaning provides a sense of purpose and direction. Achieving accomplishments, setting and working toward goals— whether personal or professional—is also seen as integral to becoming our best selves. These achievements provide a sense of mastery and efficacy, boosting our confidence and sense of self-worth.

Underpinning all these aspects is the belief in positive psychology that we can cultivate and grow our character strengths and virtues such as kindness, bravery, wisdom, and leadership. This personal growth is not seen as a fixed endpoint but a continual process of development and adaptation, contributing to our ongoing journey toward becoming the best version of ourselves.

My experience has shown me that positive psychology is an emerging science with tremendous potential for impact. In my book *YOU! The Positive Force in Change*, co-authored with my friend Eileen Rogers, I have incorporated numerous leadership practices derived from positive psychology insights.[14] One of the key insights from this field that resonates with me is the idea that personal growth is not a destination but a continuous journey of development and adaptation. This perspective aligns with the concept of constantly evolving toward the best version of ourselves.

In conclusion, each of these philosophies contributes to the understanding of why striving to become the best version of oneself is important. They collectively highlight themes of virtue, purpose, self-actualization, resilience, and the pursuit of fulfillment as central to the human experience.

HOW TO BECOME THE BEST VERSION OF YOURSELF

Drawing upon a wide range of scientific disciplines including, but not limited to, the ones I have discussed in the previous paragraph, we have crafted an all-encompassing well-being model that serves as the cornerstone of this book. This model integrates various theories and practical methodologies designed to guide you on your journey to becoming the best version of yourself.

The best version of me well-being model is structured into four key sections:

1. **Body**
2. **Mind**
3. **Purpose**
4. **Environment**

Each section comprises four or five dimensions, represented as chapters of this book. At the beginning of each section, a brief introduction to its chapters will be provided.

Figure 1.1: The best version of me well-being model

©2024. Nick van Dam et al. The Best Version of Me.

The chapters are uniquely crafted to be both independent and interconnected, allowing you the flexibility to engage with the content according to your preferences. You can either read them sequentially for a comprehensive understanding or select chapters that align with your personal interests and needs, with each offering insightful and actionable advice.

To truly embody the best version of yourself, it's crucial to consider all dimensions of the model. We view the best version of ourselves as an integrated whole rather than isolated dimensions. This means considering the synergy of body, mind, purpose, and environment.

Each dimension discussed in individual chapters also influences other aspects of the well-being model. For instance, insufficient sleep (body) can affect energy levels, eating habits, learning and memory, emotional regulation, decision-making, and the quality of relationships, potentially leading to burnout. Similarly, a lack of clarity in purpose may affect decision-making in other areas such as prioritizing physical well-being or investing in personal development and growth. Consequently, we encourage you to navigate back and forth between chapters, exploring the various dimensions and learning how they can be integrated for holistic well-being.

To facilitate an engaging and convenient reading experience, each chapter in this book follows a consistent structure. Beginning with an introduction, the chapters include a personal story related to each theme. This is followed by an exploration of how the topic supports your well-being and practical advice on enhancing your well-being based on the chapter's insights. Each chapter also features questions for self-reflection to encourage deeper thinking as well as resources for further exploration and learning. These resources include the authors' top three suggestions for articles, books, assessments and tests, videos, and podcasts.

Finally, the book is complemented by a website:
▶ thebestversionofmebook.com.

Here, you can find additional, continuously updated resources, including comprehensive assessments, an extensive knowledge center, and recommended courses. This integrated approach ensures a rich learning journey, enabling you to deeply engage with the book's content and apply its lessons in your journey toward personal well-being and becoming the best version of yourself.

THE SKY IS THE LIMIT

Humans possess an innate and remarkable potential to evolve into the best versions of themselves, similar to how a caterpillar is destined to transform into a butterfly. This potential is rooted deeply in various aspects of our being. For instance, our brainpower is colossal, with billions of neurons offering vast, untapped cognitive capabilities. Much like the unexplored depths of the ocean, the extent of our brain's potential is yet to be fully understood, suggesting immense possibilities for intellectual and creative growth. Physically, our bodies are powerhouses of strength and resilience, capable of extraordinary feats of endurance, adaptability, and transformation. In addition, our mental fortitude is profound. The human spirit has shown time and again that it can overcome tremendous challenges, endure hardship, and emerge stronger. This capacity for mental and emotional resilience allows us to navigate life's complexities and grow from our experiences. Collectively, these facets of human potential embody our capacity for flourishing, offering endless possibilities for personal development and self-actualization.

Becoming the best version of ourselves is a journey that extends beyond individual effort. It necessitates introspection, engaging in self-questioning, adopting new behaviors, and continuous personal development. Moreover, this transformation often relies on the support and input from others.

The creation of this book perfectly illustrates this collaborative process: it is the result of a team of experts working together, where the combined efforts and expertise of each contributor were essential. Individually, none of us could have crafted this book, which further highlights the importance of collective endeavor in personal growth and achievement.

I hope this book brings you a wealth of inspiration as you read it.

QUESTIONS FOR SELF-REFLECTION

- Reflecting on Stoicism's emphasis on controlling what is within our power, how can you apply this approach to your current challenges or goals?

- Considering the existentialist perspective on creating personal meaning, how do you currently define and pursue your own life's purpose and authenticity?

- How do you see the principles of positive psychology contributing to your journey toward becoming the best version of yourself, particularly in terms of personal growth and happiness?

RESOURCES FOR EXPLORATION AND LEARNING

 TOP 3: BOOKS

Clear, J. (2018). **Atomic Habits: An Easy & Proven Way to Build Good Habits & Break Bad Ones.** New York: Avery.
Description of the book from Amazon: "*Atomic Habits* will reshape the way you think about progress and success and give you the tools and strategies you need to transform your habits— whether you are a team looking to win a championship, an organization hoping to redefine an industry, or simply an individual who wishes to quit smoking, lose weight, reduce stress, or achieve any other goal."

Goldsmith, M. (2022). **The Earned Life. Lose Regret, Choose Fulfillment.** Sydney: Currency.
Description of the book from Marshall Goldsmith's website: "Marshall Goldsmith—world-renowned Executive Coach and New York Times bestselling author—offers a potent but simple approach that accommodates both our persistent need for achievement and the inescapable 'stuff happens' unfairness of life."

Maté, G. (2019). **When the Body Says No: The Cost of Hidden Stress.** London: Vermilion.
Description of the book from Gabor Maté's website: "When the Body Says No promotes learning and healing, providing transformative insights into how disease can be the body's way of saying no to what the mind cannot or will not acknowledge."

TOP 3: ARTICLES

Christensen, C. M. (2010, July-August). **How will you measure your life?**
Harvard Business Review.
▶ tinyurl.com/2jddatwd
In this article, Clayton Christensen explores questions everyone needs to ask:
How can I be happy in my career? How can I be sure that my relationship with my
family is an enduring source of happiness? And how can I live my life with integrity?

Harvard Health Publishing. (n.d.). **Positive psychology.** Harvard Medical School.
▶ tinyurl.com/mrsx8b7s
This article explores the fundamentals of positive psychology, a field focused on
what makes life most fulfilling. It addresses key pillars, including positive thinking,
self-compassion, and mindfulness, and examines the concept of mindfulness in detail.

Perrigao, B. (2020, May 22). **"Acts of kindness are really contagious."**
Historian Rutger Bregman argues for a new way of thinking about humanity. *Time*
▶ tinyurl.com/4ybeykv5
Interview with Rutger Bregman about his book *Humankind*, in which the
unconventional historian tries to unravel even more of the conventional
wisdom that, he says, actually stands on empirically shaky ground.

TOP 3: VIDEOS

The Game that Can Give You 10 Extra Years of Life. TED Talk. Jane McGonigal.
▶ tinyurl.com/5n8hwdne
From the description of the video: "When game designer Jane McGonigal found
herself bedridden and suicidal following a severe concussion, she had a fascinating
idea for how to get better. She dove into the scientific research and created the
healing game, SuperBetter. In this moving talk, McGonigal explains how a game
can boost resilience—and promises to add 7.5 minutes to your life."

How to Make Stress Your Friend. TED Talk. Kelly McGonigal.
▶ tinyurl.com/2ny4tupn
From the description of the video: "Stress. It makes your heart pound, your
breathing quicken and your forehead sweat. But while stress has been made into
a public health enemy, new research suggests that stress may only be bad for you
if you believe that to be the case. Psychologist Kelly McGonigal urges us to see
stress as a positive, and introduces us to an unsung mechanism for stress
reduction: reaching out to others."

Want to Be Happy? Be Grateful. TED Talk. David Steindl-Rast.
▶ tinyurl.com/4ymsemcx
From the description of the video: "The one thing all humans have in common is that each of us wants to be happy, says Brother David Steindl-Rast, a monk and interfaith scholar. And happiness, he suggests, is born from gratitude. An inspiring lesson in slowing down, looking where you're going, and above all, being grateful."

ENDNOTES

1 J. Barnes, ed. (1984). *Complete Works of Aristotle, Volume 1: The Revised Oxford Translation.* Princeton: Princeton University Press.

2 D. Robertson. (2018). *Stoicism and the Art of Happiness: Practical Wisdom for Everyday Life (Teach Yourself).* London: Teach Yourself.

3 I. Fischer-Schreiber, F.-K. Ehrhard, K. Friedrichs, and M. S. Diener. (1994). *The Encyclopedia of Eastern Philosophy and Religion: Buddhism, Taoism, Zen, Hinduism.* Denver: Shambhala.

4 B. Bodhi. (2023). *Noble Truths, Noble Path.* New York: Simon & Schuster.

5 L. Tzu. (2017). *Tao Te Ching.* London: Vintage Books.

6 J.-P. Sartre. (2007). *Existentialism Is a Humanism.* Translated by C. Macomber. New Haven, CT: Yale University Press.

7 J.-P. Sartre. (1957). *Being and Nothingness: An Essay on Phenomenological Ontology.* Translated by H. E. Barnes. London: Methuen, p. 20.

8 F. W. Nietzsche. (2006). *Thus Spoke Zarathustra: A Book for All and None.* Cambridge, UK: Cambridge University Press.

9 S. de Beauvoir. (2015). *The Second Sex.* Translated by C. Borde and S. Malovany-Chevallier. London: Vintage Books.

10 B. Warren. (2012). [Review of the book *The top five regrets of the dying: A life transformed by the dearly departing,* by Bronnie Ware]. Proceedings (Baylor University Medical Center) 25 (2), pp. 299–300. tinyurl.com/2t46b3th

11 C. R. Snyder, S. J. Lopez, L. M. Edwards, and S. C. Marques, eds. (2021). *The Oxford Handbook of Positive Psychology,* 3rd ed. Oxford: Oxford University Press.

12 M. Csikszentmihalyi. (1990). *Flow: The Psychology of Optimal Experience.* New York: HarperCollins.

13 M. E. P. Seligman. (2013). *Flourish.* New York: Simon & Schuster.

14 N. H. M. van Dam and E. Rogers. (2012). *YOU! The Positive Force in Change.* Morrisville, NC: Lulu Publishing.

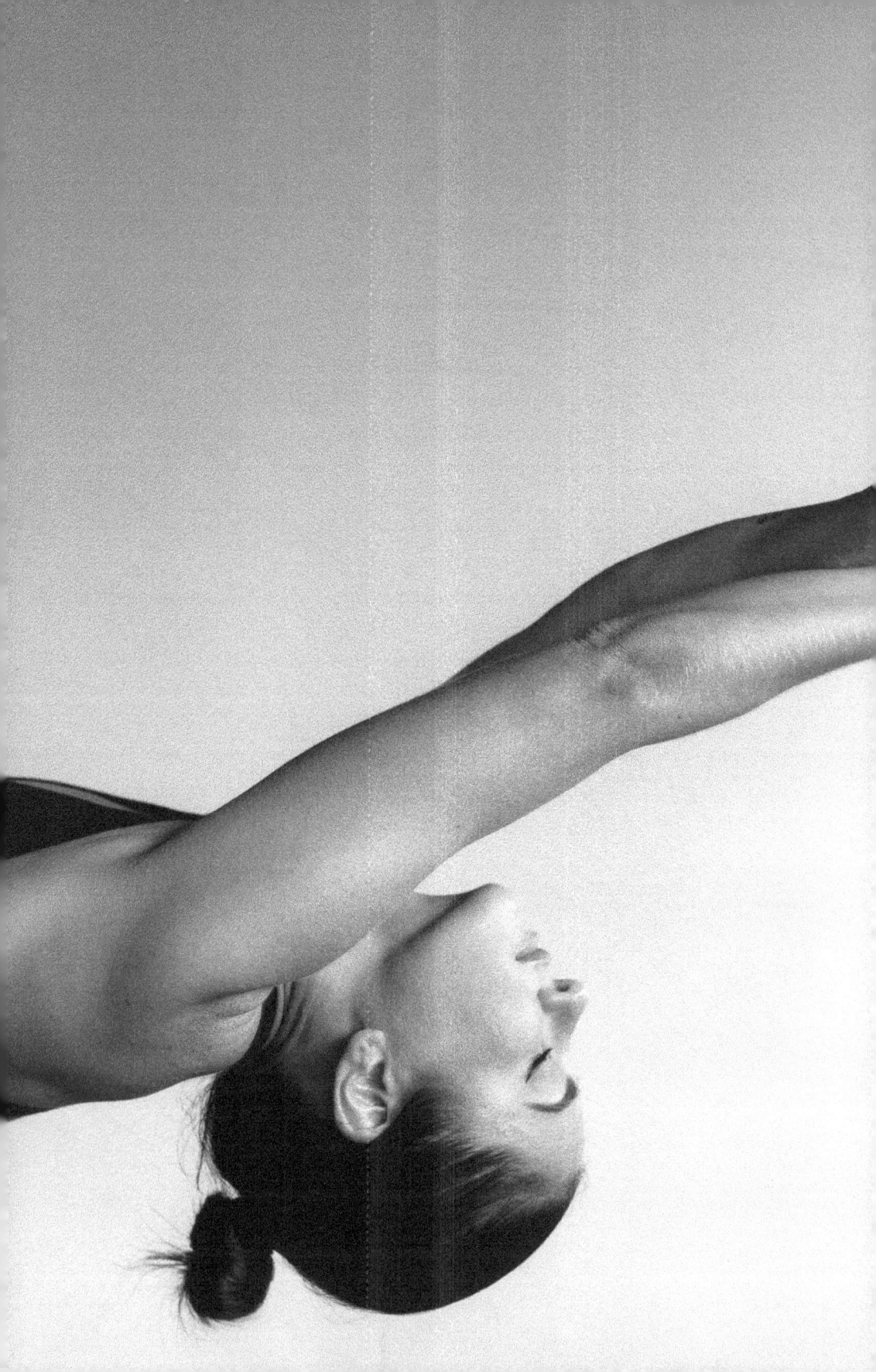

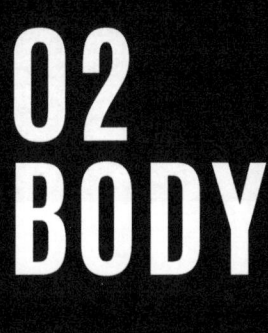

02
BODY

SLEEP
ENERGY
NUTRITION
PHYSICAL MOVEMENT
DNA

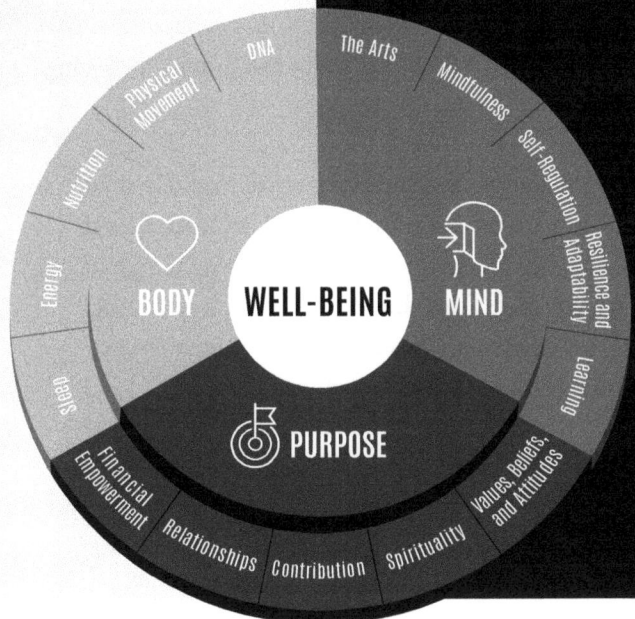

Nature Environment

Social Environment

Work Environment

Climate Environment

INTRODUCTION

Written by Dr. Nick van Dam

> "To keep the body in good health is a duty. Otherwise,
> we shall not be able to keep our mind strong and clear."
> —BUDDHA

In the first section of the book and of the Best Version of Me model—body—we examine the fundamental aspects of the cornerstone of physical well-being and health. This part of the book is structured into five comprehensive chapters, each exploring a vital component that collectively defines our bodily health and functioning.

Sleep

We explore the indispensable role of sleep in maintaining our health and well-being. Emphasizing sleep's crucial role in keeping our brain balanced, we learn how it underpins cognitive processes and emotional regulation. We address the significant consequences of sleep loss, which range from diminished mental acuity to increased vulnerability to chronic health conditions. To combat these issues, we introduce five key strategies for improving sleep quality.

Energy

An often-overlooked aspect of our well-being is the intricate dynamics of energy within the human body. Understanding how our bodies generate, use, conserve, and expend energy is pivotal for maintaining vitality and overall well-being. Here, we explore the delicate balance of energy, acknowledging that it is often challenging to maintain equilibrium in our fast-paced lives. Chronic fatigue, a common ailment in modern society, serves as a stark reminder of what happens when this balance is disrupted: the prolonged absence of energy deeply impacts our ability to function optimally.

Nutrition

Nutrition plays a powerful rule in shaping our physical and mental health. A key focus of this chapter is the concept of bio-individuality—the understanding that there is no one-size-fits-all approach to nutrition. Recognizing that each person's body has unique nutritional needs, we explore how to tailor a nutrition plan that aligns with your individual health requirements, lifestyle, and preferences. This personalized approach is essential for achieving optimal nutrition, given that what works for one person may not be effective for another. We also lay out the necessary components of a balanced nutrition plan. Last, the chapter emphasizes the importance of the importance of making sustainable changes to improve your nutrition.

Physical Movement

This chapter confronts the global crisis of physical inactivity. We explore physical activity levels, understanding the spectrum from sedentary behavior to vigorous exercise and its impact on our well-being. Highlighting the dire health effects of minimal physical movement, we examine its toll not just on our physical state but also on mental health, including stress and mood disorders. We introduce the Dance of Life model, an innovative approach designed to engage and enhance our natural regenerative abilities through movement.

DNA

We examine the complex world of DNA and its role in defining who we are, incorporating the nature versus nurture debate. We critically explore the concept of "DNA as destiny," challenging the idea that our genetic code is an unalterable path to our future. The chapter investigates the intricate connections between DNA and our physical and mental health, revealing how our genes interact with our environment, behaviors, and lifestyle choices. We also discuss the role of DNA in our overall well-being, emphasizing how understanding our unique genetic makeup can inform better health and lifestyle decisions. This exploration not only deepens our comprehension of the biological foundations of our lives but also empowers us with knowledge to positively influence our health outcomes.

SLEEP

Written by Dr. Els van der Helm

INTRODUCTION

> "Each night, when I go to sleep, I die.
> And the next morning, when I wake up, I'm reborn."
> —MAHATMA GANDHI

Personal Story

Julie was a determined and ambitious accountant climbing the ladder at her firm in record time. She worked long days at the office, then more at home in the evening, and her phone was never far from reach, including when she went to bed. Her work email was the last thing she glanced at before going to sleep and the first thing she checked after waking up. Lately, she noticed that on the weekends she felt like a zombie: fatigued, yet never able to get good-quality sleep. She felt restless and guilty when she wasn't working, unable to relax or enjoy time with friends. She felt increasingly anxious and less sharp in meetings. She had less patience with her team members, was more irritable, and had been gaining weight slowly but steadily, ever since she started this job. One day this will all be worth it, she told herself—the day she made partner.

I see clients similar to Julie all the time. When we dig into their fatigue and sleep problems, we unravel a number of maladaptive beliefs and behaviors that cause their lack of energy and poor-quality sleep. In this chapter, I will first explore two underlying beliefs people like Julie tend to have, followed by an outline of the main functions of sleep, and wrapping up with healthy habits that can lead to better sleep, greater well-being, and better performance. But first, what causes this relentless drive to perform well at work, which can actually hurt our ability to be the best version of ourselves?

Belief #1: "Just one more deadline."
Julie lived her life as if she were just one sprint away from her next career goal: "Just one more dash to the next promotion, and then I can take a break." But this is a huge misconception: often there is no peace and quiet after the next deadline or milestone. Instead, there is yet another deadline or milestone waiting to be reached. In fact, being successful in work (and in life!) is *not* a sprint—it *is* a marathon. Most people are likely to be in their career for thirty years or more, not just three years. Therefore, we need to ensure that we run at a pace we can sustain for decades. And that should start *now*, not after meeting the next deadline.

Belief #2: "The more time I spend on my work, the better I will do."
Julie often felt tempted to get extra work done in the evenings and on weekends because it felt good to cross another thing off her to-do list. She believed doing this decreased her anxiety and was the only way toward greater peace and quiet. What Julie's 24/7 mentality ended up doing was hurting her performance at work, her health, and her well-being. This notion of more time at work equals better performance is not correct; in fact, we see that most successful business leaders actively prioritize rest and recovery, not just during their holidays but throughout their careers.[1] Consider one work week or even just one day where you are building toward a peak in performance (perhaps an important deliverable, meeting, or presentation), and then factor in time for recovery. Julie had completely left out time for recovery in her life, which kept her in a state of hyperarousal caused by chronic stress. This left her tired but wired and unable to get restorative sleep.

Becoming the Best Version of Yourself
So, how can we become the best version of ourselves? When most people think about this question, topics such as exercise, healthy nutrition, mindfulness, and a sense of belonging usually come to mind. These are also featured in this book for good reason, because they indeed *are* all important elements for us to be at our best. However, a fundamental and, dare I say, *foundational* piece to our overall well-being and performance is often missing from these lists—sleep!

HOW DOES SLEEP SUPPORT YOUR WELL-BEING?

Sleep is fundamental given the impact it has not just on our well-being and performance but also on our ability to leverage other key factors such as healthy nutrition, exercise, and so on.

To give you a simple example: When we sleep just one hour less than we're used to, we eat an average of 140 calories more the next day. We also crave carbohydrates more intensely, and when we then eat sugar, our body responds differently in terms of its insulin response. As a result, just one night of sleep deprivation can increase insulin levels and make us look prediabetic. Good sleep also plays a key role in our physical activity. If we are well rested, we're much more likely to exercise, exercise more intensely, and have a lower risk of injuries.

Figure 2.1: Sleep is the foundation to our performance and well-being

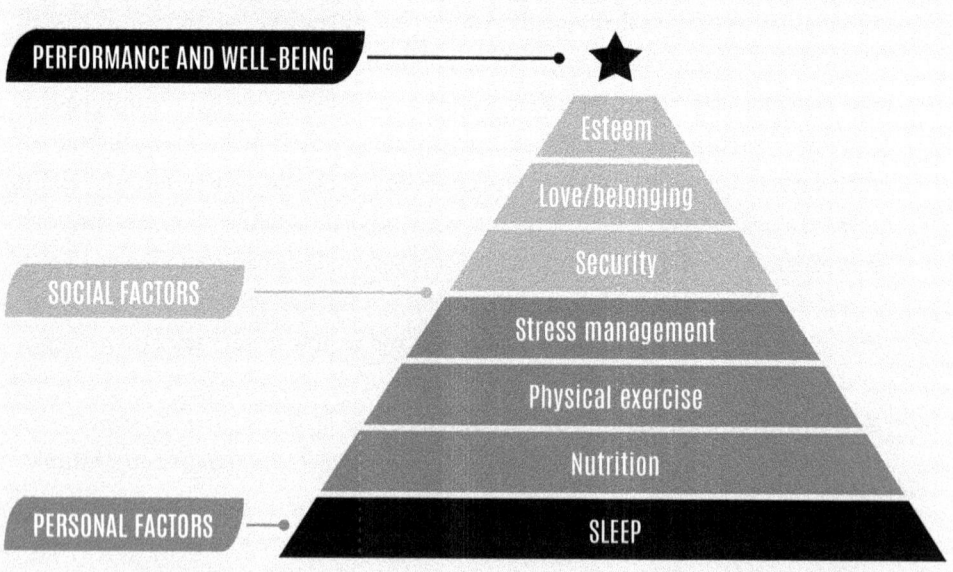

©2024. Dr. Els van der Helm. The Best Version of Me.

Sleep can also have a significant impact on job performance. When we sleep, our bodies and minds are able to rest and repair themselves, which helps us feel more alert and energized when we're awake. There is a strong link between sleep and cognitive performance, with studies showing that people who get good sleep consistently outperform those who are sleep deprived in areas such as pattern recognition, creativity, problem-solving, learning, memory, and decision-making.

> **"Studies showing that people who get good sleep consistently outperform those who are sleep deprived."**

But perhaps one of the most important effects of a good night's sleep is on our emotional well-being. When we are well rested, we are much less reactive to stressors; we can put things in perspective and see the bigger picture.

How Is It Possible that This One Thing—Sleep—Is So Fundamental?

Two key functions of sleep help explain its impact on our bodies. One function of sleep is to clean our brain. When our brain cells—our neurons—are active, they use up energy and, in this process, produce toxic byproducts. That might sound strange, but our muscles do the same thing when we exercise. Only in 2013 did scientists discover that this cleaning process occurs during sleep.[2] This means that after a good night of sleep, we wake up with a clean brain that can not only process information faster but also more accurately, and we make fewer mistakes. Even more recently, it was discovered that it is during deep sleep in particular that the cleaning process takes place.[3]

Another function of sleep is to keep us emotionally balanced.[4] A small brain structure important for emotional processing is the amygdala. Shaped like an almond, the amygdala functions as our brain's threat-detection system. If you receive a stressful email from your boss, your amygdala will be involved in the fight, flight, or freeze response. But the amygdala is not on its own; it is connected to many different brain areas, including the prefrontal cortex (PFC), the part of our brain that evolved most recently and that helps us organize, plan, and think about the consequences of our actions. Specifically, the medial PFC (mPFC) plays a regulatory role over the amygdala (Figure 2.2A); for example, the mPFC allows you to count to ten after you get that stressful email. However, this inhibitory control is only available when we are well rested! When we have not had a good night's sleep, our brain functions quite differently (Figure 2.2B).[5] For unknown reasons, the PFC is one of the brain areas most sensitive to sleep deprivation. Under conditions of sleep loss, the mPFC loses its connection with the amygdala, creating an overactive, emotional brain; as my PhD advisor, Matt Walker, used to say, "You're all gas and no brakes!"[6] This emotional imbalance explains a lot of what we see both in the lab and in real life when people are tired. They are impulsive, irritable, think only about the short term, and have a hard time managing their emotions and interpreting the emotions of others.[7] We can also feel more anxious and depressed.[8]

Figure 2.2: Sleep keeps the brain balanced

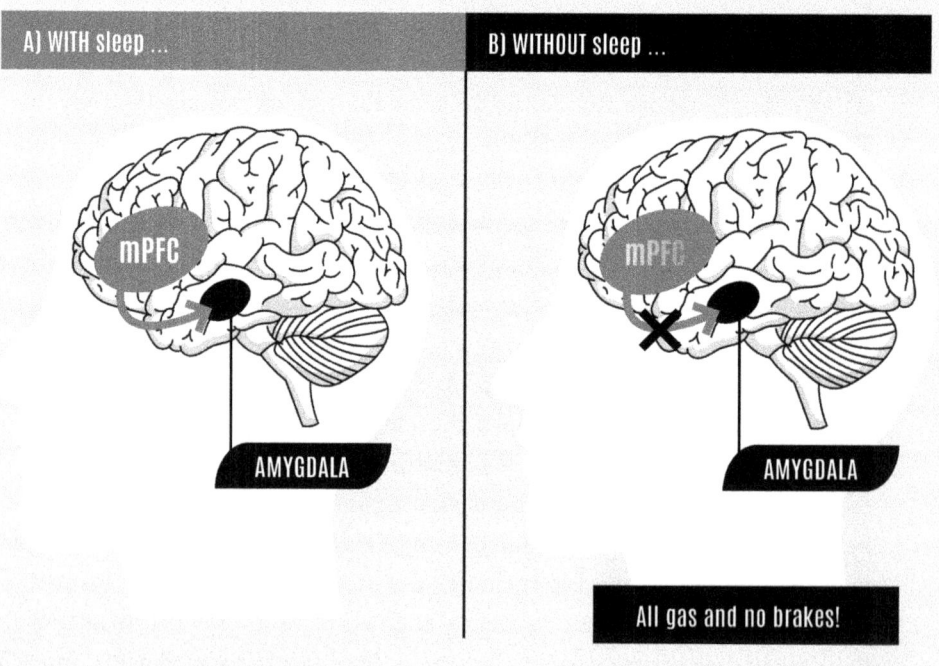

©2024. Dr. Els van der Helm. The Best Version of Me.

It is therefore no surprise that sleep loss negatively affects our ability to be a good leader.[9] One study found that leaders who had a poor night's sleep were more abusive the next day: they demonstrated "sustained ... hostile verbal and nonverbal behavior" (but were not physically abusive) toward their colleagues. This behavior led to an immediate decrease in engagement within their teams, but the reverse occurred after the same leaders had a good night's sleep.[10]

Moreover, poor sleep has been consistently identified as a causal factor for burnout,[11] depression,[12] excessive risk-taking,[13] increased unethical behavior, and decreased moral awareness in the workplace.[14] See Figure 2.3.

Figure 2.3: Consequences of sleep loss

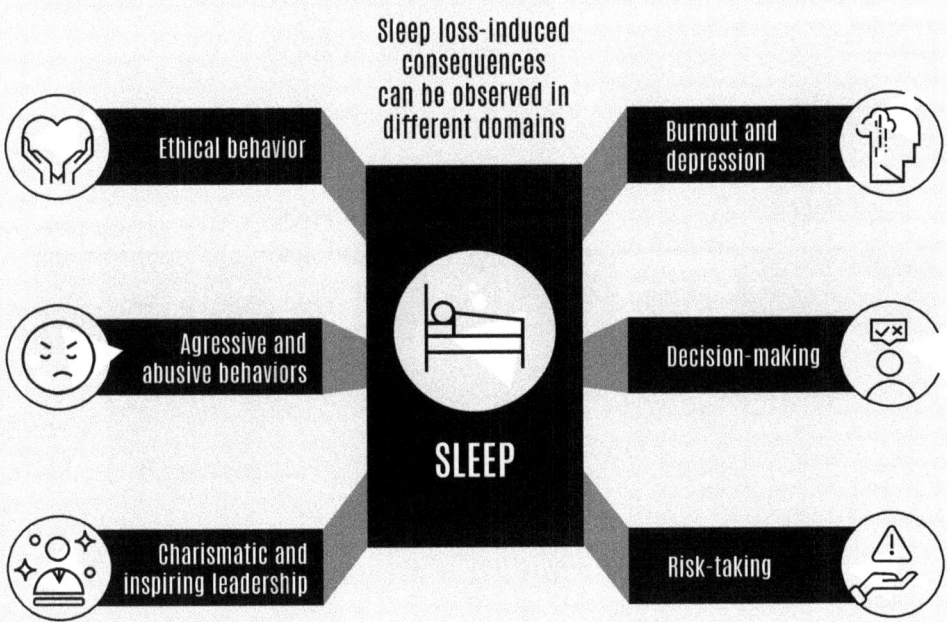

Sleep loss-induced consequences can be observed in different domains

Ethical behavior

Burnout and depression

Agressive and abusive behaviors

Decision-making

Charismatic and inspiring leadership

Risk-taking

SLEEP

©2024. Dr. Els van der Helm. The Best Version of Me.

Understanding Sleep

We sleep for about a third of our lives, yet most of us have no idea how we can get the very best sleep. This is surprising given how much we try to optimize parts of our waking life. In order to improve our sleep, it helps to first understand what a good night of sleep actually is. Figure 2.4 presents an example of the sleep patterns of a young and healthy person (approximately twenty-five years old). As the figure shows, it is normal to take up to thirty minutes to fall asleep. On one hand, if it takes you longer than thirty minutes to fall asleep, that may be an issue. On the other hand, if you fall asleep within only a minute or so, that may be a sign that you are sleep deprived and could benefit from more sleep. Waking up at night is also completely normal, as long as you can fall back to sleep within roughly five minutes (don't look at the clock for this!). We get most of our deep sleep during the first half of the night, and most of our dream or rapid eye movement (REM) sleep in the second half. If you are well rested, you can wake up without an alarm. If you absolutely *need* an alarm, set it as late as you can in order to get as much consolidated sleep as possible. Finally, one way to ensure you have good sleep quality in the morning is to stop hitting the snooze button.

Figure 2.4: Healthy sleep patterns (architecture)

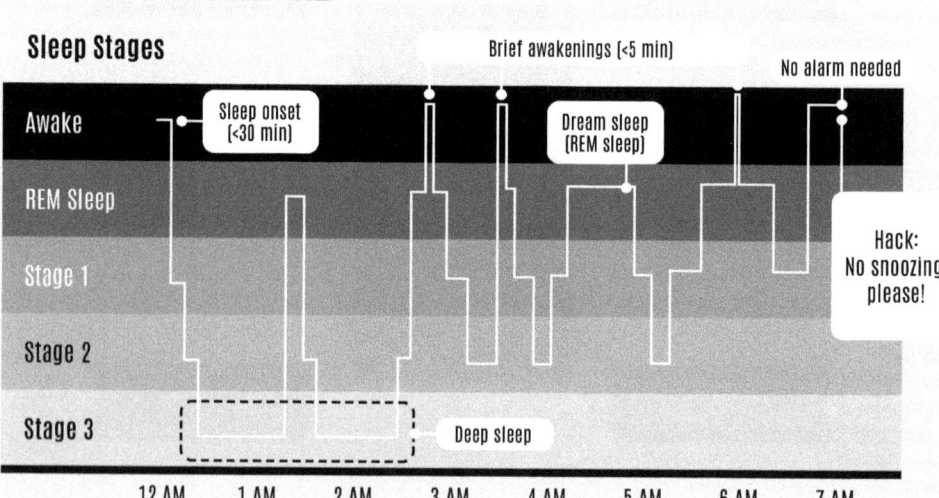

©2024. Dr. Els van der Helm. The Best Version of Me.

BOOSTING YOUR WELL-BEING THROUGH SLEEP

Many of us believe that to improve sleep, we only need to focus on what we do right before bed. If only our bodies had a hidden switch we could simply flip at night! On the contrary, our sleep at night is a mirror of our entire day. A good night's sleep starts with how we wake up and what we do during the day.

Try focusing on the following five areas to start improving your sleep:

1. Concentrate on sleep quality instead of sleep duration.
With my clients, I always work on improving sleep quality before moving on to potentially extending sleep duration. I want to ensure that every hour of sleep is the best it can be before extending the number of hours of sleep. This means that unless you have great sleep quality, I wouldn't recommend suddenly going to bed much earlier than you are used to, because this can lead to trouble falling or staying asleep. Any shifts in your sleep rhythm are best to make at a gradual pace. For example, try going to bed fifteen minutes earlier for a week before moving on to an earlier time.

2. Lower stress in any way that works for you.
Usually, the first target for improving sleep quality is stress. Stress hormones are a primary cause of having trouble falling asleep, waking up at night and not being able to fall back to sleep quickly, and early morning wakeups. It makes sense: stress signals our brain to be on high alert and run away from a lion around the corner. Sleep is less important when you think you're fighting for survival.

Lowering stress is more easily said than done, but here are a few tips:

- Explore which relaxation techniques and habits work best for you and at which time of the day. These are needed for the next two steps.

- Build in micro-breaks during your workday, even as short as one to five minutes. Use these breaks to concentrate on anything not related to work. Try focusing on your breath, stretching, walking, meditating, or simply staring out the window.

- Wind down before going to bed using any ritual or activity that helps you relax and finish off your day. I personally write in my journal for five to ten minutes, then read in bed for five to ten minutes. I keep my phone outside my bedroom to prevent disruptions to my sleep.

Finally, timing is everything, as the next three suggestions show.

3. Sleep at the right time.

In addition to duration and quality, another important element is timing. We all function at our best when we can align our sleep with our biorhythm. However, there is no one-size-fits-all when it comes to sleep timing because we all have a different optimal biorhythm. The simplest way to figure out your own biological rhythm is to think about a situation without any obligations, whether work or personal. What would be your preferred bedtime and wake-up time? Morning types prefer an earlier bedtime than night owls. Whatever your rhythm, you want to be as consistent as possible with your sleep timing in order to create a strong rhythm with a clear contrast between night and day.

4. Get light at the right time; avoid light at the right time.

It is important to get enough bright light during the day, especially early in the morning. Humans spend more than 90% of their time indoors, meaning we often are exposed to very dim light, which our biological clock interprets as nighttime. As a result, this makes our biological rhythm less strong and can decrease our ability to sleep at night because our clock is confused about what time it actually is. To counteract this, ensure you get bright light (>10k Lux; Lux is the unit used in light, where 1 Lux equals the brightness of one candle) for at least thirty minutes before noon each day. For example, go outside, even on a cloudy day, or sit in front of or under a bright therapy light. However, you should avoid bright light in the roughly three hours before you go to bed. We only produce melatonin, the sleep hormone, in dim lighting. In the summer, for example, this might mean closing the blinds or curtains or wearing blue light-blocking glasses for a few hours before you go to bed.

5. **Eat at the right time.**

In addition to getting and avoiding light at the right times, our biorhythm also responds to the timing of our meals. Studies show that not eating in the three to four hours before your bedtime improves sleep quality and leads to fewer wakeups.[15] Over time, eating late in the day may also contribute to obesity. Perhaps surprisingly, the less you eat at night, the *fewer* calories you eat the next day.

QUESTIONS FOR SELF-REFLECTION

- Can I wake up naturally?

- Do I feel refreshed when I wake up in the morning?

- Do I feel energized throughout the day, or am I compensating for fatigue by drinking caffeine, checking my phone, and eating snacks?

RESOURCES FOR EXPLORATION AND LEARNING

TOP 3: ARTICLES

Barnes, C. (2018, August 27). **You know you need more sleep. Here's how to get it.** *Harvard Business Review.*
▶ tinyurl.com/2vcdwm4c
Acknowledging that one would feel and perform better with better sleep is much easier than actually leaving work early enough to get a good night's sleep. This article gives simple tips to help you change your behavior and improve your sleep.

Hougaard, R., and C. Carter. (2018, February 28). **Senior executives get more sleep than everyone else.** *Harvard Business Review.*
▶ tinyurl.com/z8z49vcw
Clever research on more than 35,000 leaders dispels the myth that successful leaders hardly sleep, or that the only way to get to the top is to cut back on your sleep in order to do more work.

van der Helm, E., and N. van Dam. (2016, February 1).
The organizational impact of insufficient sleep. *McKinsey Quarterly.*
▶ tinyurl.com/3w73pwjk
This article describes the direct impact of sleep on leadership quality through four key pathways and provides actionable tips to improve sleep in a demanding job.

 TOP 3: BOOKS

Huffington, A. (2016). **The Sleep Revolution: Transforming Your Life, One Night at a Time.** Chatsworth, CA: Harmony.
This book is a call to action for people to prioritize sleep. It describes how sleep is essential for our health, productivity, and overall well-being. The book provides practical advice on how to get more sleep, as well as stories from celebrities and other high achievers who have found success by prioritizing sleep.

Pink, D. (2018). **When: The Scientific Secrets of Perfect Timing.** New York: Riverhead.
This book is all about timing, including timing your sleep and your work across the day, depending on your mood and cognitive functioning. It is a very practical "when to" (versus "how to") book that gives concrete advice on how to structure your day.

Walker, M. (2017). **Why We Sleep.** New York: Scribner.
Explores the science of sleep, including what happens when you don't sleep enough. The book provides a wealth of information on the benefits of sleep, as well as practical tips on how to improve sleep habits. It is aimed at people who still need a bit of convincing for why sleep is critical to health, well-being, and performance.

 TOP 3: VIDEOS

 The Science of Sleep. Dr. Els van der Helm.
▶ tinyurl.com/dvdykbhz
Many of us live by the slogan "work hard, play hard" in our hyper-connected, 24/7 world, where our demanding lives keep us glued to digital screens. In this talk, Dr. Els van der Helm outlines why your slogan should instead be "work hard, play hard, AND sleep hard!" She shares what science has taught us about the benefits of sleep and why you should place sleep at the top of your priority list.

How to Succeed? Get More Sleep. Arianna Huffington.
▶ tinyurl.com/45uncb2e
In this short talk, Arianna Huffington shares a small idea that can awaken much bigger ones: the power of a good night's sleep. Instead of bragging about our sleep deficits, she urges us to shut our eyes and see the big picture: we can sleep our way to increased productivity and happiness—and smarter decision-making.

Sleep and Work. Christopher Barnes.
▶ tinyurl.com/55yx4dcm
Today we hear leaders boast about how little they sleep, claiming it signifies their dedication and work ethic. But what if this is the wrong way around; what if this lack of sleep is causing us (and them) to make poor decisions? Chris Barnes explores how our chronic lack of sleep makes us less efficient and hurts our productivity and health.

TOP 3: PODCASTS

Get Sleepy.
▶ tinyurl.com/mrwu2k7p
Sleep meditation and stories. Fall asleep more easily to this story-telling podcast.

Lancefield on the Line.
▶ tinyurl.com/45x6wpwn
Leadership expert and podcast host David Lancefield interviews Dr. Els van der Helm on topics of sleep, leadership, well-being, and performance.

The Matt Walker Podcast.
▶ tinyurl.com/yc4ju289
A podcast about sleep, the brain, and the body. Matt Walker is a professor of psychology at the University of California, Berkeley, and the author of the book *Why We Sleep*.

TOP 3: APPS

Headspace and Calm. Two great apps to help you relax and practice mindfulness, meditation, and breathing exercises, or just listen to a relaxing story before bed.

Light Meter. A handy tool with which you can measure light intensity. For example, use Light Meter to determine where to put your desk in your home office or measure the intensity of light in an office.

Timeshifter. A useful app to help you adjust to a new time zone faster and minimize jet lag.

 TOP 3: PRODUCTS

Bright Light Therapy Lamps. Helpful if your office isn't at least 500 Lux during the day (you can use the Light Meter app to find out). Ensure you choose a lamp that can reach at least 10,000 Lux.

Sleep Trackers. Some examples depending on the form you prefer: a ring (OURA), a wristband (Apple Watch or WHOOP), or on your bed (Withings).

Sunrise Alarm Clock. Helpful if you re a snoozer or a strong evening type who struggles to get sleepy at night or wake up in the morning. There are many products on the market, so be sure to choose one where the light attains at least 10,000 Lux.

ENDNOTES

1   R. Hougaard and J. Carter. (2016, February 28). Senior executives get more sleep than everyone else. *Harvard Business Review*. tinyurl.com/z8z49vcw

2   L. Xie, H. Kang, Q. Xu, M. J. Chen, Y. Liao, M. Thiyagarajan, J. O'Donnell, D. J. Christensen, C. Nicholson, J. J. Iliff, T. Takano, R. Deane, and M. Nedergaard. (2013). Sleep drives metabolite clearance from the adult brain. *Science 342* (6156), pp. 373–77. tinyurl.com/2s4bmkyz

3   A. W. Varga, M. E. Wohlleber, S. Giménez, S. Romero, J. F. Alonso, E. L. Ducca, K. Kam, C. Lewis, E. B. Tanzi, S. Tweardy, A. Kishi, A. Parekh, E. Fischer, T. Gumb, D. Alcolea, J. Fortea, A. Lleó, K. Blennow, H. Zetterberg, L. Mosconi, L. Glodzik, E., O. E. Burschtin, M. J. de Leon, D. M. Rapoport, S.-E. Lu, I. Ayappa, and R. S. Osorio. (2016). Reduced slow-wave sleep is associated with high cerebrospinal fluid Aβ42 levels in cognitively normal elderly. *Sleep 39* (11), pp. 2041–48. tinyurl.com/4uc3ykr9

4   M. P. Walker and E. van der Helm. (2009). Overnight therapy? The role of sleep in emotional brain processing. *Psychological Bulletin 135* (5), pp. 731–48. tinyurl.com/fwtxtnw8

5   S. S. Yoo, N. Gujar, P. Hu, F. A. Jolesz, and M. P. Walker. (2007). The human emotional brain without sleep—a prefrontal amygdala disconnect. *Current Biology 17* (20), pp. R877–78. tinyurl.com/3achu4yv

6   E. van der Helm, J. Yao, S. Dutt, V. Rao, J. M. Saletin, and M. P. Walker. (2011). REM sleep depotentiates amygdala activity to previous emotional experiences. *Current Biology 21* (23), pp. 2029–32. tinyurl.com/4s6wpre8

7   E. van der Helm, N. Gujar, and M. P. Walker. (2010). Sleep deprivation impairs the accurate recognition of human emotions. *Sleep 33* (3), pp. 335–42. tinyurl.com/nzxkmksu

8   K. A. Babson, C. D. Trainor, M. T. Feldner, and H. Blumenthal. (2010). A test of the effects of acute sleep deprivation on general and specific self-reported anxiety and depressive symptoms: An experimental extension. *Journal of Behavior Therapy and Experimental Psychiatry 41* (3), pp. 297–303. tinyurl.com/zc8a5xf5

9   N. van Dam and E. van der Helm. (2016, February 16). There is a proven link between effective leadership and getting enough sleep. *Harvard Business Review.* tinyurl.com/5n6jm85d; N. van Dam and E. van der Helm. (2016, February 16). The organizational cost of insufficient sleep. *McKinsey Quarterly.* tinyurl.com/3w73pwjk; C. Barnes. (2018, September 16). Sleep well, lead better. *Harvard Business Review.* tinyurl.com/ztkmymmk

10 C. M. Barnes, L. Lucianetti, D. P. Bhave, and M. S. Christian. (2014). You wouldn't like me when I'm sleepy: Leader sleep, daily abusive supervision, and work unit engagement. *Academy of Management Journal 58* (5), pp. 1419–37. tinyurl.com/ycdsfbyy

11 M. Söderström, K. Jeding, M. Ekstedt, A. Perski, and T. Akerstedt. (2012). Insufficient sleep predicts clinical burnout. *Journal of Occupational Health Psychology 17* (2), pp. 175–83. tinyurl.com/yws6f7yc

12 D. Riemann, L. B. Krone, K. Wulff, and C. Nissen. (2020). *Sleep, insomnia, and depression. Neuropsychopharmacology 45* (1), pp. 74–89. tinyurl.com/yckb5ezu

13 S. D. Womack, J. N. Hook, S. H. Reyna, and M. Ramos. (2013). Sleep loss and risk-taking behavior: A review of the literature. *Behavioral Sleep Medicine 11* (5), pp. 343–59. tinyurl.com/3yje7bm7

14 C. M. Barnes, E. Awtrey, L. Lucianetti, and G. Spreitzer. (2020). Leader sleep devaluation, employee sleep, and unethical behavior. *Sleep Health 6* (3), pp. 411–17.e5. tinyurl.com/2tb6r27s; C. M. Barnes, B. C. Gunia, and D. T. Wagner. (2015). Sleep and moral awareness. *Journal of Sleep Research 24* (2), pp. 181–88. tinyurl.com/2rju2fpj

15 S. I. Iao, E. Jansen, K. Shedden, L. M. O'Brien, R. D. Chervin, K. L. Knutson, and G. L. Dunietz. (2021). Associations between bedtime eating or drinking, sleep duration and wake after sleep onset: Findings from the American time use survey. *British Journal of Nutrition 127* (12), pp. 1–10. tinyurl.com/4avdd2b4; C. A. Crispim, I. Z. Zimberg, B. G. dos Reis, R. M. Diniz, S. Tufik, and M. T. de Mello. (2011). Relationship between food intake and sleep pattern in healthy individuals. *Journal of Clinical Sleep Medicine 7* (6), pp. 659–664. tinyurl.com/ywzz53xy

ENERGY

Written by Hebe Boonzaaijer

INTRODUCTION

Perhaps the most precious thing in life is our energy. It's also the most mysterious. Our personal energy is the seat of our creation, because it literally defines everything else in our life. When we're always tired but wired, life can be a dreadful struggle. But when we're inspired and filled with energy, every minute of every day can be an exciting and even magical experience, where we feel ready to take on the world. In this chapter, I invite you to explore the dynamic energies that stream through your body, mind, and spirit, in an eternal dance with the unseen forces within and outside you. With knowledge, awareness, and intentional practice, you can form a conscious partnership with each, helping you optimize your body's natural capacity to bring renewed vigor to a tired body, fresh vitality to an exhausted mind, and new fuel to a sagging spirit. You can balance your energy to effectively meet stress and reduce anxiety, and use your energy to become a source of healing for others, too. Uncovering the sources and fluctuations of your energy is a priceless gift to yourself and those around you in the journey of becoming the best version of yourself.

> "You are the universe in ecstatic motion."
>
> —RUMI

Personal Story

I was sitting with my eyes closed when I realized there was not a tiny bit of energy left in me. I just couldn't do anything anymore; my body had almost completely shut down. The weeks before my burnout hit, there were some clear signs. I often worked twelve-hour days and prioritized productivity, self-improvement, and meeting others' expectations above my body's call for rest and nourishing self-care. I brushed off the need for nutritious food, moments of relaxation, and regular movement. At home, where my husband was recovering from cancer, my urge to stay strong for our young children, coupled with the fear of losing him, was emotionally exhausting. I felt like a tense machine rather than a living, breathing being. I couldn't stop my mind from planning, thinking, judging, and worrying, as if I were trapped in a mental bubble. I slept poorly; my immune system was compromised; I felt irritable, anxious, unable to concentrate; and I cried a lot. Relationships that had previously filled me with joy now felt like stressful obligations to avoid.

My recovery from burnout started with a great therapist, who gave me the structure and tools to bring my mentally and emotionally overstimulated nervous system back into balance. We also worked on expanding my awareness of fixed beliefs, negative self-talk, and mindsets that undermined my energy. With the support of a holistic doctor, I attended to my nutritional deficits and took up both a meal plan and daily exercise routine.

As I regained control over my health, I threw myself into understanding the intricacies of human energy—physically, emotionally, mentally, and spiritually. I learned that the body's circadian rhythm and hormones are closely linked to the regulation of our energy levels throughout the day. I started wearing a smartwatch to help me manage my energy through fitness tracking and sleep analysis. Through reading books, utilizing free apps, and studying different modalities, I experimented with Eastern and Western approaches to holistic health and well-being, adding one new healthy habit at a time. I discovered that mindfulness and breathing were powerful techniques to balance my energy and started teaching this in my work and to my children at home.

Now, I am grateful this collapse set me on a path of deeper devotion to serve people in their journey toward becoming their best self while remaining a student myself, which has brought a sense of purpose and joy to my existence. A profound shift in my energy occurred when I started to regularly focus my mind; tune in to my body with slow, intentional breath and an awareness of feeling centered in my core; and bring into consciousness a tender, loving presence of universal energy surrounding me. By practicing this meditative state on a daily basis, I started to learn how my emotions, thoughts, actions, and environment all affected my energy. This state of consciousness—in deep union with my spirit and body—brought me a sense of homecoming, where I could show up for myself as a friend, responding with kindness and care to my body's whispers, aches, contractions, and bursts of bliss. I began to make intuitive decisions about how to spend my energy and with whom.

I am humbled not only by the vastness of science and knowledge "out there" but also by the wisdom of my own body "in here." I found that with discipline, curiosity, and self-compassion, it is possible to not just manage my energy but to live as a conscious energy being, in connection with an intelligent universal life force, and create experiences filled with awe, wonder, love, and trust.

Human Energy Crisis

In my work on human performance and well-being over the last twenty years, I have met almost daily with people experiencing fatigue or exhaustion. They're tired, distracted, and anxious, and feel alienated from a state of flourishing, vibrant aliveness, calm, joy, inner love, and fulfillment. So many people in our modern world are plagued by low energy that having more energy has become a common health goal.

The energy crisis is real. The Gallup Organization found in 2023 that stress among workers was at a record high for the second year in a row, and employee stress has been rising for over a decade.[1] Though it's perfectly normal to experience fluctuating energy levels due to daily demands, persistent and chronic stress can lead to fatigue and burnout if not successfully managed.[2] In addition, according to a recent study by the McKinsey Health Institute of people across thirty countries, almost a quarter of employees (22%) experience burnout symptoms at work.[3] As a result, it's not surprising that employers are investing in the energy of their employees. According to Tony Schwartz, author of well-known *Harvard Business Review* article "Manage your energy, not your time," the best measure of productivity is not the number of hours we work but how much focused energy we bring to whatever hours we work.[4] But we aren't designed to be robots and can't operate at high speeds for long periods while running multiple programs at the same time.

A Conscious Partnership with Our Energy

There is a straight line from our inner life to the actions we take, the relationships we build, and the impact we create. In order to become your best self and do your most meaningful work, you need to bring your awareness to what's going on inside of you and build a trusted, conscious partnership with your own energy. The fascinating thing about energy is that it is regulated by our central nervous system, and 99.99% of bodily functions are autonomous—in other words, they run independently of our conscious actions. They happen beyond our notice, at the level of the cell. Inside every cell, a thousand processes have changed in the time you took to read this sentence. Donna Eden and David Feinstein, pioneers of energy regulation, explain that your energy system animates millions of processes in your body every second. Each cell emits and responds to electrochemical signals in an unimaginably complex and coordinated dance that keeps your lungs breathing, your heart pumping, your food digesting, your eyes blinking, and your tissue safe when microorganisms invade. Your mind is not actually required to assist the highly intelligent operation of your energy systems.[5]

The problem, however, is that our central nervous system isn't adapted to cope with the frenetic pace of modern life. The automatic responses inherited from our prehistoric ancestors—our default settings in the brain—are no longer able to return the body to a normal state of balance.[6] To be more specific, the daily pressure, information overload, distraction, and uncertainty that we've learned to accept as normal is constantly activating the sympathetic nervous system. This drives the "fight-or-flight" response, which is meant to last for only a matter of minutes—not all the time. This chronic response to our environment results in a range of physical and mental disorders and disease.[7] Ideally, the sympathetic nervous system is in harmony with its opposite, the parasympathetic nervous system, which regulates our "rest-and-digest" or "tend-and-befriend" response, creating a homeostatic balance.[8] But with our default design adjusting poorly to today's demands, such balance requires a conscious partnership among the body, emotions, mind, and spirit. The dramatic increase in medical prescriptions to help us calm down, especially in young adults, signals the call for action.[9] Calm is the new cool, and bookstores even sell quirky paperback notebooks with phrases such as "the true measure of success is a calm nervous system" emblazoned on front. But before learning strategies to achieve this state of inner harmony, where the realms of calm and vibrancy blend, let's first get a better understanding of the sources of energy available to us.

HOW DOES ENERGY SUPPORT YOUR WELL-BEING?

Energy and well-being are intricately linked, offering profound opportunities to overcome fatigue and pulsate with boundless energy. You've probably felt this at times, experiencing deep reservoirs of energy, and feeling positive, engaged, resilient, creative, laser focused, and fully open to what life offers. You may have felt more resolve and greater generosity of spirit. Your true and radiant self was peeking through in these moments. The goal is to create the consciousness that leads these glimpses to become lasting and permanent, as a constant undercurrent running through your life.

In physics, energy is described as the capacity to do work. It means having the strength and vitality to do what we want to do—move, think, work, play. Though our energy can decline as a result of aging or illness, much of our energy can be influenced through lifestyle adjustments, requiring us to move rhythmically between its expenditure and its intermittent renewal.[10] In humans, energy is derived from four sources: the body, the mind, the emotions, and the spirit. According to researchers Tony Schwartz and Jim Loehr, these four dimensions can be seen as batteries that are all necessary and complementary to sustainably thrive; not one is sufficient by itself. In each, energy can be systematically expanded and regularly renewed by establishing specific rituals or habits—behaviors that we carefully practice and schedule so that they become our way of life. Our best energy is pleasant and positive energy—meaning that it flows from the perception of opportunity, adventure, and challenge.[11]

Here's a short explanation of each of the sources of energy:

1. **Physical energy** is about the quantity of your energy and is the foundation on which everything else rests. For the highest quantity of energy, you will need to regularly top up your physical energy with restorative sleep, a healthy and wholesome diet with a diverse range of nutrient-dense foods, a regular exercise routine that includes cardiovascular and strength training, and regular breaks built into the day to renew and recharge. Our modern lifestyle has distanced us from nature's nourishing benefits in the physical realm since the 1950s, with most people now spending up to 90% of their time indoors, with sedentary lifestyles and eating artificial foods.[12] Connecting more closely with nature using all our senses, physical movement, and primarily eating foods with high nutritional value, has been proven to positively impact our energy in many ways.[13]

2 **Emotional energy** governs the way you feel, which dramatically influences how you perform, how you lead, and how you interact with others. For the highest-quality emotional energy, we need to experience the positive emotions of approaching life with a sense of opportunity, adventure, and challenge. It allows us to create experiences that are associated with enjoyment. Insight into our default emotional responses is crucial for channeling our energy effectively. If our energy is constantly triggered by the perception of threat, danger, fear, or survival, our vision becomes confused and conflicted. Our default setting then works against us, directing us toward protection and avoidance, which swiftly leaves us feeling burned out. Being aware of how you feel, satisfying and expressing your core emotional needs, healing from trauma, and releasing negative emotions are ways to influence your emotional energy in a positive way.[14]

3. **Mental energy** is about the focus of our attention. It means that we bring appropriate focus and realistic optimism to the work at hand, with a clear and sharp mind. We need this energy for thinking, reasoning, decision-making, creativity, problem-solving, and concentration. For the best focus, we need to do one thing at a time. Smartphones and other devices keep us "switched on": accessible and interruptible every second of the day. Distraction and constant fragmentation of our time and concentration have therefore become the new normal, but these deplete our mental energy drastically.[15] Optimizing your physical and emotional state, single tasking, and learning to focus your attention through mindfulness meditation are ways to boost your mental energy.

4. **Spiritual energy** is an unseen, non-physical life force or essence that connects us to a higher power, the universe, or our own inner consciousness, which can be derived from the sense of living with purpose. To experience a force of spiritual energy, your daily experiences should validate your highest personal values. Deepak Chopra describes three paths to follow through which to connect more profoundly with your values and purpose, based on various wisdom traditions. These are the paths of love and devotion, action and service, and knowledge and truth. By following these paths, you can connect with an underlying essence or life force that unites all existence, bringing you a sense of inner completeness and wholeness. Once you find the path that fits you best, it will become the easiest and most natural one for you to follow.[16]

To get a sense of how well you are balancing your energy across the four dimensions, I invite you to do an energy audit. Review each of the sources of energy in the following figure, asking yourself which, if any, feel over or under stressed. Although the examples are not meant to be comprehensive, they will give you an immediate window of awareness into what requires your dedicated focus.

Figure 2.5: Sources of energy

THE BODY
PHYSICAL: THE QUANTITY OF YOUR ENERGY

- Good quality of sleep
- Regular exercise routine
- Hydration and nutritious, healthy food
- Regular breaks during the day
- Taking in nature using all your senses

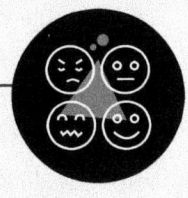

THE EMOTIONS
EMOTIONAL: THE QUALITY OF YOUR ENERGY

- Have compassion toward self and others
- Become aware of how you feel
- Control emotions and reactions
- Express emotions, incl. appreciation
- Release negative emotions, incl. trauma

Sources of Energy

THE MIND
MENTAL: THE FOCUS OF YOUR ENERGY

- Focus attention
- Take one thing at a time
- Quiet the mind chatter (seek stillness)
- Condition the mind (beliefs, expectations, perspectives)
- Leverage long-term activities

THE SPIRIT
SPIRITUAL: THE FORCE OF YOUR ENERGY

- Demonstrate core values in everyday behaviors
- Prioritize meaningful and purposeful experiences, relationships, and goals
- Explore the paths of love and devotion, action and service, and knowledge and truth
- Expand consciousness

Western and Eastern Approaches to Energy

To build a trusted, conscious partnership with your energy, I encourage you to explore the vast science and wisdom on energy balancing from both Western and Eastern approaches. The Western approach typically focuses on metabolism, integrating nutrition and diet, caloric balance, hydration, exercise and physical activity, rest and sleep, circadian rhythms, hormonal balance, stress reduction, lifestyle choices, and medical interventions that promote optimal energy levels and overall health. The Eastern approach provides greater insight into the laws of inner energy, based on traditional philosophies and thousands of years of empirical knowledge, particularly of Chinese and Indian origin. Systems such as the chakras (India) and dantians (China) are described as the centers of energy in our bodies, and healing practices focus on balancing and activating the vital flow of energy in the body, which is referred to as Qi. Examples of practices include mindfulness, stillness meditation, yoga poses (asanas), breathing techniques (pranayama), Tai Chi, Qigong, acupuncture, acupressure, aligning to natural rhythms, herbal remedies, and a nourishing diet that is in harmony with one's constitution or with the season. Both Western and Eastern approaches incorporate elements rooted in scientific understanding, but they may differ in their methodologies and philosophical foundations.

BOOSTING YOUR WELL-BEING THROUGH BALANCING YOUR ENERGY

With greater awareness, the right mindset, and small changes in behavior, we can learn to optimize our body's natural capacity to bring renewed vigor to our body, mind, and spirit. Though all the chapters in this book illuminate different paths toward achieving this goal, I want to focus here on three foundational strategies to balance your energy. These strategies are aimed at addressing the most significant hurdles we may experience when on the journey. Remind yourself that success is in incorporating the following strategies into your daily habits with discipline and self-compassion, so that the desired energy comes not just in glimpses but becomes lasting and permanent.

1. **Awareness: Anchor into your body.**
Energy Hurdle: You feel overwhelmed by the advice on energy "out there."
Energy Strategy: Anchor into your body for awareness about what is needed "in here."

Knowledge is power, but the vast science, wisdom traditions, information from smart wearables that track your energy data, and advice "out there" may also be overwhelming. You may wonder where to start changing your habitual patterns to gain greater energy. Therefore, the first strategy is to build a trusted relationship with your body, creating awareness about what's needed "in here." This strategy is about anchoring into your body and assessing your energy levels two or three times a day for ten to fifteen minutes. In his book *Quantum Body: The New Science of Living a Longer, Healthier, More Vital Life,* Deepak Chopra describes how this process, called interoception, concerns a sixth sense for how our bodies feel on the inside. Your body is constantly sending signals that usually stay below the radar. Understanding what's going on inside will increase the sensitivity of your interoception, expanding your ability to respond with the restorative and nourishing energy practices that work for you.[17]

For this practice, find a spot where you can sit or lie quietly with your eyes closed without interruption. Take a few deep, abdominal breaths to become more centered in your body by activating the vagus nerve, which governs the relaxation response of your parasympathetic nervous system.[18] Now, begin to scan your body, following the steps in the figure on the next page. As you observe all these parts of your physical, emotional, and mental self, it is as if you are switching on a light. First, notice what's changing, such as your heart rate, breathing, muscle tension, or stomach contraction. Second, use these physical sensations as triggers to an emotion, which can be negative or positive. A faster heart rate may indicate anxiety, nervousness, sexual stimulation, or an impulse of love; be curious about what you find. Resist the urge to escape the sensation if it is unpleasant. Take deep, easy breaths, and let loving awareness soothe the emotion or area that beckons attention. Third, identify the emotion, and give it a name. Allow every emotion the dignity of its existence. Then you can decide if you take it to heart or let it go. As you are opening up to all your body's signals, ask your body what it needs to be in an optimal state for what you've set out to do, and

Figure 2.6: Tuning in to your body

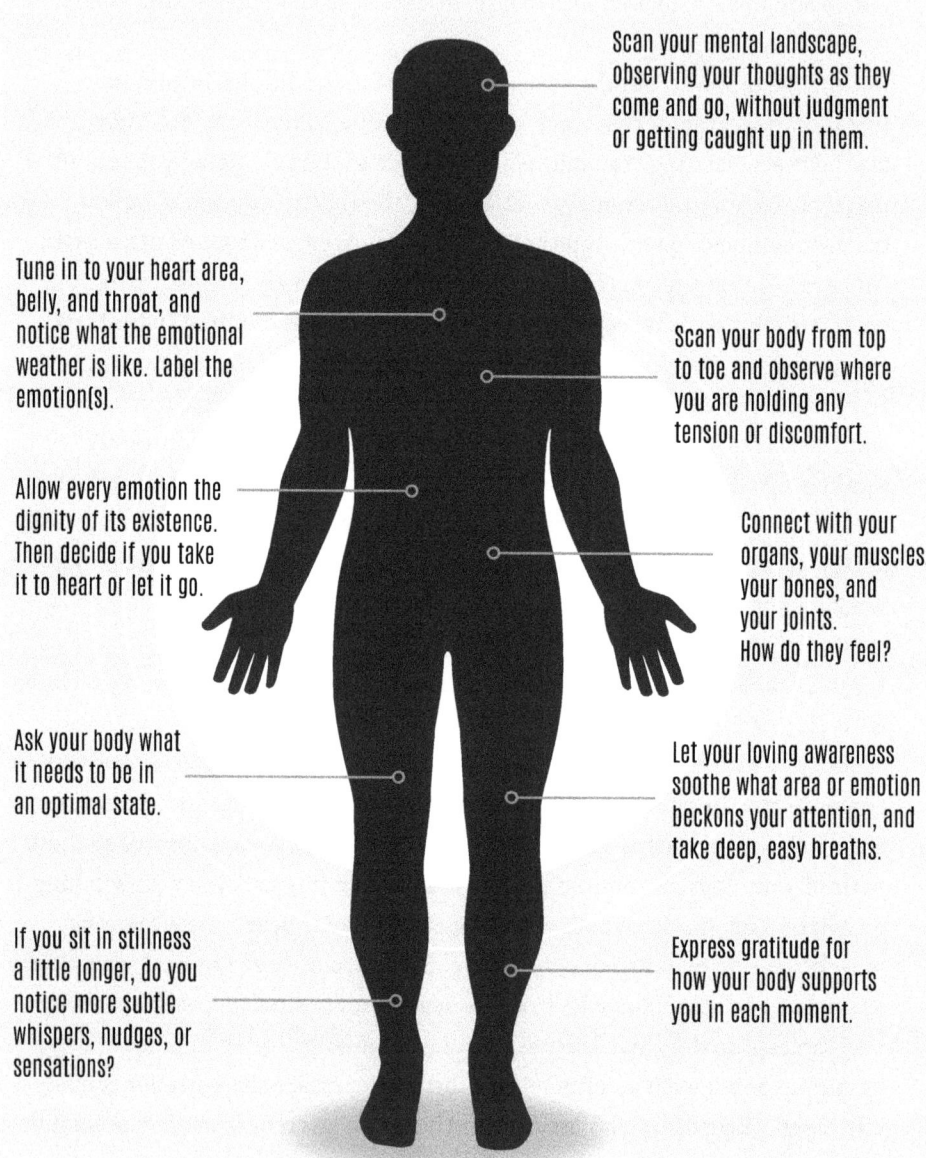

Scan your mental landscape, observing your thoughts as they come and go, without judgment or getting caught up in them.

Tune in to your heart area, belly, and throat, and notice what the emotional weather is like. Label the emotion(s).

Scan your body from top to toe and observe where you are holding any tension or discomfort.

Allow every emotion the dignity of its existence. Then decide if you take it to heart or let it go.

Connect with your organs, your muscles, your bones, and your joints. How do they feel?

Ask your body what it needs to be in an optimal state.

Let your loving awareness soothe what area or emotion beckons your attention, and take deep, easy breaths.

If you sit in stillness a little longer, do you notice more subtle whispers, nudges, or sensations?

Express gratitude for how your body supports you in each moment.

what you can let go of. At the end of this practice, express gratitude for your body, as you are making it a sanctuary for well-being and vitality.

When you make this internal sensory awareness a daily habit, you build new circuitry within your body and brain that enables the mind to perceive your energy in more subtle ways, allowing for an optimal response to life from a more deeply embodied and integrated state. This is how you can begin to eliminate the imbalances that are the basis of (chronic) fatigue and restore a natural energy flow where you feel more soft, open, pliable, relaxed, and joyful. Remind yourself that you can't go wrong. Merely, the non-judgemental observation of the energy that is in you boosts its natural flow. It allows you to accept the ebb and flow of your energy with understanding and compassion. Over time, this non-judgemental awareness should make you feel more comfortable in your body and ready to pick up on signs of internal distress.

2. Mindset: From victimhood to creatorship.
Energy Hurdle: You feel stuck in survival mode.
Energy Strategy: Shift your mindset from victimhood to creatorship.

A massive game changer in managing your energy is to transform your inner perspective from victim to creator. As harsh as it may sound, your life reflects that choice. Your energy arises not just from the circumstances of your life but from the conditioning of your mind. You are the creator of your own life, and what can you imagine that is more beautiful than stepping into your full energetic power? In *The Energy Codes: The 7-Step System to Awaken Your Spirit, Heal Your Body, and Live Your Best Life*, Sue Morter explains that we can operate from three different perspectives.[19] It's up to us which perspective to choose, as illustrated in Figure 2.7 on the next page.

In reviewing these three perspectives, or stages, ask yourself where you spend most of the time. How does this impact your energy?

Figure 2.7: Three distinct levels of consciousness to reclaim your energy

 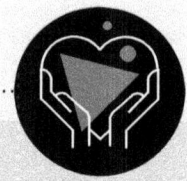 

VICTIMHOOD

- Life is happening *to* me.
- Opposing outside forces seem to be beyond my control. I am unable to do what I want most of the time.
- Operating in survival mode (fatalism, resignation).
- Characterized by fear, anger, hopelessness, helplessness and struggle: "protecting myself."

SELF-HELP

- Life is happening *to* me but I choose to make the best of it.
- Something is broken and needs fixing, but there is something I can do about it.
- Operating on the level of "doing" (problem-solving).
- Characterized by feelings of inadequacy and lacking.

CREATORSHIP

- Life is happening *for* me.
- Every challenge is an opportunity for expansion, mastery, and growth.
- Operating on the level of "being" (embodiment).
- Characterized by feelings of trust and empowerment, inspiration, and fulfillment: "creating life."

Consciously choosing creatorship sheds a completely different light on how you can be present with life's stressful events. With this mindset, every hinderance becomes an opportunity for expansion and growth, and every effort is a path to mastery. What if your greatest pain was actually hiding the greatest gift you would ever receive? What if your greatest challenges uncovered your truest talents? You're essentially working with all that you are in the present moment, feeling empowered by the thought that every life experience is a meaningful step that takes you deeper into your wholeness, your true self, or the light of your own being. You spend less energy seeking outside approval or validation because it wells up from within instead. This state of mind enables you to experience the highest quality of emotions, which leads to positive and balanced energy.

3. **Change: Become a healer of stress.**
Energy Hurdle: You slip back into your old routines.
Energy Strategy: Maintain restful alertness to become a healer of stress.

Sometimes external demands bring you out of balance, and you resort to old routines. You can't exist in both a peaceful, meditative state and a stressful state at the same time. By meditative state, I mean a state of restful alertness in which you feel calm and centered, but also very awake, like you practiced using the first strategy. The goal is not to become perfectly stress free but to consider areas in your professional and private life where you can reduce stress. In this vein, Deepak Chopra poses three questions[20] you can ask yourself every day:

- Am I creating stress?

- Am I reacting to stress from outside?

- Am I helping to reduce and heal the stress?

When you move past creating and reacting to stress, you reject the role of the victim and become an active healer of strain or pressure we suffer from. Each of us is a creator of our own stress, and it can spread like a virus. Energy moves through people. By reversing your behavior in relation to stress, you can both heal stress and break free from toxic workplace behaviors and harmful dynamics in your home environment. A positive and loving environment will contribute to maintaining balanced energy more sustainably.

CLOSING THOUGHTS

Life is a process of endless renewal. Every moment brings a new opportunity to step into the best version of you. With loving awareness, an empowered mindset, and small changes of behavior, we shine more brightly. Our energy radiates outward, inspiring others to do the same. I will leave you with the words of Rumi, the Persian poet who testified to the hidden beauty behind all things: "You are the universe in ecstatic motion."

RESOURCES FOR EXPLORATION AND LEARNING

TOP 3: ARTICLES

Creary, S., and K. Locke. (2021, November 16). **To reduce the strain of overwork, learn to listen to your body.** *Harvard Business Review.*
▶ tinyurl.com/bdzzvjam
We can learn to engage with our body differently to help with adverse symptoms of overwork. This article draws upon research to bring some practical advice to let go of work stress due to excess workloads and harmful work norms by bringing awareness to your body.

Maslach, C., and M. P. Leiter. (2021, March 19). **How to measure burnout accurately and ethically.** *Harvard Business Review.*
▶ tinyurl.com/4hdakjne
To better understand fatigue and burnout, and to diagnose it, this article provides insight into the first scientifically developed measure of burnout, called the Maslach Burnout Inventory (MBI), used for individual diagnosis or organizational metrics.

Schwartz, T., and C. McCarthy. (2007, October). **Manage your energy, not your time.** *Harvard Business Review.*
▶ tinyurl.com/mtjwk7sd
A well-known article discussing how managing your energy, not your time, leads to greater productivity and better performance. It describes how habits are the foundation to systematically expand and renew energy in the context of an organization.

TOP 3: BOOKS

Chopra, D., J. Tuszynski, and B. Fertig. (2022). **Quantum Body: The New Science of Living a Longer, Healthier, More Vital Life.** New York: Harmony Books.
This book tackles how to build a conscious relationship with your body and spirit, based on concepts of quantum physics and the fundamental nature of consciousness. It provides a combination of prescriptive exercises and scientific research on how we can shift our sense of reality to achieve a new level of whole-body energy and well-being.

Eden, D., and D. Feinstein. (2008). **Energy Medicine: Balancing Your Body's Energies for Optimal Health, Joy, and Vitality.** New York: TarcherPerigee.
At nearly 400 pages, this book is a comprehensive guide for gaining insight into our energy systems, providing many practical tips for balancing our body's energies for optimal health, joy, and vitality.

Komaroff, A. L., and S. Clifford-Higby. (2020) **Boosting Your Energy: How to Jump-Start Your Natural Energy and Fight Fatigue.** Boston: Harvard Medical School.
To obtain a science-based and medical approach to increasing your energy through foundational lifestyle adjustments, this guide from Harvard Medical School is a good place to start.

 TOP 3: VIDEOS

 Daily Energy Routine. Donna Eden.
▶ tinyurl.com/mpkvk8hu
Daily Energy Routine: This is a quick and easy "energy habit" that you can perform in five to seven minutes to build your immune system, gain energy, feel younger, and relieve pain, by Donna Eden, a pioneer of energy medicine.

 The Mind-Body Connection: A Guided Meditation. Deepak Chopra.
▶ tinyurl.com/ycyh5v5a
Coming from the fundamental notion that our minds and bodies are connected, this guided meditation by Deepak Chopra will help you to learn more about the mind-body connection and strengthen that connection within yourself for more energy.

 The Mind-Body Connection: Is Your Brain Making You Sick? Eckhart Tolle.
▶ tinyurl.com/52nav8r2
This twelve-minute video with spiritual teacher and author Eckhart Tolle explains how our state of mind can greatly affect our physical and mental well-being, and how the practice of being present in the moment, through awareness and acceptance, can lead to improved health and overall energy.

 TOP 3: APPS

 Aura
▶ tinyurl.com/ufxeu4kw
This app leads you to specific, personalized content to boost your energy, offering not just meditations, courses, and sound healing but also prayers, energy healing, hypnosis, and cognitive behavioral therapy.

 Calm
▶ tinyurl.com/28xcdr23
This app is known for its guided meditations and sounds to find calm and sleep better, but it also offers some great content to sharpen your focus, tune out distractions, and tap into a state of flow.

Insight Timer
▶ tinyurl.com/s38e428f
To balance your energy and strengthen the body-mind connection, this app provides an endless library for guided meditations, music, courses, and talks, led by the world's top meditation and mindfulness experts, neuroscientists, psychologists, and teachers.

TOP 3: PRODUCTS

Inner Balance Coherence Plus Sensor
▶ tinyurl.com/muj7pyjr
The Inner Balance Coherence Plus sensor is a clip-on wearable that translates your heart rhythm patterns into a real-time coherence score and supporting visuals that help you establish more wholesome breathing patterns for better overall energy.

NOWATCH: Personalized Health Tracking for Stress, Sleep, and Habits
▶ tinyurl.com/b59aptwn
The NOWATCH is a wearable that helps you grow your energy awareness with biosensing technology, reading your heart rate, physical movements, sleep patterns, respiratory rate, and your "cognitive zone" (mental focus). It helps you build habits to feel more calm, strong, and present in the now.

Oura Ring
▶ tinyurl.com/3drwxu37
The Oura Ring is an energy awareness wearable in the form of a ring. Precise sensors provide accurate reading for over twenty biometrics, including heart rate, heart rate variability, body temperature, oxygen, activity, sleep monitoring technology, and more, helping you to adapt your lifestyle to experience more energy and better sleep.

ENDNOTES

1   Gallup. (2023). State of the global workplace: 2023 report. tinyurl.com/yc3yfky6

2   World Health Organization. (2019, May 28). Burn-out an "occupational phenomenon": International Classification of Diseases. tinyurl.com/mpu6jawp

3   J. Brassey, B. Herbig, B. Jefferey, and D. Ungerman. (2023, November 2). Reframing employee health: Moving beyond burnout to achieving physical, mental, social, and spiritual health. McKinsey Health Institute. tinyurl.com/4sra5nxw

4   T. Schwartz and C. McCarthy (2007). Manage your energy, not your time.
    Harvard Business Review. tinyurl.com/mtjwk7sd

5   D. Eden and D. Feinstein. (2008). *Energy Medicine: Balancing Your Body's Energies for
    Optimal Health, Joy, and Vitality.* New York: TarcherPerigee, pp. 2-3.

6   D. Chopra, J. Tuszynski, and B. Fertig. (2022). *Quantum Body: The New Science of Living
    a Longer, Healthier, More Vital Life.* New York: Harmony Books.

7   A. Kandola and A. Sharon. (2023, February 17). What is chronic stress and what are its
    common health impacts? Medical News Today. tinyurl.com/u46rsc68

8   C. Bergland. (2017, May 15). A vagus nerve survival guide to combat fight-or-flight urges.
    Psychology Today. tinyurl.com/y7e8h3mm

9   E. Bird. (2022, April 5). Anxiety prescriptions on the rise among young adults.
    Medical News Today. tinyurl.com/v5ams9cn

10 H. Godman. (2023). Ways to maximize your energy. Harvard Health Publishing.
    tinyurl.com/2p9z83zb

11 T. Schwartz and J. Loehr. (2003). *The Power of Full Engagement: Managing Energy,
    Not Time, Is the Key to High Performance and Personal Renewal.* New York: Free Press.

12 J. Allen and J. Macomber. (2020). *Healthy Buildings: How Indoor Spaces Drive Performance
    and Productivity.* Cambridge, MA: Harvard University Press; R. Lovell. (2022).
    How modern food can regain its nutrients. BBC. tinyurl.com/5fn8t72n

13 Q. Li. (2018, May 1). "Forest bathing" is great for your health. Here's how to do it. *Time.*
    tinyurl.com/37a77eyy

14 T. Pychyl. (2009, February 8). Approaching success, avoiding the undesired:
    Does goal type matter? Psychology Today. tinyurl.com/3pp8jruz

15 H. Griffey. (2018, October 14). The lost art of concentration: Being distracted in a digital
    world. *Guardian.* tinyurl.com/2tractma

16 D. Chopra and K. Snyder. (2016). *Radical Beauty: How to Transform from the Inside Out.*
    New York: Harmony Books, pp. 258-60.

17 Chopra, Tuszynski, and Fertig 2022, pp. 50-58.

18 C. Bergland. (2017, May 16). Diaphragmatic breathing exercises and your vagus nerve.
    Psychology Today. tinyurl.com/2t3r3apr

19 S. Morter. (2019). *The Energy Codes: The 7-Step System to Awaken Your Spirit, Heal Your Body,
    and Live Your Best Life.* New York: Atria Books.

20 Chopra and Snyder 2016, p. 279.

NUTRITION

Written by Marcella Sarno

INTRODUCTION

Over the past fifty years, the field of nutrition has undergone a profound transformation, driven by scientific advancements, shifting societal attitudes, and changing food production systems. The concept of nutrition has transcended mere sustenance to become a holistic approach to wellness, encompassing physical, mental, and emotional well-being. This evolution has been reflected in the foods we consume, the dietary guidelines we follow, and the advertising campaigns that have shaped our perceptions of what constitutes a healthy diet.

> **"Let food be thy medicine and medicine be thy food."**
> —HIPPOCRATES

Personal Story

John's Digestive Health:

For years, John had been silently battling digestive issues that left him feeling uncomfortable and frustrated. Bloating and irregular bowel movements had become a regular part of his life, affecting his mood and overall well-being. Tired of feeling this way, John consulted a nutritionist who specialized in digestive health.

The nutritionist carefully analyzed John's diet and lifestyle to identify potential triggers for his digestive issues. It became evident that John's diet lacked sufficient fiber, a vital component in promoting a healthy gut, and that he was consuming processed foods more often than nutrient-rich options.

The nutritionist recommended a dietary plan that incorporated fiber-rich foods such as fresh fruits, leafy vegetables, and whole grains. With determination, John embraced these dietary changes, welcoming colorful salads, hearty bowls of oatmeal, and a variety of fresh produce into his meals. In addition to the increased fiber intake, the nutritionist proposed an elimination diet to identify potential food intolerances that might be aggravating John's digestive system. Following the plan, John temporarily excluded certain foods commonly known to cause sensitivities, including gluten and dairy, from his diet.

Through the process of gradually reintroducing specific foods, John attentively monitored his body's response. Surprisingly, he discovered that certain foods he had considered staples were causing adverse reactions.

As the weeks passed, John's digestive symptoms began to subside. The bloating decreased, and his bowel movements became more regular, providing him with a newfound sense of relief. His energy levels increased, and he noticed improvements in his overall health.

With time, John's perseverance paid off. The newfound freedom from discomfort and improved gut health brought about a sense of empowerment and joy that radiated into other aspects of his life.

John's journey taught him the significance of nourishing his body with the right foods. The positive results inspired him to continue with a fiber-rich diet and making conscious choices about the foods he consumed. From that moment on, John's digestive health no longer held him back, and he embraced each day with newfound vitality and enthusiasm.

In the 1970s, nutrition researchers linked diet to diseases and blamed fat for weight and heart issues, leading to the development of low-fat products. One of the most prominent examples from this era was the advertising campaign by the margarine industry that promoted the switch from butter to margarine. But science showed the fat story was more complex.[1]

The 1980s brought a more comprehensive understanding of nutrition, with a particular focus on the balance of macronutrients. The introduction of the Food Guide Pyramid by the United States Department of Agriculture in 1992 was a milestone in nutrition education. The pyramid underscored the importance of consuming a variety of foods from different food groups, with a strong emphasis on carbohydrates as the primary source of energy. This led to the increased consumption of processed grains such as refined bread and pasta, which were marketed as healthy choices. Around the same time, Italy saw a notable rise in Mediterranean diet awareness, highlighted by TV ads endorsing olive oil's health benefits. In addition, a charismatic Italian chef became the face of a campaign linking olive oil to the traditional Mediterranean diet, further boosting its adoption across Italy.

In the twenty-first century, nutrition has become a subject of increasing complexity and scrutiny, spurred by mounting evidence of the impact of diet on health outcomes. The emergence of social media and the rise of wellness influencers has also fueled a shift toward personalized nutrition and the popularity of fad diets. One notable example is the rise of gluten-free diets, propelled by the perception that gluten consumption is detrimental to overall health. Food companies quickly capitalized on this trend, flooding supermarket shelves with gluten-free alternatives and labeling products as gluten-free even when gluten was never present in the original formulation.

In recent years, there has been a growing focus on whole, minimally processed foods for optimal health, moving away from fixation on specific nutrients. Campaigns such as "Know Your Food, Know Your Farmer" highlight local, organic produce and sustainable farming, thus connecting nutrition, sustainability, and responsibility.

Instead of strict diets, people now consider broader factors that affect their food choices, recognizing how environment and lifestyle impact well-being. Nutrition is seen as interconnected with stress, sleep, activity, and social interactions. This holistic approach promotes balanced, unprocessed meals; mindfulness; and sustainable choices for lasting health.

HOW DOES NUTRITION SUPPORT YOUR WELL-BEING?

The relationship between nutrition and well-being has garnered increasing attention from researchers, health professionals, and the general public. It is now widely recognized that our dietary choices play a crucial role in determining our physical and mental well-being. The science behind how nutrition impacts well-being is a complex and multifaceted field that encompasses various disciplines, including biochemistry, physiology, and psychology.

This section aims to delve into the scientific evidence that elucidates the relationship between nutrition and well-being, emphasizing the importance of maintaining a healthy and balanced diet for optimal physical and mental health.

Nutrition and mental health. One of the most significant aspects of the impact of nutrition on well-being is its effect on mental health. Numerous studies have established a strong association between inadequate nutrient intake and the development of mental disorders such as depression, anxiety, and cognitive decline.[2] For instance, deficiencies in omega-3 fatty acids, B vitamins, zinc, and magnesium have been linked to an increased risk of depression and anxiety disorders.[3] Similarly, insufficient intake of iron, iodine, and vitamin B12 can impair cognitive function, affecting memory, concentration, and overall cognitive performance. Increasingly, researchers have concluded that the diets of people with mental health disorders lack key nutrients for brain health, and that replenishing these nutrients can play an important role in treating those disorders.

> **"... Diet is as important to psychiatry as it is to cardiology, endocrinology, and gastroenterology."**
> —Jerome Sarris et al.[4]

The emerging field of nutritional psychiatry is a fast-growing approach that uses food and supplements in the treatment of mental health conditions.[5] Nutritional psychiatry has shed light on the intricate connection between the gut and the brain, known as the gut-brain axis.[6] The gut microbiota, or the diverse community of microorganisms residing in our digestive tract, plays a crucial role in regulating brain function and mental health. A healthy and balanced diet rich in fiber, whole grains, fruits, and vegetables promotes the growth of beneficial gut bacteria, which produce neurotransmitters and metabolites that positively influence mood and cognition.[7] Conversely, a diet high in processed foods, sugar, and unhealthy fats disrupts the gut microbiota, leading to inflammation and an increased risk of mental health disorders.

Nutrition and physical health. Nutrition plays a pivotal role in our overall well-being, and its profound impact on our physical health cannot be overstated. Nutrition has been shown to possess remarkable qualities for combating inflammation, a key driver of various chronic diseases.[8] Through a balanced and nutrient-rich diet, we can harness the power of food to modulate our body's inflammatory response, thereby promoting optimal health. Foods such as fruits, vegetables, whole grains, and fatty fish rich in omega-3 fatty acids are known to possess anti-inflammatory properties. They contain a wide array of bioactive compounds, including antioxidants and phytochemicals, which help reduce inflammation at the cellular level. Additionally, proper nutrition supports the body's immune system, thus ensuring efficient defense against harmful pathogens and aiding tissue repair and recovery.[9] By embracing the principles of nutrition, we can empower ourselves to nurture our bodies from within, fostering a harmonious balance and vibrant physical health.

When discussing the relationship between nutrition, inflammation, and physical health, it is important to mention the work of Dan Buettner, a renowned researcher and *New York Times* best-selling author known for his expertise in longevity and healthy aging.[10] Buettner has extensively studied populations in areas of the world known as blue zones, where people live exceptionally long and healthy lives. One of the key factors he has identified in these blue zones is the presence of a plant-based, nutrient-dense diet that naturally combats inflammation and promotes overall well-being. Buettner's findings emphasize the importance of adopting dietary patterns rich in fruits, vegetables, whole grains, and healthy fats, which have been scientifically proven to reduce chronic inflammation and contribute to enhanced physical health. By incorporating Buettner's research into our understanding of nutrition, we can further appreciate the profound impact of a healthy diet on inflammation and its role in optimizing our overall health and longevity.

BOOSTING YOUR WELL-BEING THROUGH NUTRITION

Evidence-based practices play a crucial role in promoting improved, sustainable nutrition given that they consider the well-being of both people and the planet and provide a reliable foundation for making informed dietary choices. To achieve sustainable nutrition, it is essential to acknowledge the concept of bio-individuality. Bio-individuality recognizes that each person has unique nutritional needs, preferences, and genetic factors. Tailoring nutrition plans to individual requirements can optimize health outcomes and ensure long-term adherence. By considering bio-individuality and incorporating evidence-based practices such as consuming a plant-based diet, choosing organic and locally sourced foods, minimizing food waste, and supporting sustainable farming methods, we can foster a healthy and sustainable relationship with food, benefiting both our own well-being and the environment.

A nutrition plan using the bio-individuality approach may include the following components:

- **Assessment.** Review a person's health status, medical history, dietary habits, lifestyle, and specific health goals. Gather information on any allergies, intolerances, or health conditions that may influence dietary choices.

- **Identify bio-individual factors.** Recognize that each person has unique bio-individual factors such as metabolism, genetic makeup, gut health, and nutrient needs. Consider these factors while designing a nutrition plan.

- **Personalized macronutrient ratios.** Determine the most suitable macronutrient ratios (carbohydrates, proteins, and fats) based on the person's health status, activity level, and body composition goals.

- **Food preferences.** Take into account the person's food preferences and cultural background. Design a plan that includes foods they enjoy and are willing to incorporate into their daily routine.

- **Identify nutrient-rich foods.** Focus on nutrient-dense foods that provide essential vitamins, minerals, and antioxidants.

- **Address special dietary needs.** Consider any special dietary needs such as vegetarian or vegan preferences, gluten intolerance, or lactose intolerance, and adjust the plan accordingly.

Implementing evidence-based practices and following practical tips are essential for achieving sustainable nutrition improvement. By incorporating scientifically supported strategies into our dietary habits, we can promote long-term health and well-being. The figure below provides some evidence-based practices and tips for fostering sustainable nutrition improvement.

Figure 2.8: Dietary habits promoting long-term health and well-being

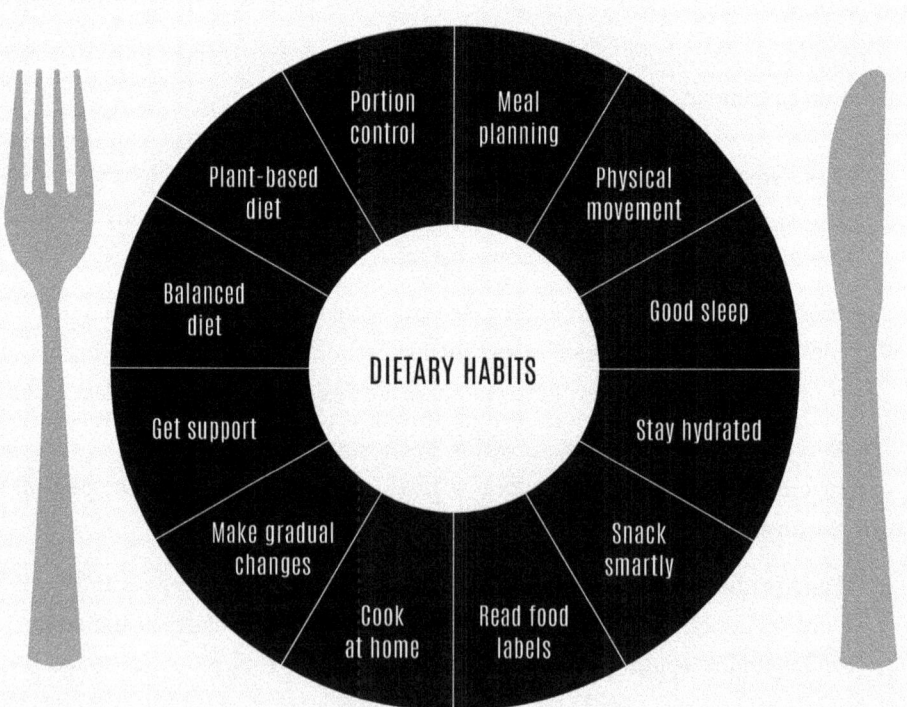

Balanced diet. A balanced diet includes a variety of whole foods from different food groups, ensuring the intake of essential nutrients. Emphasize the consumption of fruits, vegetables, whole grains, lean proteins, and healthy fats while minimizing processed and sugary foods.

Plant-based diet. Plant-based diets are rich in fiber, vitamins, minerals, and phytonutrients while simultaneously lower in saturated fat and cholesterol. Moreover, a plant-based diet promotes sustainability by minimizing the ecological footprint, conserving water, and curbing deforestation. From enhancing heart health and managing weight to supporting biodiversity and mitigating climate change, the advantages of a plant-based diet extend far beyond the plate, making it a compelling choice for a healthier future.

Portion control. Managing portion sizes is crucial for maintaining a healthy weight and preventing overeating. Be mindful of portion sizes, listen to your body's hunger and fullness cues, and avoid super-sized servings.

> 腹八分目に医者いらず
> —*Hara hachi bun me ni isha irazu.*

This Japanese proverb translates to "Eating to only 80% full keeps the doctors away." *Hara hachi bun me* is a 2,500-year old Japanese Confucian teaching that means "stomach eight parts full."

Meal planning. Plan your meals in advance to ensure a well-rounded diet. Incorporate a mix of macronutrients (carbohydrates, proteins, and fats) and include a colorful variety of fruits and vegetables. Meal planning can also help save time and money by reducing impulsive food choices and decreasing food waste. Meal prepping can be a game changer in a nutrition journey.

Physical movement. Regular exercise complements a healthy diet by boosting metabolism, improving cardiovascular health, and promoting weight management. Engaging in activities such as walking, jogging, swimming, or strength training for at least thirty minutes a day can greatly enhance overall health (see chapter 2.5: Physical Movement).

Good sleep. Inadequate sleep is consistently linked to negative impacts on diet, metabolism, and overall nutrition. In particular, numerous studies have revealed that insufficient sleep leads to consuming more calories, especially from high-fat and high-carb foods.[11] Sleep loss disturbs appetite hormone controls such as leptin and ghrelin, thereby triggering hunger and cravings for unhealthy foods. Enhancing sleep is supported by certain nutrients. Tryptophan-rich foods (e.g., turkey, nuts, dairy) boost serotonin for sleep regulation. Magnesium in foods such as greens, nuts, and whole grains calms the nervous system (refer to chapter 2.2: Sleep).

Good hydration. Stay hydrated by drinking adequate water throughout the day, approximately 32 ounces or 2.5 liters per day.[12] Water is essential for maintaining bodily functions, regulating body temperature, and supporting digestion. Carry a reusable water bottle and make water your primary beverage choice.

Snack smartly. Opt for nutritious snacks such as fruits, vegetables, nuts, and seeds instead of processed snacks high in added sugars and unhealthy fats. Keep healthy snacks readily available at home, work, or on the go to avoid reaching for unhealthy options.

Read food labels. Pay attention to food labels to make informed choices. Check for added sugars, artificial additives, and excessive sodium content. Choose products with simple and recognizable ingredients.

Cook at home. Cooking at home allows you to have control over the ingredients and cooking methods used. Experiment with healthy recipes, try new flavors, and involve family or friends in meal preparation.

Make gradual changes. Making gradual changes is more sustainable than drastic dietary overhauls. Start by incorporating small, achievable goals such as adding an extra serving of vegetables to your meals or swapping sugary beverages for water.

Get support. Enlisting the support of friends, family, or a nutrition specialist can provide accountability and motivation in achieving and maintaining a healthy diet. Sharing goals, progress, and challenges can make the journey more enjoyable and sustainable (see chapter 5.3: Social Environment).

Finally, as an integrative nutrition health coach, I wholeheartedly embrace the holistic approach to nutrition. I firmly believe that sustainable nutrition is essential, and it should be tailored to each individual's unique circumstances and aspirations. By adopting this comprehensive strategy, individuals can gain the power to make informed choices, develop positive routines, and foster a seamless link between their dietary selections and their overall well-being. This approach emphasizes the importance of considering not only the physical aspects of nutrition but also its impact on mental, emotional, and spiritual dimensions of health. It is through this holistic perspective that people can achieve lasting and transformative changes in their lives.

RESOURCES FOR EXPLORATION AND LEARNING

 TOP 3: ARTICLES

 Kolata, G. (2023, August 17). **We know where new weight loss drugs came from, but not why they work.** *New York Times.*
▶ tinyurl.com/ntemse3j
The article delves into the complex and multifaceted process that led to the development of drugs aimed at addressing obesity from a new perspective.

 Munteanu, C., and B. Schwartz. (2022). **The relationship between nutrition and the immune system.** *Frontiers in Nutrition 9.*
▶ tinyurl.com/3ye32xkh
This article explains how nutrition and health are highly interrelated and how the consumption of specific nutrients has a profound impact on human health.

 Selhub, E. (2022, September 18). **Nutritional psychiatry: Your brain on food.** Harvard Health Publishing.
▶ tinyurl.com/2544tsax
This article shows how what you eat directly affects the structure and function of your brain and, ultimately, your mood.

TOP 3: BOOKS

Buettner, D. (2023). **The Blue Zones Secrets for Living Longer: Lessons from the Healthiest Places on Earth.** Washington, DC: National Geographic.
From Amazon's description of the book: In his latest book, "Buettner returns to Sardinia, Italy; Ikaria, Greece; Okinawa, Japan; Costa Rica's Nicoya Peninsula; and Loma Linda, California, to check in on the super-agers living in the blue zones and interprets the not-so-secret sauce of purpose, faith, community, down-time, natural movement, and plant-based eating that has powered as many as 10 additional years of healthy living in these regions. And Buettner reveals an all-new blue zone—the first man-made blue zone yet explored."

Hyman, M. (2023). **Young Forever: The Secrets to Living Your Longest, Healthiest Life.** Boston: Little, Brown Spark.
From Amazon's description of the book: "To uncover the secrets to longevity, [Dr. Mark Hyman] explores the biological hallmarks of aging, their causes, and their consequences—then shows us how to overcome them with simple dietary, lifestyle, and emerging longevity strategies."

Sinclair, D. (2019). **Lifespan: Why We Age—and Why We Don't Have To.** London: Harper Collins.
From the Cielito Lindo senior living community's description of the book: "In this paradigm-shifting book from [an] acclaimed Harvard Medical School doctor and one of TIME magazine's 100 most influential people on earth, Dr. David Sinclair reveals that everything we think we know about aging is wrong, and shares the surprising, scientifically-proven methods that can help readers live younger, longer."

 TOP 3: ASSESSMENTS AND TESTS

 Circle of Life
▶ integrativenutrition.com/circle-of-life
From the Institute for Integrative Nutrition's website: "This exercise is a valuable tool for better understanding your unique needs and how to find balance when you're feeling stuck. By becoming more self-aware of what areas feel nourished and which could use more attention, you will discover how to continuously take care of your body, mind, and soul."

 My Plate: What's on your plate? Are you making every bite count?
▶ myplate.gov/myplate-quiz
MyPlate is a tool to find your healthy eating style and build it throughout your lifetime.

Vitamin Deficiency Test: What vitamins does your body need?
▶ freevitamindeficiencytest.com
This test examines about 300 deficiency symptoms related to about 50 vitamins and minerals.

TOP 3: VIDEOS

How to Live to Be 100+. Dan Buettner.
▶ tinyurl.com/46pfsxs2
From the description of the video: "To find the path to long life and health, Dan Buettner and team study the world's 'Blue Zones', communities whose elders live with vim and vigor to record-setting age. In his talk, he shares the 9 common diet and lifestyle habits that keep them spry past age 100."

How Nutrition Impacts Brain Development and Mental Health. The Dr. Axe Show.
▶ tinyurl.com/tjdnhvk2
From the description of the video: "Psychiatrist and New York Times best-selling author Dr. Daniel Amen discusses the importance of nutrition and the gut-brain connection. Dr. Amen shares his experience working with patients to determine how brain development and mental well-being can be optimized with proper nutrition and shares his tips on foods, supplements and daily habits."

How to Reduce Inflammation, Heal Your Gut, and Prevent Disease. Dr. Mark Hyman.
▶ tinyurl.com/48x7bd6z
In this episode, Dr. Hyman talks about the "gut-immune and gut-brain connection, what imbalances our gut health, and his top strategies for reducing inflammation and healing the gut."

TOP 3: PODCASTS

How Do Foods Affect Your Health? Daniel Amen.
▶ tinyurl.com/yuaf3rd9
This podcast is about the ways a poor diet can disrupt your health.

Merging Science with the Mystical. Dr. Andrew Weil.
▶ tinyurl.com/bdces4yc
The godfather of integrative medicine and a true pioneer of health,
Dr. Andrew Weil is a legend in the realm of mind-body healing.

The Silent Killer: Inflammation and Chronic Disease. Dr. Mark Hyman.
▶ tinyurl.com/mvhb7hs6
This podcast is about the top inflammation-fighting foods and what lifestyle
changes we can make to mitigate the effects of inflammation.

TOP 3: ONLINE COURSES

Eating Disorders. Oxford Home Study.
▶ tinyurl.com/3b4r66ut
In this course, learn how several different types of eating disorders impact the
health and well-being of those affected, while considering potential causes and
triggers of common eating disorders.

Human Health—Diet and Nutrition. Alison Empower Yourself.
▶ tinyurl.com/45z7vprc
In this diet and nutrition course, learn about making good food choices,
recommended dietary intakes (RDI), and the serious effects of diet-related diseases.

Stanford Introduction to Food and Health at Stanford. Careers 360.
▶ tinyurl.com/yc88we7c
This course aims to provide learners with the right knowledge and practical skills
required to optimize food consumption and cultivate dietary habits.

ENDNOTES

1   Harvard Health Publishing. (2020, January 29). Butter vs. margarine.
    tinyurl.com/5ywe3h45

2   T. S. Sathyanarayana Rao, M. R. Asha, B. N. Ramesh, and K. S. Rao. (2008). Understanding
    nutrition, depression and mental illnesses. *Indian Journal of Psychiatry 50* (2), pp. 77–82.
    tinyurl.com/2t9unddz

3   G. Deacon, C. Kettle, D. Hayes, C. Dennis, and J. Tucci. (2017). Omega 3 polyunsaturated
    fatty acids and the treatment of depression. *Critical Reviews in Food Science and Nutrition 57*
    (1), pp. 212–23. tinyurl.com/3knsep39; J. Sarris, A. C. Logan,
    T. N. Akbaraly, G. P. Amminger, V. Balanzá-Martínez, M. P. Freeman, J. Hibbeln, Y. Matsuoka,
    D. Mischoulon, T. Mizoue, A. Nanri, D. Nishi, D. Ramsey, J. J. Rucklidge, A. Sanchez-Villegas,
    A. Scholey, K.-P. Su, and F. N. Jacka. (2015). Nutritional medicine as mainstream in
    psychiatry. *Lancet Psychiatry 2*, pp. 271–74. tinyurl.com/5n82sjst

4   Sarris et al. 2015.

5   R. A. H. Adan, E. M. van der Beek, J. K. Buitelaar, J. F. Cryan, J. Hebebrand, S. Higgs,
    H. Schellekens, and S. L. Dickson. (2019). Nutritional psychiatry: Towards improving
    mental health by what you eat. *European Neuropsychopharmacology 29* (12), pp. 1321–32.
    tinyurl.com/2xdhdkdw

6   M. Carabotti, A. Scirocco, M. A. Maselli, and C. Severi. (2015). The gut-brain axis:
    Interactions between enteric microbiota, central and enteric nervous systems.
    Annals of Gastroenterology 28 (2), pp. 203–9. tinyurl.com/4zufx7jx

7   K. Berding, C. Carbia, and J. F. Cryan. (2021). Going with the grain: Fiber, cognition,
    and the microbiota-gut-brain-axis. *Experimental Biology and Medicine 246* (7), pp. 796–811.
    tinyurl.com/y9yke7fb

8   L. Galland. (2010). Diet and inflammation. *Nutrition in Clinical Practice 25* (6), pp. 634–40.
    tinyurl.com/6wcdks59

9   A. F. Gombart, A. Pierre, and S. Maggini. (2020). A review of micronutrients and the
    immune system—Working in harmony to reduce the risk of infection. *Nutrients 12* (1),
    p. 236. tinyurl.com/mute7udk

10 D. Buettner. (2008). *The Blue Zones: 9 Lessons for Living Longer from the People Who've Lived the
    Longest.* Washington, DC: National Geographic.

11 P. Prinz. (2004). Sleep, appetite, and obesity—What is the link? *PLoS Medicine 1* (3), p. e61.
    tinyurl.com/28xucykc

12 H. E. LeWine. (2023, May 22). How much water should you drink? Harvard Health Publishing.
    tinyurl.com/bdpzh4ub

PHYSICAL MOVEMENT

Written by Dr. Sanae Tabnaoui

INTRODUCTION

Picture yourself out for a walk. You notice someone moving slowly, shoulders hunched, gaze fixed on the ground. Their movement seems to narrate their distress. In contrast, imagine yourself walking upright, steps light and free with joyful exuberance. It is like you are dancing down the street, with your infectious smile and rhythm conveying a story of joy and vitality. These scenarios illustrate how physical movement (PM) reveals our profound emotions and experiences in ways words fall short of expressing.

> "Movement is the poetry of the body;
> it expresses what words cannot."
> —MARTHA GRAHAM

Personal Story

PM is a vital force that has guided me through life's toughest challenges and has sculpted my identity. In my adolescent years, marked by the loss of my parents, I found an unexpected sanctuary in my cultural roots—folk dance. Dancing to tunes that once echoed with my parents' laughter was an homage to them and a release for my sorrow. Using the feelings that arose, I let my body move me through dance, helping my grief pass through me. Discovering the joy of movement, both alone and in a group, was a source of freedom and peace that filled the void of my parents' absence and served as a reminder that amid the pain, I am alive.

Movement is my life's rhythm, a state of being rather than doing. Simple acts include stretching beside the coffee machine, subtly shifting while seated, and opting for the floor or a wobble board instead of a chair. I nod my head while listening and clarify my ideas through gestures that allow me to engage with others through many micro-movements. These daily dance steps infuse a joyful vitality into the routine.

Off the clock, the soccer field is my stage, where a group of us moves in sync with the game's tempo. This bond transcends the game, underlining the power of shared PM. When I dance or play soccer, it is like a reset button. PM sharpens my mind, opening fresh perspectives and imbuing life with renewed optimism. Each step, stretch, or shift in stance is part of our unique dance of life. As I continue my dance, it remains my joy, strength, and link to the world around me.

To help you enrich your unique personal narrative of movement, it is essential to challenge common beliefs about PM. Lines of evidence offer a fresh perspective, especially the research by Daniel E. Lieberman and colleagues, which focuses on understanding the evolution of human physical activity, especially human biomechanics and physiology, and has shed light on the complex nature of our evolutionary tendencies toward PM.[1]

In 2012, global health authorities described the health effects of physical inactivity as a pandemic. This stark warning reminds us that PM is one of the most potent preventive medicines to shield us against leading noncommunicable diseases, also known as chronic diseases. In fact, engaging in PM could prevent up to 8% of global mortality as well as provide social and economic benefits that directly contribute to achieving many of the United Nations Sustainable Development Goals (SDGs), which serve as a "universal call to action to end poverty, protect the planet, and ensure that by 2030 all people enjoy peace and prosperity."[2]

According to a 2022 World Health Organization (WHO) report, one in four adults is inactive, missing out on the chance to decrease up to 30% of their risk of dying prematurely compared to those who engage almost daily in thirty minutes of moderate-intensity PM.[3] However, PM has taken a backseat as we advance economically; urbanization and modern technology have turned us into inert bodies. Moreover, demands on professional performance further add to a sedentary lifestyle.

Despite being constantly bombarded with messages nudging us to "just do it," many people feel guilty about not following the recommended WHO prescriptions for PM (at least 150 minutes per week of moderate-intensity activities and two days per week of muscle-strengthening activities for adults).[4] But far from being lazy, we are in fact trapped in an "exercise paradox": we know that PM is good for us, yet we tend to avoid it. There is no reason to feel bad, however, because the central principle governing our dance of life is our biological imperative to conserve energy for reproduction, even if the trade-off leads to ill health or shorter life spans. For nearly two million years, we lived and evolved as hunter-gatherers adapted to be PM endurance athletes, who only moved out of necessity, playfulness, or survival. Hunter-gatherers never needed to undertake voluntary, planned, repetitive PM to improve their health and fitness—known today as exercise. But grasping our evolutionary realities enables us to enrich our movement narratives with the natural rhythm of our being.

Intriguingly, we burn the same number of daily calories as our ancestors, though they were six to ten times more active than we are and sat almost as much as we do: around 9.9 hours against 11 hours, on average.[5] This suggests that the real issue with sitting—which has been called the "new smoking"—is our prolonged, uninterrupted stillness combined with excessive caloric intake, which sets our bodies on fire. Excess fat accumulates in and around organs such as the heart, which can trigger chronic inflammation in the long term. Each hour spent sitting like a couch potato is a missed opportunity to engage in PM.

Characteristics of Physical Movement

Because energy is a cornerstone of human evolution, it is imperative to understand the different physical activity levels (PALs) of modern lifestyles, as shown in Table 2.1.[6] PAL is the total energy you spend in a day divided by the energy you spend on keeping your body alive while you do nothing, called the basal metabolic rate. Many people may not realize that just staying alive is expensive, requiring about 60% to 70% of daily caloric intake.

Table 2.1: Different physical activity levels (PALs) of modern lifestyles

Lifestyle	Description	Physical Activity Levels
Sedentary	Predominantly sitting still, reclining, or lying down.	1.2
Lightly active	Light body movements or office work, assuming six hours sitting and two hours standing.	1.6
Physically inactive	Describes adults who do not meet WHO recommendations for PM.	Less than 1.7
Moderately active	**a)** Predominantly standing work. **b)** Office work with active lifestyle: 90 minutes resting, or 30 minutes shopping and one hour of light activity at home (domestic tasks, light gardening), or one hour walking rather than going by car.	1.7 1.9
Vigorously active	**a)** Physical work or dancing two hours per day. **b)** Professional athletes such as a Tour de France cyclist.	2.3 4.5

HOW DOES PHYSICAL MOVEMENT SUPPORT YOUR WELL-BEING?

Life is a constant flow of energy, a perpetual dance that is expressed on a molecular level and impacts each cell of your body. Unsurprisingly, many root causes of chronic diseases have a connection to this energy flow choreographed by your metabolism. When the dance is off, metabolic syndromes such as high cholesterol, high blood sugar, high blood pressure, and persistent inflammation can take over. These intertwined factors roll out the red carpet for the leading causes of death in high-income countries: cardiovascular diseases and cancers. They also significantly contribute to diabetes, hypertension, obesity, osteoporosis, and depression.

So, why move? Well, imagine hitting the regenerative button on your body with a chance to make it even better than before—PM is free, personalized medicine! Moreover, PM is the most effective way of turning on a marvelous range of the body's repair processes and disrupting the body's evolutionary tendency to conserve energy in order to have children.

"What dramatically affects your health is how your calories are allocated toward different physiological functions."

Depending on your age and energy budget, what dramatically affects your health is how your calories are allocated toward different physiological functions. When you move, energy is diverted from reproduction and energy storage (as fat) toward growth, body maintenance (resting metabolism), and being active. A well-studied example of these energy trade-offs is the significant drop in female hormones after ovulation when women walk about one hour a day, reducing by approximately 55% their risk of developing breast cancer.[7] Moreover, proper hormonal regulation leads to a 30% lower cancer risk for all genders.[8]

In addition to increasing caloric demand, PM is also physiologically stressful: you sweat, you get hot—reasons why some people do not like it! PM pushes your cells' power engines, called mitochondria, to their full capacity to generate energy. However, this creates harmful oxidative stress—think of a fresh-cut apple that turns brown. If left unchecked, oxidative stress damages DNA and other body molecules. To understand why the destructive side-effect of PM is so healthy, we need to explore the virtuous cycle of damage and restoration.

Reduce chronic inflammation. Until recently, people had scarce unallocated energy available, and as a result, PM was not avoidable. So, we evolved to match the capacity needed to maintain our body's systems ability to function properly while adjusting the energy demand and supply. Thanks to PM, energy is channeled toward your muscles and other tissues, producing antioxidants and anti-inflammatory proteins that regulate your immune system.

In an energy-abundant environment, these shifts in energy allocation offset excess fat accumulation, helping you combat the silent chief cause of inflammation—organ fat. This cycle enables your body to restore whatever harm is triggered by PM. In addition, it even repairs damage accrued elsewhere during physical inactivity.

Lower blood sugar and cholesterol. Repeated bouts of PM improve body composition independent of your body weight by reducing harmful organ fat. PM increases good cholesterol and lowers unhealthy cholesterol in the bloodstream, which stiffens the arteries and increases your blood pressure. Because PM stimulates your muscles and bones, they grow and strengthen, demanding more fuel, which induces a proliferation of mitochondria, thus enhancing your cardiovascular fitness and reducing the risk of osteoporosis. The ability to reverse insulin resistance, which helps to prevent and treat type 2 diabetes, may be the most remarkable benefit of PM. Indeed, PM restores your cells' ability to deliver, transport, and use as much as fifty times more blood sugar compared to when cells are insulin resistant.[9]

Lower blood pressure. Aerobic PM, commonly called cardio, increases the push of your blood flow—the blood pressure as your heart beats faster to supply more oxygen and sugar to every part of your body to match the demand. That leads to micro-damage of the walls of your arteries. Yet over time, cardio stimulates the growth of capillaries and arterioles, and your arteries subsequently adapt, becoming more robust and elastic, keeping blood pressure low and preventing hypertension during rest. Your heart then can pump more blood with each stroke, becoming more energy efficient.

After stopping PM, the afterburn state keeps you diverting energy away from reproductive and organ fat for a few hours up to two days to repair and restock depleted energy reserves. That may help explain how and why PM can slow down your body's senescence (biological aging), thus extending your healthspan— your quality of life as you age.

Improve mental health. Could PM be more effective than medication? In some cases, the answer is yes. For example, people with depression and anxiety typically experience lethargy and hopelessness, as well as low motivation to engage in PM. However, research has shown that PM is one-and-half times more effective at reducing mild to moderate symptoms of depression and anxiety than medication, and that short, high-intensity exercise produces the greatest effect.[10] The primary reason for this is that every time you move, you give your body a "wonderful bubble bath of neurochemicals," according to neuroscientist Wendy Suzuki.[11] In other words, your body secretes several essential neurotransmitters to keep up with PM despite its stressful effects. One such neurotransmitter, glutamate, helps spread information efficiently throughout your brain, and is often depleted in people with depression and anxiety. Engaging in PM leads to the production of glutamate, thereby enhancing your learning, memory, and decision-making abilities. In addition, your brain gains greater clarity for detecting threats and generating appropriate stress responses. Another neurotransmitter, anandamide, reduces pain, regulates your immune function, and manages stress responses. Anandamide is further involved in appetite, sleep, and balancing your mood. Interestingly, it is named after the Sanskrit word for bliss, *ananda*. As another result of PM, your body turns on growth factors that induce brand-new brain cells, especially in regions related to memory. Moreover, you can better shift and focus your attention while ameliorating mood and delaying the onset of dementia by modulating neuroinflammation.[12] Imagine what good can happen to your body and mind when you give yourself this "neurochemical bubble bath" regularly.

BOOSTING YOUR WELL-BEING THROUGH PHYSICAL MOVEMENT

The Innate Elements of the Dance of Life

How can we view PM as a part of being rather than as an onerous task to complete? Despite knowing the benefits of PM, many people still do not incorporate it into their lives. As discussed earlier, our ancestors moved to survive, play, and celebrate. You can harness the power of these innate elements to build a bridge between what you desire and what you can accomplish.

First, turn the voice in your head into a motivational coach by following your inherent nature to move when necessary, pleasurable, or otherwise rewarding. For 41% of people, time is the primary barrier that keeps them from engaging in

PM; for 25%, it is the lack of motivation.[13] As you go over your daily schedule, build upon meaning and creativity to reconnect with your body's vital force in motion. To help you craft a joyful and rewarding narrative of movement, build upon your character strengths,[†] do what you enjoy, and build upon these micro-moments to feel positive emotions and a sense of achievement.[14] Second, humans are a social species and rely on each other to survive and thrive. Build upon your community to find your "play zone" and enhance your PM experience. Play-oriented forms of PM engage you with others and constitute a neural exercise that strengthens your nervous system's ability to transition between stress (defense state) and calm, promoting feelings of safety and trusting relationships.

You can also find a supportive community online using #MyDanceOfLife on social networks. Browse the hashtag, connect with fellow dancers, and let their stories inspire and motivate you. Every dance tells a story; let's write ours together! Remember, every step counts. Let's create a community that moves, supports, and dances through life.

The Dance of Life Challenge

The PM lifestyle continuum, depicted in Figure 2.9, shows how PM can be tailored to your unique needs. The Dance of Life Challenge will help you activate your natural regenerative abilities. As you ramp up your PM routine, neurochemicals will flow, supporting you along the way. Remember, your body maintenance is energetically expansive, and no one-size-fits-all dose or type of PM is prescribed by nature. To help you confidently sustain your effort as you strengthen your body to move through life with ease and flexibility, reframe the maxim "no pain, no gain" to "use it or lose it until you work it again."[15] In addition, it is imperative to include equal time for body recovery, adequate sleep, and balanced nutrition.

> **"It is imperative to include equal time for body recovery, adequate sleep, and balanced nutrition."**

---

† Seligman and Peterson (2004) define character strengths as "strong capacities in you and they are probably engaging, energizing, and comfortable to use."

Figure 2.9: Dance of Life: Your regenerative medicine

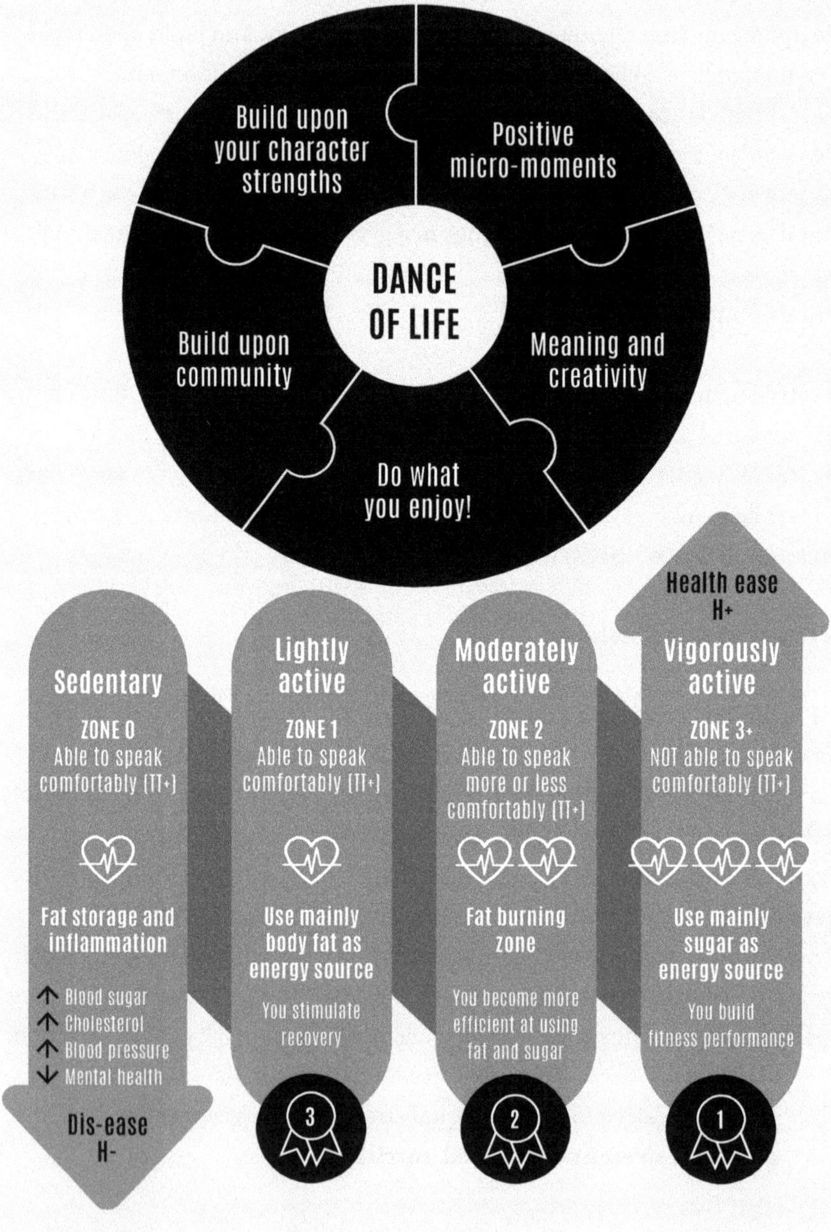

DANCE OF LIFE

Build upon your character strengths

Positive micro-moments

Build upon community

Meaning and creativity

Do what you enjoy!

Sedentary

ZONE 0
Able to speak comfortably (TT+)

Fat storage and inflammation

↑ Blood sugar
↑ Cholesterol
↑ Blood pressure
↓ Mental health

Dis-ease
H-

Lightly active

ZONE 1
Able to speak comfortably (TT+)

Use mainly body fat as energy source

You stimulate recovery

3

Moderately active

ZONE 2
Able to speak more or less comfortably (TT+)

Fat burning zone

You become more efficient at using fat and sugar

2

Vigorously active

ZONE 3+
NOT able to speak comfortably (TT+)

Use mainly sugar as energy source

You build fitness performance

1

Health ease
H+

©2024. Dr. Sanae Tabnaoui. The Best Version of Me.

Bronze Medal—The Awakening

- *Goal:* Shift from an exclusively sedentary lifestyle to being lightly active. Regardless of age, moving from an inactive to an active state has the greatest health benefits.[16] Remember, there are no wrong movements; there is only your unique expression.

- *PM intensity:* Zone 1—you are able to speak comfortably (Talk Test+, or TT+). Your metabolism mainly uses fat as an energy source.

- *Activity examples:* If you cannot move, use motor imagery as neural exercise to strengthen your muscles. If you are limited or disabled by health circumstances, use mindfulness-based movement or dance movement therapy.[17] Train your balance and coordination, adopt active sitting, a dynamic workstation through upright postural shifting every twenty minutes, fidgeting, and movement "snacking" (stand up and stretch, doing two sets of thirty seconds for each muscle group over the course of six days).[18]

 Silver Medal—The Momentum

- *Goal:* Progress to being moderately active. Whether you are out of shape or not, remember, you are—by design—an endurance athlete. Prefer realistic goals based on time, not performance. A mere eleven minutes of PM per day has been linked to a lower risk of early death.[19]

- *PM intensity:* Zone 2—you are able to more or less speak comfortably (TT±). Your metabolism becomes more efficient at burning fat as fuel. To aid recovery, return to Zone 1 activity.

- *Activity examples:* Any aerobic (oxygen-burning) and resistance (muscle-strengthening) activity, whether brisk walking or enthusiastic cleaning (think of Robin Williams's Mrs. Doubtfire!).

 Gold Medal—The Zenith

- *Goal:* Include short bouts of vigorous activities in your healthy lifestyle. Your lungs are overbuilt by design. Therefore, the goal is mainly to strengthen your heart and intercostals.

- *PM intensity:* Zone 3+—you are not able to speak comfortably (TT-). This zone is the best for building fitness performance, as your metabolism uses fat, sugar, and oxygen more efficiently. Revisit Zone 2 to get better at high-intensity interval training (HIIT, or above 85% to 90% of your maximum heart rate).

- *Activity examples:* HIIT, such as sprinting for a short period, makes you stronger faster and improves your maximum oxygen uptake, called VO2 max. Although vigorous activities have vast health benefits for virtually everyone, it is essential to confirm with your doctor that you can engage in PM at such intensity.

In conclusion, as much as possible, don't sit if you can walk; don't walk if you can dance. There is always a new rhythm to embrace.

QUESTIONS FOR SELF-REFLECTION

Consider the following questions to reflect on how movement positively impacts your health and daily experience to create a sense of coherence and purpose in life.

- Think of a moment when movement shifted your mental state.
  How can you use this connection for better mental well-being?

- Reflect on a time when shared PM such as dancing or playing with others deepened your social connections. How can you regularly incorporate such social activities into your life?

- Recall a time when movement made a day special.
  How can you make such moments a regular part of your life?

RESOURCES FOR EXPLORATION AND LEARNING

TOP 3: ARTICLES

Allison, M. (2022, May 30). **How our feelings of safety guide our behavior.** Psychology Today.
▶ tinyurl.com/v376jzkk
Discover the transformative power of recognizing and fostering feelings of safety in our lives, from the tennis court to everyday interactions.

Bendix, A. (2023, March 1). **Just 11 minutes per day of moderate exercise linked to lower risk of early death, study finds.** NBC News.
▶ tinyurl.com/yvv6bafh
Do you think 150 minutes of exercise a week is too much? Discover how just eleven minutes daily might change your life.

Menda, S. (2022, March 14). **Is dance the best form of exercise? Health benefits of dance explained.** Mya Care.
▶ tinyurl.com/e2jjyvsn
Discover how dance, from the grace of ballet to the rhythm of tap, has been enhancing human well-being for ages.

TOP 3: BOOKS

Bowman, K. (2017). **Move Your DNA Expanded Edition: Restore Your Health through Natural Movement.** Carlsborg, WA: Propriometrics Press.
Through this book, discover the power of natural movement and how it can transform your health in profound ways.

Lieberman, D. (2020). **Exercised: The Science of Physical Activity, Rest and Health.** London: Allen Lane.
This book blows up the myth-busting science behind our modern attitudes to exercise: what our bodies really need, why it matters, and its effects on health and well-being.

Ratey, J. J. (2013). **Spark: The Revolutionary New Science of Exercise and the Brain.** Boston: Little, Brown.
This book reveals the surprising and transformative effects of exercise on our brains and its benefits for mental health and cognitive function.

TOP 3: ASSESSMENTS AND TESTS

The Behavioural Regulations in Exercise Questionnaire (BREQ).
Uncover your intrinsic motivation by identifying what encourages or discourages you from being more active.
▶ tinyurl.com/bdktmv3z

Exercise Benefits/Barriers Scale.
Being aware of your perceptions of the benefits of and barriers to physical movement help to shift from sedentary to lightly active lifestyle.
▶ tinyurl.com/bdz29s96

Physical Activity Enjoyment Scale (PACES).
Use this assessment to get a sense of your level of enjoyment of physical movement.
▶ tinyurl.com/mt99xh3x

TOP 3: VIDEOS

The #1 Way to Strengthen Your Mind Is to Use Your Body.
With Wendy Suzuki. BigThink.com.
▶ tinyurl.com/5y6tspyk
Unlock the secret to brain health with just ten minutes of walking daily.

Regulating the Nervous System with Movement.
With Deb Dana.
▶ tinyurl.com/4bfd68h2
If physical movement is a challenge, engage in a neural exercise and navigate life's hurdles with Deb Dana's insights.

Why Some People Find Exercise Harder than Others.
With Emily Balcetis.
▶ tinyurl.com/46tmbhve
Discover the power of perception and how visual tactics can transform your approach to physical movement goals.

TOP 3: PODCASTS

Depression. With Dr. Charles Raison. FoundMyFitness.
▶ tinyurl.com/mrxnb7dx
Unravel the intricate relationship between inflammation and depression.

Get Up! Our Potential. With Dr James Levine. HumbleWorks.
▶ tinyurl.com/k42prwfk
Discover the secrets of standing versus sitting and explore the transformative power of the energy we expend in every action outside of sleeping, eating, or sports-like exercise.

The Science and Practice of Movement. With Ido Portal. Huberman Lab.
▶ tinyurl.com/383rjf74
Dive into the intricate link between mind and body, uncovering the profound benefits of weaving movement into your everyday routine.

TOP 3: FREE ONLINE COURSES

The Body Matters: Why Exercise Makes You Healthy and How to Stay Uninjured. edX, McGill University.
▶ tinyurl.com/mr2jyn49
Discover the essential benefits of stretching, explore the psychological effects of injury, and learn strategies for injury prevention and recovery.

A Guide to Physical Activity. University of Minnesota Libraries.
▶ tinyurl.com/5ad5pynw
This course provides a breakdown of key topics in the field of physical activity, including a comprehension check.

Managing Your Health: The Role of Physical Therapy and Exercise. Coursera, University of Toronto.
▶ tinyurl.com/29y33ac6
Explore the role of physical therapy and exercise in enhancing health, from combating cardiovascular disease to managing arthritis.

ENDNOTES

1   D. E. Lieberman, T. M. Kistner, D. Richard, I. M. Lee, and A. L. Baggish. (2021). The active grandparent hypothesis: Physical activity and the evolution of extended human healthspans and lifespans. *Proceedings of the National Academy of Sciences of the United States of America 118* (50), e2107621118. tinyurl.com/3su9mx4z

2   P. T. Katzmarzyk, C. Friedenreich, E. J. Shiroma, and I. M. Lee. (2022). Physical inactivity and non-communicable disease burden in low-income, middle-income and high-income countries. *British Journal of Sports Medicine 56* (2), pp. 101-6. tinyurl.com/4h59uuxz; United Nations. (n.d.). Sustainable development goals. tinyurl.com/4mykntc2

3   World Health Organization. (2022, October 5). Physical activity. tinyurl.com/pr22uv6e

4   World Health Organization. (2022).

5   D. A. Raichlen, H. Pontzer, T. W. Zderic, J. A. Harris, A. Z. P. Mabulla, M. T. Hamilton, and B. M. Wood. (2020). Sitting, squatting, and the evolutionary biology of human inactivity. *Proceedings of the National Academy of Sciences of the United States of America 117* (13), pp. 7115–21. tinyurl.com/7bktec67

6   Food and Agriculture Organization of the United Nations. (2004). Energy requirements of adults. tinyurl.com/4fxnvaar

7   J. Shi, L. C. Kobayashi, A. Grundy, H. Richardson, S. Sengupta, C. A. Lohrisch, J. J. Spinelli, and K. J. Aronson. (2017). Lifetime moderate-to-vigorous physical activity and ER/PR/HER-defined post-menopausal breast cancer risk. *Breast Cancer Research and Treatment 165* (1), pp. 201-13. tinyurl.com/34tet5vn

8   H. Arem, S. Moore, A. V. Patel, P. Hartge, A. B. De Gonzalez, K. Visvanathan, P. T. Campbell, M. Freedman, E. Weiderpass, H. O. Adami, M. S. Linet, I. M. Lee, and C. E. Matthews. (2015). Leisure time physical activity and mortality. *JAMA Internal Medicine 175* (6), p. 959. tinyurl.com/435ne6ev

9   L. Sylow, M. Kleinert, E. A. Richter, and T. E. Jensen. (2017). Exercise-stimulated glucose uptake: Regulation and implications for glycaemic control. *Nature Reviews Endocrinology 13* (3), pp. 133-48. tinyurl.com/3vzsfx6j

10 B. Singh, T. Olds, R. Curtis, D. Dumuid, R. Virgara, A. Watson, K. Szeto, E. O'Connor, T. Ferguson, E. Eglitis, A. Miatke, C. E. Simpson, and C. Maher. (2023). Effectiveness of physical activity interventions for improving depression, anxiety and distress: An overview of systematic reviews. *British Journal of Sports Medicine 57*, pp. 1203-9. tinyurl.com/mr3rty85

11 W. A. Suzuki. (2023). The #1 way to strengthen your mind is to use your body. BigThink.com. tinyurl.com/mr3hsw2b

12 B. K. Pedersen and B. Saltin. (2015). Exercise as medicine—Evidence for prescribing exercise as therapy in 26 different chronic diseases. *Scandinavian Journal of Medicine & Science in Sports 25*, pp. 1-72. tinyurl.com/4dy3mbwn

13 European Union. (2022). Sport and physical activity.
    tinyurl.com/bdezasav

14 D. E. R. Warburton and S. S. D. Bredin. (2019). Health benefits of physical activity:
    A strengths-based approach. *Journal of Clinical Medicine 8* (12), 2044. tinyurl.com/3krtczn3;
    C. Peterson and M. E. P. Seligman. (2004). *Character Strengths and Virtues:
    A Handbook and Classification.* Oxford, UK: Oxford University Press.

15 D. Beres. (2019, January 28). The maxim "use it or lose it" is wrong, researchers say. Here's
    why. BigThink.com. tinyurl.com/2jre9aa4

16 D. E. R. Warburton. (2006). Health benefits of physical activity: The evidence. *Canadian
    Medical Association Journal 174* (6), pp. 801–9. tinyurl.com/y7xt8uyd

17 A. R. Lucas, H. D. Klepin, S. W. Porges, and W. J. Rejeski. (2016). Mindfulness-based
    movement: A polyvagal perspective. *Integrative Cancer Therapies 17* (1), pp. 5–15.
    tinyurl.com/2b4w9522

18 E. Thomas, A. Bianco, A. Paoli, and A. Palma. (2018). The relation between stretching
    typology and stretching duration: The effects on range of motion. *International Journal of
    Sports Medicine 39* (4), pp. 243–54. tinyurl.com/mrxcs2fw

19 A. Bendix. (2023, March 1). Just 11 minutes per day of moderate exercise linked to lower risk
    of early death, study finds. NBC News. tinyurl.com/2s3bbxjc

INTRODUCTION

> "... The curious paradox is that when I accept myself as I am, then I change."
> —CARL ROGERS

Why are you who you are? Why do you make the choices that you do? And on a deeper level: are you actually choosing? Or could it be that you are just the product of a predetermined set of instructions based on your genetic blueprint?

When trying to become the best version of yourself, understanding what you can and what you can't control is paramount. By focusing on the aspects of our life that are within our circle of influence, we shift our mindset from reactive to proactive. The belief that we can impact and influence our future provides us with a sense of agency.

Agency is the power to act and the ability to make choices that affect your life. It is the belief that you are in control of your own destiny, and that you have impact and can create the life you want. It motivates us to transform intentions into actionable strategies. It allows us to shape our future rather than to simply endure it.

Agency is a core concept of many models around motivation, and expanding our (subjective) agency is the key to happiness, well-being, and high performance.[1] As long as we are convinced that the choices we make and the actions we take significantly drive life's outcome, we are empowered and take ownership in creating meaningful change. This cultivates resilience and helps us deal with uncertainty by putting us back in the driver's seat of our personal and professional growth. Indeed, it is the key to unlocking our full potential. Just like Confucius said: Those who think they can, and those who think they cannot, are usually both right.

So, when you think about your well-being, ask yourself this question first: "To what extent do I feel I am in control of my physical and mental health, my happiness, and my future?"

Personal Story

Liam had always been told that he bore an uncanny resemblance to his grandfather, both in appearance and temperament. Stories of Grandpa Joe's legendary athleticism, his vigor, and his magnetic charisma were woven into the family folklore. Liam had also inherited from his grandfather a susceptibility to certain health conditions. Every family gathering, every comment from distant relatives, every glance in the mirror was a reminder that he was Grandpa Joe's living reflection.

But when Liam reached his twenties, he noticed something. Despite regular workouts, his physique wasn't developing as he'd imagined, nor did he possess the stamina described in the tales of his grandfather's youthful exploits. The genetic hand he'd been dealt seemed a far cry from that of the legendary Grandpa Joe. Discouraged and questioning his potential, Liam sought out a renowned geneticist, Dr. P. Rotein, hoping to understand more about his DNA and perhaps uncover some hidden potential. The results surprised him. Though he did share a significant genetic overlap with his grandfather, he was, of course, unique. Dr. Rotein emphasized, "Your DNA might provide a foundation, Liam, but it's not your fate. Lifestyle, mindset, environment—they all play pivotal roles."

Heartened by this, Liam sought guidance from a wellness coach named Maya. Together, they began the process of transformation, of working on new habits and ways of thinking. Specifically, Maya introduced Liam to the concept of self-expansion, explaining how beliefs can either limit or unleash potential. The journey was not easy. There were setbacks and self-doubt, and Liam spent countless hours reshaping his mental model about himself and the world around him.

A year later, after hard work and introspection, Liam participated in a local marathon. As he crossed the finish line, exhausted but ecstatic, he realized something profound. He might not be the mirror image of the legendary Grandpa Joe, but he had forged his own path, transcending the constraints he'd once believed his DNA had imposed.

Liam's transformation wasn't merely physical—it was deeply mental. His journey exemplified that although genes might influence the starting line, determination, resilience, and a growth mindset defined the race's outcome.

Nature versus Nurture

Liam's story brings us to the nature versus nurture debate: how much of our personality, behavior, and mental state is determined by our genes? And how much can we learn (from others) and change over time (a process called self-expansion)?[2] These questions directly tap into what many of us think makes us human: our ability to quickly adapt to a rapidly changing environment. At the same time, we all realize that there are limits to our potential and that we all develop within a set of predefined boundaries and limitations.

The nature-nurture debate has been going on for centuries among philosophers, psychologists, and biologists, and there yet is no easy answer. However, recent advances in genetics and neuroscience have shed new light on the issue. We now know that our genes play a significant role in shaping who we are. Our genes are a gift from our parents and—technically speaking—all the ancestors who came before them. We are born with a genetic blueprint consisting of billions of pieces of code we call DNA. This DNA is at the foundation of every cell in our body and contains the instructions for the color of our eyes, the texture of our hair, and even our height.

Beyond physical traits, DNA determines our risk for certain diseases and disorders, as well as our personal and professional aspirations, work ethic, job satisfaction, and even entrepreneurial tendencies.[3]

Is DNA Your Destiny?

But DNA is not our destiny. Life experiences impact how much of our genetic potential will actually develop during our lifetime. For example, a person with a genetic predisposition for tallness may not reach their full height potential if they experience malnutrition during childhood. Stressful life events and the availability of our caretakers during our early childhood rewire our brains and change how we handle social interactions later in life, sometimes even in contradiction to our genetic predispositions.

To understand how we can improve our well-being, increase our longevity, and enhance our mental health, we need to leverage the intricate interplay between what we are born with and what we can develop later in life. In other parts of this book, you will find paradigms, models, tips, and insights that are related to your nurture and the context you grow up and live in. However, in this chapter, we will zoom in on how our genetic makeup influences and impacts who we are and who we can become. By understanding the role of genes as our point of origin, we can better understand ourselves and our future potential. It also helps us develop more effective strategies to (re)take the reins on our lives and improve our future well-being. Indeed, by understanding our past, we will seize control of our future.

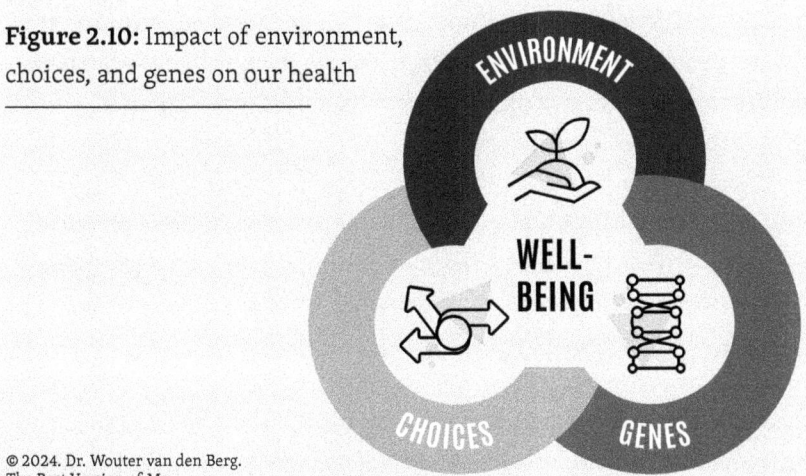

Figure 2.10: Impact of environment, choices, and genes on our health

© 2024. Dr. Wouter van den Berg.
The Best Version of Me.

Humans are emergent creatures. We could see ourselves as a combination of characteristics that grow when specific conditions are present and combine into something greater than the individual components themselves. The key concept of emergence is that the end-state situation cannot be derived from, or could not have been predicted from, the individual parts before its emergence.

Smartphone

Imagine that you are like a brand new smartphone right out of the box. Your DNA is analogous to the phone's hardware: the processor, memory, camera quality, screen size, and battery capacity. Just as each smartphone model has a certain set of specifications, every individual has a genetic blueprint that determines certain physical attributes, predispositions, and inherent talents. However, a smartphone is much more than its hardware. What truly unlocks its potential is the software—the operating system, apps, settings, and the data you feed into it. In the same way, though your DNA provides a foundational structure, it's your experiences, environment, learning, choices, and mindset that determine how you function, adapt, and grow.

Two smartphones with identical hardware can perform quite differently based on their software and user settings. One might be optimized for productivity with office apps, cloud integrations, and time-management tools, whereas another could be tailored for entertainment with games, movies, and music apps. Similarly, two people with a similar genetic makeup—such as twins—can have vastly different personalities, skills, and life trajectories based on their upbringing, experiences, and choices.

In essence, though your DNA—like a smartphone's hardware—sets certain parameters, it doesn't strictly determine your destiny. It's the "software updates" of life—education, experiences, relationships, and especially mindset—that play a critical role in shaping who you become.

Going through the process of self-expansion means you allow yourself to keep updating, optimizing, and exploring new facets of yourself, pushing the boundaries of what you might have thought possible based on your "factory settings."

How Is DNA Linked to Body and Mind?

DNA is the genetic material that makes up all living things. It contains the instructions for building proteins, the fundamental building blocks of every cell in our body. Through these proteins, DNA impacts both our physique and our ways of thinking. DNA is passed down from parents to their offspring at the moment of conception. We inherit 50% of our genes from our father and 50% from our mother. Though DNA was discovered in the late 1860s, a first map of the full human genetic blueprint was not completed until 2003.

When thinking about how our genes influence our well-being, we typically focus on the physical- and health-related aspects. Indeed, genetic variations can make some individuals more prone to certain conditions such as heart disease, diabetes, or cancer. Genetic variation between individuals either up- or down-regulates the cellular processes that underlie these diseases. For example, there are single-gene disorders, where one genetic mutation has a causal impact on the disorders we develop. There are also genetic predispositions—when genes interact with each other or with the environment—that, when combined with environmental factors such as diet, exercise, or exposure to toxins, can increase or decrease the likelihood of developing these diseases.

However, because our DNA also codes for the proteins that impact how our brain cells function, our genes also impact our mind. Our brain governs most of our more complex behavior and feelings such as our responses to adversity and stress but also to pleasure and joy.

Brain cells communicate with each other through releasing a chemical signal we call neurotransmitters. Neurotransmitters travel from the "sending" neuron, cross the interneuronal space, and bind to a receptor on the "receiving" neuron. In doing so, they transmit a signal. For example, this could be a signal from a tastebud in your mouth when you taste a raspberry to the pleasure center in your emotional brain that labels this flavor as tasty and delicious.

Signals that occur more often form more stable connections through increased receptor density or neurotransmitter release, thereby turning independent neurons into interlinked networks of memories, thoughts, and emotional responses. The baseline existence of these connections, and their effectiveness, efficiency, and stability over time, are influenced by our genes.

To conclude: our genes don't only impact who we are when we enter this world; they also impact how we perceive, process, and adapt to the world and our experiences.

HOW DOES DNA SUPPORT YOUR WELL-BEING?

DNA and Physical Well-Being

One of the most significant findings in the field of genetics is the association between specific DNA variations and disease susceptibility. There is a limited set of genes that have a causal and determinant role in shaping who we are. These are the genes that underlie so-called monogenic diseases. Having the genetic variant means a guaranteed development of the disease. Huntington's disease, for example, is one of the most well-known monogenic diseases.

In most cases, however, there is no full causal connection, and your genetics simply increase the likelihood of developing certain conditions such as diabetes, cardiovascular diseases, and certain types of cancers. For example:

- Studies have shown that certain variations in the BRCA1 and BRCA2 genes are associated with a significantly higher risk of developing breast and ovarian cancers.[4] These genetic markers can be inherited from either parent and can increase the lifetime risk of developing these cancers by up to 80%. Identifying these genetic variations can help individuals and their health care providers make informed decisions about screening and preventive measures such as regular mammograms and prophylactic surgeries.

- Researchers have identified specific DNA variations that increase the risk of developing type 2 diabetes.[5] These variations affect the body's ability to regulate blood sugar levels, leading to insulin resistance, which is at the core of the disease.

- Cardiovascular diseases such as heart disease and stroke have also been found to have a genetic component.[6] Certain DNA variations can affect cholesterol levels, blood pressure regulation, and blood clotting, all of which are important factors in cardiovascular health.

By identifying the genes involved, we have learned a lot about the underlying biological mechanisms of these diseases. This has enabled health care providers to develop targeted screening strategies and preventive measures. Early detection and intervention can dramatically improve treatment outcomes and potentially save lives.

Moreover, advancements in genetic research have led to the development of personalized medicine. This approach takes into account an individual's genetic makeup to tailor treatment plans that are more effective and have fewer side effects. For example, certain genetic variations can affect how an individual metabolizes medications, making them more or less effective. By considering these genetic factors, health care providers can prescribe medications that are more likely to work for a particular individual, leading to better treatment outcomes.

In conclusion, the relationship between DNA and disease risk is a fascinating area of study in genetics. The identification of genetic markers associated with various diseases has revolutionized health care by allowing for targeted screening, preventive measures, and personalized treatment plans. As research continues to uncover more about the intricate connections between our DNA and disease susceptibility, the potential for improving health outcomes and saving lives grows exponentially.

DNA and Mental Well-Being

Our well-being is not limited to our bodily health. In fact, research suggests that how our brain processes our experiences is the real driver of our well-being. In that sense, our well-being is more like a subjective judgment rather than an objective depiction of our experiences. To be able to dive a bit deeper in how that works, we need to understand more about how our brain works. With a weight of only 1,350 grams (3 pounds), the brain is the most complex, sophisticated, and efficiently built machine ever known. Shaped by an exceptionally long history of adaptive evolutionary forces, the brain is optimized to deal with the ever-changing, uncertain world around us. Our brain plays a central role in who we are. It is responsible for everything from our basic survival instincts to the most complex thoughts, feelings, and emotions that drive our behavior. As such, our brain has a significant impact on our sense of well-being.

Earlier we learned how our genes impact how our brain functions and the way we process what we see, hear, and taste. When our brain experiences a world that is safe, manageable, and meaningful, we feel happy, healthy, and engaged with the environment around us. However, when those elements are absent, we may experience anxiety, depression, or other mental health problems.

Research has found a clear link between genes and different aspects of our mental well-being. For example, studies indicate that 20% to 50% of variability in well-being can be attributed to our genetic makeup. In addition:

- Studies have shown that genes can influence our risk for developing certain mental disorders such as schizophrenia and depression;

- We know that the way our body responds to stress is partly regulated by genetics. Some people are genetically predisposed to produce more of the stress hormone cortisol, which can make them more vulnerable to stress-related issues, trauma, and uncertainty;

- Our genes also influence cognitive functions such as memory and attention, which can in turn affect mental well-being. For example, poor cognitive function can make it more challenging to perform tasks, climb the corporate ladder, and maintain good mental health;

- Studies on personality suggest that traits such as resilience, extraversion, and openness are partly influenced by genetics. These traits can help individuals cope with life's challenges, thereby promoting mental well-being. Finally, our genes impact some of our behavioral tendencies, which can predispose individuals to behaviors that indirectly impact mental health such as substance abuse, risk-taking behavior, and poor sleep habits.

BOOSTING YOUR WELL-BEING THROUGH UNDERSTANDING YOUR DNA

1. **Go against nature.** Your DNA determines your starting point. To elaborate, let's say that you have a gene that makes you more likely to be anxious. This gene will increase your baseline level of anxiety. If you adhere to your genetic predisposition, you may avoid stressful situations such as speaking in public or meeting new people. But by purposefully going against what feels natural to you, you broaden your developmental path and self-expand rather than live life as a self-fulfilling prophecy.

2. **Accept that we are all different.** We are all equal but not identical. Our genetic makeup offers each of us a different starting point. Or, put differently, we are all in the same storm, in the same ocean, yet not all sailing in the same boat. When we acknowledge that everyone has unique strengths and weaknesses, we can be more forgiving of our own imperfections. This fosters self-esteem and self-compassion, which are vital components of mental well-being. Constant comparison with others can lead to chronic stress and anxiety. Accepting individual differences can reduce these stressors, contributing to emotional and psychological stability.

3. **Leverage your strengths.** Recognizing your unique skills can help you focus on what you excel at, leading to personal growth and a sense of accomplishment. This, in turn, improves self-esteem and happiness. In practical terms, different talents and skills are often complementary. When we appreciate the diverse abilities of others, it can lead to more effective collaboration, both professionally and personally.

CONCLUSION

In the intricate dance of life, our DNA sets the rhythm, but we choose the steps. DNA provides the notes, but we create the music. Remember, our genetic blueprint might offer a starting point, but it's our beliefs, actions, and continuous growth that shape the path ahead.

We invite you to embrace the boundless possibilities that build on, but are not limited by, your genetic blueprint; to investigate and accept the things that inherently define you; and to also choose the path of self-expansion and step into the vastness of your potential. The journey of self-discovery is ever evolving, and with a growth mindset, you are equipped to transcend any perceived limits, forging ahead to become the best versions of yourself.

QUESTIONS FOR SELF-REFLECTION

- What preconceptions did you have about the role of genetics in your well-being before reading this chapter? How have they changed?

- Are there specific diseases or conditions that run in your family that you should be more aware of or actively take steps to prevent?

- How do you currently interact with your environment (e.g., diet, exercise, stress levels), and what might that reveal about your genetic predispositions?

- What ethical considerations arise when thinking about genetic predispositions, both for yourself and society at large?

RESOURCES FOR EXPLORATION AND LEARNING

TOP 3: ARTICLES

Fryer, B. (2001, April). **DNA: Handle with care.**
Harvard Business Review.
▶ tinyurl.com/w8xr3ftm

Hutson, M. (2023, August 9). **The race to save the world's DNA.**
New Yorker.
▶ tinyurl.com/38pt8r73

Markel, H. (2021, September 13). **The ugly truth behind the discovery of DNA.** *Washington Post.*
▶ tinyurl.com/mwu3jtsk

TOP 3: BOOKS

Rutherford, A. (2017). **A Brief History of Everyone Who Ever Lived: The Human Story Retold through Our Genes.** New York: The Experiment.

Sapolsky, R. M. (2023). **Determined: A Science of Life without Free Will.** London: Penguin Press.

Watson, J. D. (2017). **DNA: The Story of the Genetic Revolution.** New York: Knopf.

 TOP 3: VIDEOS

 How to Read the Genome and Build a Human Being. Riccardo Sabatini, TED Talk.
▶ tinyurl.com/2jshyrpz
From the TED description of the video: "Secrets, disease and beauty are all written in the human genome, the complete set of genetic instructions needed to build a human being. Now, as scientist and entrepreneur Riccardo Sabatini shows us, we have the power to read this complex code, predicting things like height, eye color, age and even facial structure—all from a vial of blood. And soon, Sabatini says, our new understanding of the genome will allow us to personalize treatments for diseases like cancer. We have the power to change life as we know it. How will we use it?"

 Perspective Is Everything. Rory Sutherland, TED Talk.
▶ tinyurl.com/5n79pnkh
Reframe the way you see yourself. According to Rory Sutherland, "The circumstances of our lives may matter less than how we see them." In this TEDxAthens talk, Sutherland "makes a compelling case for how reframing is the key to happiness."

 What Is DNA and How Does It Work? Stated Clearly.
▶ tinyurl.com/3f5vkjs7
This animated short film has been made for those wanting a simple introduction (or even a refresher) on how DNA creates a living creature. In this video, you will learn a bit about genetic code, DNA transcription and translation, and the importance of proteins in the chemistry of life.

TOP 3: FREE ONLINE COURSES

DNA Decoded. McMaster University.
▶ tinyurl.com/yb7nj42e
From the course website: "If you're curious about DNA, join Felicia Vulcu and Caitlin Mullarkey, two biochemists from McMaster University, as they explore the structure of DNA, how scientists cracked the genetic code, and what our DNA can tell us about ourselves. Along the way, you'll learn about the practical techniques that scientists use to analyze our genetic risks, to manipulate DNA, and to develop new treatments for a range of different diseases. Then, step into our virtual lab to perform your own forensic DNA analysis of samples from a crime scene and solve a murder."

GeneCards®: The Human Gene Database.
▶ tinyurl.com/nheerv7w
Not a real course, but in this database you will discover all there is to know about a specific gene or genetic mutation. Think about biological pathways, genomic locations, phenotypes, functional implications, and much more.

Introduction to Biology—The Secret of Life. MITx.
▶ tinyurl.com/3e8x4npe
From the course website: "Join Professor Eric Lander and the MITx Biology team in an exciting learning experience. This course is an introductory level biology course hosted by professor Eric Lander, who was one of the leaders of the Human Genome Project. The course content reflects the topics taught in the MIT introductory biology courses and many biology courses across the world. As a learner, you will first focus on the structure and function of macromolecules such as DNA, RNA and proteins. You will discover how changes in the structure of some of these macromolecules alter their functions and what the implications of such changes have on human health."

TOP 3: PODCASTS

Culture, Consciousness, Diet, Drugs, Sleep, Dating & Evolution with Heather Heying & Bret Weinstein (Episode 36). Mind & Matter Podcast. Nick Jikomes.
▶ tinyurl.com/bdhyrhkn
From the episode description: "Nick talks to evolutionary biologists Bret Weinstein and Heather Heying about using evolutionary thinking to understand humanity's predicaments in the 21st century. They discuss a variety of topics related to their new book, *A Hunter Gatherer's Guide to the 21st Century*, including modern medicine, dieting and health, sleep and light, dating and mating systems, and questions related to consciousness and the state of civilization at large. The book is meant to provide an evolutionary toolkit for understanding the modern human condition by understanding our past."

The Hidden Truths in Your DNA with TEDx Speaker Kashif Khan. Personalizing Your Health Plan, How DNA Testing Can Prevent Disease, Slow Aging, and Optimize Performance. The Gabby Reece Show.
▶ tinyurl.com/yjh65j9s
From the episode description: "... The co-founder of the DNA Company, Kashif [Khan]'s journey into genomics is fascinating—he faced some serious physical ailments and was able to use his DNA to understand what he needed to avoid, what environments were best for him, and even what supplements could support him in his work and family life. He's here to talk about how DNA testing can impact our health and wellbeing."

 The Nature of Human Nature: A Conversation with Robert Plomin (Episode 211). Making Sense. Sam Harris.
▶ tinyurl.com/yc4befhp
From the episode description: "In this episode of the podcast, Sam Harris speaks with Robert Plomin [a research professor in behavioral genetics] about the role that DNA plays in determining who we are. They discuss the birth of behavioral genetics, the taboo around studying the influence of genes on human psychology, controversies surrounding the topic of group differences," and much more.

ENDNOTES

1   R. M. Ryan and E. L. Deci. (2017). *Self-Determination Theory: Basic Psychological Needs in Motivation, Development, and Wellness. New York:* Guilford Press.

2   A. Aron and E. N. Aron. (1997). Self-expansion motivation and including other in the self. In S. Duck (Ed.), *Handbook of Personal Relationships: Theory, Research and Interventions* (pp. 250-70). Hoboken, NJ: John Wiley & Sons.

3   J. P. Beauchamp, D. Cesarini, M. Johannesson, M. J. H. M. van der Loos, P. D. Koellinger, P. J. F. Groenen, J. H. Fowler, J. N. Rosenquist, A. R. Thurik, and N. A. Christakis. (2011). Molecular genetics and economics. *Journal of Economic Perspectives* 25 (4), pp. 57–82. tinyurl.com/ye23z8nw

4   S. A. Narod and W. D. Foulkes. (2004). BRCA1 and BRCA2: 1994 and beyond. *Nature Reviews Cancer* 4 (9), pp. 665-76. tinyurl.com/4435kh36

5   I. Prokopenko, M. I. McCarthy, and C. M. Lindgren. (2008). Type 2 diabetes: New genes, new understanding. *Trends in Genetics* 24 (12), pp. 613-21. tinyurl.com/mr3w25zd

6   C. Wallace, S. J. Newhouse, P. Braund, F. Zhang, M. Tobin, M. Falchi, M., ... and P. B. Munroe. (2008). Genome-wide association study identifies genes for biomarkers of cardiovascular disease: serum urate and dyslipidemia. *American Journal of Human Genetics* 82 (1), pp. 139-49. tinyurl.com/2ts6tck3

03
MIND

THE ARTS
MINDFULNESS
SELF-REGULATION
RESILIENCE AND ADAPTA
LEARNING

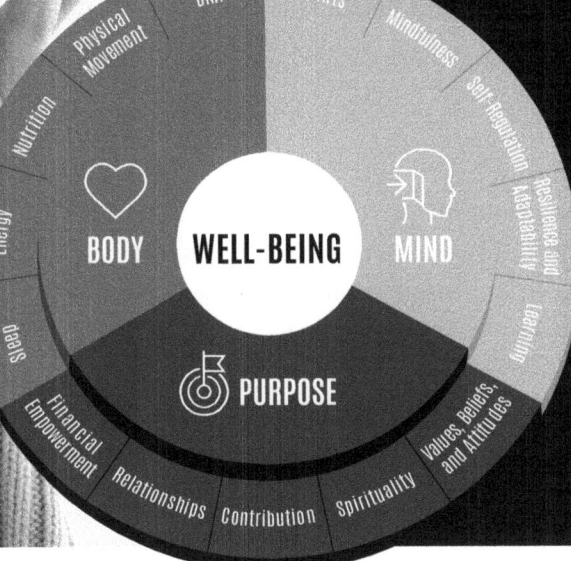

- DNA
- Physical Movement
- Nutrition
- Energy
- Sleep
- Financial Empowerment
- Relationships
- Contribution
- Spirituality
- Values, Beliefs, and Attitudes
- Learning
- Resilience and Adaptability
- Self-Regulation
- Mindfulness
- The Arts

BODY

WELL-BEING

MIND

PURPOSE

Nature
Environment

Social
Environment

Work
Environment

Climate
Environment

INTRODUCTION

Written by Dr. Nick van Dam

"It is not enough to have a good mind;
the main thing is to use it well."
—RENÉ DESCARTES

In the enlightening Mind section of this book, we shift our focus to the tangled and fascinating world of mental health and cognitive well-being. This section, integral to the comprehensive Best Version of Me model, is dedicated to unraveling the complexities of the human mind. It is structured into five insightful chapters, each delving into key aspects that collectively shape our mental landscape.

The Arts

We explore the profound impact of the arts on cognitive, emotional, and mental well-being. This chapter considers how engagement with various art forms can significantly enhance mental health, sharpen cognitive abilities, and enrich emotional experiences. We examine the therapeutic power of the arts in reducing feelings of loneliness, a pervasive issue in today's fast-paced world. We discuss how artistic pursuits can bolster confidence, foster resilience, and provide valuable tools for dealing with anxiety and depression.

Mindfulness

This chapter introduces the concept of mindfulness not as a fleeting trend but as a fundamental tool for personal growth and mental clarity. We explore five dimensions of mindfulness, each offering a unique perspective and approach: simple knowing, care and compassion, curiosity and inquisitiveness, wise discernment, and grounding ourselves by using the anchor of the six senses.

In addition, this chapter provides practical mindfulness practices, which may be particularly valuable in times of stress.

Self-Regulation

We look into the multifaceted concept of self-regulation, an umbrella term that encompasses a range of skills, abilities, and internal psychological processes that play an important role in our lives. This chapter demystifies the often-conflated concepts of self-regulation and self-control, highlighting their distinct yet interconnected roles in shaping our behavior and mental processes. We explore self-regulation in a multidimensional context, recognizing its complexity and the various ways it manifests in our lives. The impact of self-regulation extends far beyond the individual, affecting our interactions with others and our overall contribution to our environment.

Resilience and Adaptability

We investigate the pivotal roles resilience and adaptability play in personal growth and well-being. These qualities are not just buzzwords; they are fundamental traits that enable us to navigate life's challenges and changes with grace and strength. This chapter explores resilience and adaptability within the framework of four elements of holistic health: physical, emotional, mental, and spiritual. Each element showcases how resilience and adaptability manifest and can be strengthened in these different dimensions of our lives.

Learning

In this chapter, we explore the expansive and dynamic concept of learning, not as merely an academic exercise but as a continuous, life-enriching process that significantly impacts various facets of our lives. We delve into how learning profoundly influences personal growth, enriches our perspectives, and enhances our understanding of ourselves and the world around us. We also address the impact of learning on social life, revealing how learning improves communication and empathy, leading to stronger and more meaningful relationships. Additionally, we consider learning's crucial role in career development, where continual skill acquisition and adaptability are key to professional success and satisfaction. This chapter also offers a range of evidence-based practices that boost well-being through learning.

THE ARTS

Written by Judith Grimbergen

INTRODUCTION

"Art washes away from the soul the dust of everyday life."
–PABLO PICASSO

Personal Story

As long as I can remember, I've felt kind of nervous when entering a museum. I know I am entering a candy store: overwhelmed by the beauty, the choices, the colors, the shapes of the art pieces. Sometimes it even feels that every piece of art is screaming for attention: "Don't forget to look at me—I am here!" Slowly, I feel at ease with my surroundings and the great enjoyment can begin. Looking at art makes my brain happier; my brain starts to look for patterns, shapes, and anything else that makes me feel more connected to the piece. Artists already know the mental benefits of creating art, but did you know that simply viewing art can be beneficial as well?

Art for me means an escape from the everyday. A museum always leaves me awestruck. I come back enriched, curious, and eager to learn. But art is so many things. It enriches our lives. It brings out feelings and emotions. Art is everywhere in our lives and in everything we do: almost every aspect of our lives incorporates some form of art.

According to the great artist Picasso, the purpose of art, among other things, is washing the dust of daily life off our souls. It is easy, in everyday life, to feel overwhelmed by the numerous things we are supposed to do in twenty-four hours. But if you take just a couple of minutes and sit down, in front of your favorite piece of art, often you can clear your mind. Even looking at a nice picture in an art book or a visual of a work of art online will most likely help you destress. For example, color can brighten up your day, and abstract images can be calming and might encourage you to reflect, contemplate, and associate. Overall, art can pique your curiosity and make you wonder about the artist's inspiration.

If we go back to the artwork of Picasso, we can ask ourselves the question: what made his paintings so original and, for most of us, so great to look at? He changed the goal that European painters had subscribed to for centuries by staying away from painting true to life. His goal was to produce something extraordinary. He generated novelty by bending, breaking, and blending what he knew. Through this, he made history with his groundbreaking art.

How do we define the art or the arts? There is no generally agreed definition of what constitutes art, but I like the following: art can be defined as "an act of expressing feelings, thoughts, and observations through different resources,"[1] including:

- **The visual arts** (architecture, ceramics, drawing, filmmaking, painting, photography, video, digital art, and sculpting)
- **The literary arts** (fiction, drama, poetry, and prose)
- **The performing arts** (dance, music, and theater)

In this chapter I concentrate mainly on the visual arts, but this approach can easily be applied to other disciplines of art as well.

HOW DO THE ARTS SUPPORT YOUR WELL-BEING?

The arts serve as a multifaceted bridge to individuals' well-being.

Figure 3.1: The arts and well-being

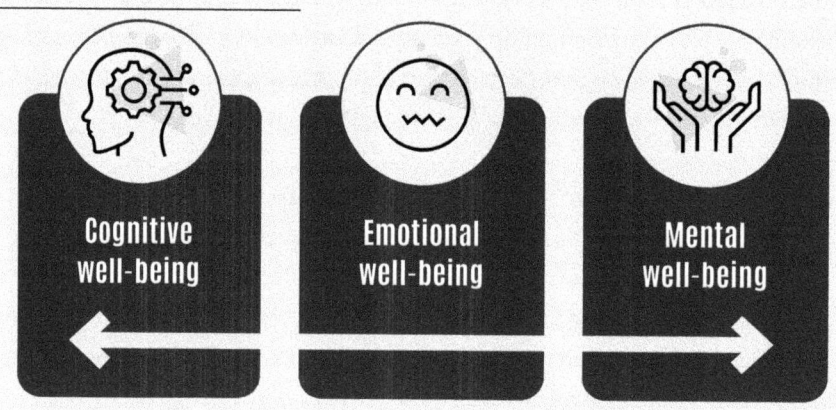

The Arts and Cognitive Well-Being

Most likely, we look after our bodies through exercise and the food we eat, so why do we fail to give the same attention to our minds? We simply do not always take the time for ourselves to engage with creativity. If you look back to your childhood you might remember finger painting, pasta collages and necklaces, toilet roll sculptures: activities ending up as artwork using household materials, still rooted in our memories. So, at what point did we put the scissors and glue stick down and, at the same time, stop looking after our own mental health? As Christianne Strang, a professor of neuroscience, has said: "Creativity in and of itself is important for remaining healthy, remaining connected to yourself and connected to the world."[2] In addition, several studies have found clear evidence that self-expression helps with attention and focus and improves cognitive well-being. Both art production and passive engagement are effective: looking at art activates the reward circuitry found in the prefrontal cortex, helping improve functional connectivity, cognitive processes, and cognitive flexibility.

The Arts and Emotional Well-Being

"The hardest thing to see is what is in front of your eyes."
—Friedrich Schiller (1759-1805)

Humans are visual creatures: in fact, 90% of information transmitted and processed by our brain is visual.[3] That means people do not just appreciate visualizations, but they are etched in our minds, which is why we often remember the things we have seen for a long time. One central feature of aesthetic experiences is their ability to trigger emotions in observers. If an artwork does not appeal to us, this often means that it does not connect to our emotions. It feels natural to experience joy, pleasure, and awe in front of grandiose artworks, or sometimes even negative emotions of fear, anger, or disgust in front of visually challenging stimuli, because art is not always happy. Edvard Munch's painting *The Scream* (1893), for example, expresses anxiety, whereas Gustav Klimt's *The Kiss* (1907-1908) reveals intimacy and joy. The arts influence our lives because of their emotional connection and their predestination to be remembered. The visual appeal becomes a memorable experience and is meant to be shared. Sharing experiences tackles emotions. Our bodies play a significant role in the aesthetic experience. Bodily sensations can draw people to art: art evokes feelings in the body, and such stimulations feel pleasant to the viewer. Every fiber of your being—your senses, your intellect, your emotions, even your physical body—responds to works of art.

Biological scientist Abigail Tucker has concluded that art does in fact have the ability to make people feel and interpret things differently, which means it can make people change their opinions.[4] This is why the emotions and bodily sensations evoked by art can be used, for example, in mental health rehabilitation and care. Cathy Malchiodi, a psychologist who specializes in the treatment of traumatic stress, has cited multiple studies that confirm that being creative can increase positive emotions, lessen depressive symptoms, reduce stress, decrease anxiety, and even improve immune system functioning.[5]

The Arts and Mental Well-Being

> "I fight pain, anxiety, and fear every day, and the only method I have found that relieves my illness is to keep creating art. I followed the thread of art and somehow discovered a path that would allow me to live."
> —Yayoi Kusama, Infinity Net: The Autobiography of Yayoi Kusama

Japanese contemporary artist Yayoi Kusama works primarily in sculpture and installation but is also active in painting and various other art disciplines. She became internationally famous for her use of brightly colored polka dots, influenced by the Pop Art movement. From a young age she created artwork she saw in hallucinations; these fantastic visions became the origin of her artistic style. Kusama has always been open about her mental well-being and has lived since the 1970s in a mental health facility that she leaves daily to walk to her nearby studio. She says that art has become her way to express her mental problems.

Getting involved in the arts has powerful and lasting effects on well-being. It can help to protect against a range of mental health conditions, manage ill mental health, and boost recovery. Besides these benefits, engagement with art also alleviates and lowers anxiety, depression, and stress. The arts' valuable role in mental well-being is recognized, and several studies have demonstrated the benefits of art museums as settings for therapy. Benefits include improved memory, lower stress levels, and enhanced social inclusion. I would like to emphasize the following conditions in particular[6]:

Reducing the feeling of loneliness. By getting involved in arts programs, people later in life can rebuild their social connections and extend existing support in their communities. Through the loss of social connections, including friends, family, and—importantly—the workplace (due to retirement), the feeling of remaining relevant is important for mental health. Getting in touch with others helps to alleviate loneliness and isolation. Time spent on creative hobbies has been associated with increased life satisfaction and decreased symptoms of depression and anxiety. This is also true for care homes, where arts activities can help increase social interactions between residents and staff, which can improve mood and well-being.

Building confidence and resilience. Looking at and creating art can help boost confidence and make us feel more engaged and resilient in recovering quickly from stress. Regular creative practice fosters confidence and a strong sense of self in many ways, especially for children. Furthermore, creating art provides a safe space for thoughts and feelings, encourages people to express their ideas to others, and leads to opportunities to turn vision into reality. Creating art will give you a sense of pride and self-worth, and through art you'll connect with others. As for becoming more resilient, art provides a nonverbal space for self-reflecting, processing difficult emotions, and envisioning a better future. Art also engages the part of the brain that reduces stress, enhances positive emotions, and builds connections between self and others.

Dealing with depression and anxiety. The title of the documentary film *I Remember Better When I Paint: Treating Alzheimer's through the Creative Arts* sums up the findings of a growing body of research into the cognitive, conscious effects of making art. The film demonstrates how drawing and painting have stimulated memories in people with dementia and enabled them to reconnect with the world. However, people with dementia aren't the only ones to benefit: studies have shown that expressing themselves through art can help people dealing with depression and anxiety, and that doing so has been linked to improved memory, reasoning, and resilience in healthy older people.

BOOSTING YOUR WELL-BEING THROUGH THE ARTS

A visit to a museum or art gallery can sometimes be an overwhelming experience. Entering a museum gallery can feel like walking into a crowded classroom: everyone wants to pull your focus to what they have to say. Where do you go, and what do you look at when everything looks appealing? With so many works available, trying to see everything can feel like a race against the clock.

How long do you usually spend looking at art in a gallery? Studies have found that visitors to art galleries spend an average of only eight seconds looking at each work on display.[7] What if, instead of looking briefly at many artworks, we look slowly at a few? The act of looking slowly at (art) objects affects the way we understand them. You will be amazed by the discoveries you can make when you look for longer at art. What happens when we spend five minutes, fifteen minutes, an hour, or a whole afternoon (although the last one will be quite a challenge!) really looking in detail at an artwork? This concept is called "slow looking." It is an approach based on the idea that, if we really want to get to know a work of art, we need to spend time with it. It is like human relationships: the more time you invest in them, the more flourishing and satisfying the relationships will be.

Slow looking is not about curators, (art)historians, or even artists themselves telling you how you should look at art. Slow looking is about the interaction between you and the artwork, allowing yourself time to make your own discoveries and form a more personal connection with it. You may be doing this alone, but you are also surrounded by other art lovers. You are connected not only to the reality of the artist who made it but also to the millions of other people who have seen it.

Start, for example, with a figurative painting such as the *Garden of Earthly Delights* by Hieronymus (Jeroen) Bosch (1450–1516).

Scan the QR code and dive into the whimsical and imaginary world of Jeroen Bosch.
▸ tinyurl.com/4u23dnta

Because little is known about Bosch's life or his intentions, most interpretations of his artistic intent behind the work are assumptions made over centuries. There is much to see in the painting, especially in the center panel, but you can also start with the left (the Garden of Eden) or right (Hell) panels. In a work so busy and complex, it can take some time to unravel the different stories taking place. In only eight seconds, you might spot numerous nude figures, parades of many different animals, or the green grass surrounded by water. But have a closer look. Notice the mountains, fountains, palm trees, strange objects, that the right panel is darker, and so on. By looking even more slowly and closely, you'll see whimsical scenes of people and animals interacting with each other. You will identify, perhaps, biblical scenes. Let your eyes and mind wander.

The next step could be trying to spend ten minutes in front of an abstract painting, a photograph, an installation, or a sculpture. Perhaps you could lose yourself in the photographs of one of my favorite photographers, Andreas Gursky (b. 1955), which are often digitally manipulated to create dense and complex depictions of modern life. You will probably find some things in common between the two works of art. What do you see?

Scan the QR code and dive into the disorienting, meticulously detailed world of Andreas Gursky.
▸ tinyurl.com/bdc3uk7u

TIPS FOR VISITING A MUSEUM

- **Prepare** for your visit. Consider what you want to see, and read some background information that will help you to understand the artwork and artist. However, sometimes it is better not to do this, and instead start with an open view and mind.

- **Limit yourself** to a maximum of three or four pieces of art.

- **Make yourself comfortable.** Find a bench or space on the floor that gives you a good view of the work. Feel free to stand or move around the artwork in order to explore it from different perspectives.

- **Close your eyes** for a short time. Be mindful in the moment; forget your plans for the day.

- **Focus.** Put quiet music on (use headphones or ear buds); try not to be distracted by your surroundings.

- **Don't worry** if nothing comes to mind at first. Be patient. Try to focus on a particular detail. If you are still struggling, consider one of the following themes as a starting point: color, shape, texture, symbols, story or narrative aspect, perspective. Or just simply follow the lines with your eyes, toward the direction the artist wants you to look.

- **Dream and fantasize, wonder and wander.** What is the story of the specific artwork? Unravel further meanings. Try to understand the inner life of the characters and their relationships to each other, if there are any. Your eyes and mind will make connections between elements of the work. Try to spot details that are hidden in plain view.

- **Ask yourself questions.** What do I like about this piece of art? How do I feel? Pay attention to how your mind and body respond. This might be in a subtle way. Most likely the art helps you feel calm, or maybe it irritates or excites you. Does it trigger any memories?

- **Trust your intuition.** Pay attention to your first impressions and why you were drawn to the work in the first place.

- **Spend a maximum of one hour** in a museum or gallery so that you are not overloaded by visual information.

- **Buy a museum pass**—the best investment ever.

- **Come back and look again.** Try a different artwork or the same artwork, straight away, after a coffee break, or on a different day. How does it look in other conditions?

CONCLUSION

Being involved in the arts benefits you in many different ways: with greater peace of mind, improved relaxation, being less withdrawn or apathetic, greater prevention of mental health problems, and increased ability to connect. For example, as demonstrated in the aforementioned documentary, people remember better when they paint: it helps them engage, come alive, and regain a certain quality of life. Creating art enables people to take greater responsibility for their own health and well-being by helping maintain independence and curiosity and improve the quality of their life by bringing greater joy.

Unfortunately, I see the lack of support for the arts. In many countries, the importance of the arts and culture is undervalued and underestimated; our investment in creative infrastructure reflects our investment in creative learning. If we do not work to support these industries, they will not, in turn, be able to support us and have an impact on our well-being. A world without the arts is desolate; we need art to communicate thoughts, feelings, and emotions that are otherwise hard to explain and understand.

QUESTIONS FOR SELF-REFLECTION

- What role does art play in your life?
- How does art affect your well-being?
- Does art evoke certain emotions and bodily sensations within you?
- Does slowly looking at art change your point of view toward a quick or fast look at a piece of art?

RESOURCES FOR EXPLORATION AND LEARNING

TOP 3: ARTICLES

Beckett, S. W. (n.d.). **The art of looking at art.** *Encyclopedia Britannica.*
▶ tinyurl.com/2p97e38r
Written by Sister Wendy Beckett, a nun and presenter of the BBC television art
series *Sister Wendy's Story of Painting*, this article addresses how to look at and
engage with art in museums.

Tucker, A. (2012, November). **How does the brain process art?** Smithsonian.com.
▶ tinyurl.com/2x6nmbxs
This article explores the results of a study conducted by neuroscientists and an art
historian in which participants' brains were monitored while looking at art. The
article further delves into the field of neuroaesthetics, or how the brain processes art.

Watts, J. P. (2019, June 25). **Slow art in an age of speed.** Tate.

▶ tinyurl.com/3e6pzdsd
In this article, English writer Jonathan P. Watts discusses the benefits of looking
slowly at art.

TOP 3: BOOKS

Cowan, B., R. Laird, and J. McKeown. (2021). **Museum Objects, Health and Healing:
The Relationship between Exhibitions and Wellness.** Abingdon, UK: Routledge.
This book provides an innovative and interdisciplinary study of the relationship between
objects, health, and healing. Shedding light on the primacy of the human need for relationships
with objects, the book explores what kind of implications these relationships might have on
the exhibition experience.

Malchiodi, C. (2013). **Art Therapy and Health Care.** New York: Guilford Press.
This book provides a complete, practical introduction to medical art therapy. It presents evidence-
based strategies for helping people of all ages—from young children to older adults—cope with
physical and cognitive symptoms, reduce stress, and improve their quality of life.

Tishman, S. (2017). **Slow Looking: The Art and Practice of Learning through
Observation.** New York: Routledge.
This book provides a robust argument for the importance of slow looking in learning
environments both general and specialized, formal and informal, and its connection to major
concepts in teaching, learning, and knowledge.

TOP 3: ASSESSMENTS AND TESTS

Artistic Preferences Scales.
The APS measures individual differences in what people enjoy about visual art.
▶ tinyurl.com/2z4rt3nz

Obelisk Art History.
Competitive art history quizzes
▶ tinyurl.com/yc88ecec

RISE ART's Art Personality Test.
Just a fun test to discover your art personality.
▶ tinyurl.com/4ymsv2jy

TOP 3: VIDEOS

Art of Healing. Currier Museum, Manchester, New Hampshire
▶ tinyurl.com/y8v5ffhf
Engaging with art and artmaking can profoundly impact our mental, emotional, and physical health. The Currier Museum's art and wellness programs turn this truth into action, transforming the lives of individuals, their families, and entire communities.

It's Official: Art Makes You Happy. *The Guardian.*
▶ tinyurl.com/mrxuwr3j
This video from the *Guardian* talks about scientists who have discovered that looking at art induces the same feelings of pleasure as being in love.

The Healing Powers of Art. Domingo Zapata.
▶ tinyurl.com/3xhvjwaw
In this TEDx talk, Domingo Zapata discusses how art can be a means of personal therapy all while painting his concepts onto a large canvas. His concepts include the healing powers of art for the artist and the viewer.

TOP 3: FREE ONLINE COURSES

Art through Time: A Global View. Annenberg Learner.
▶ tinyurl.com/3nr3fav3
This course examines themes connecting works of art created around the world in different eras. The thirteen-part series explores diverse cultural perspectives on shared human experiences.

Contemporary Art. The Art Explora Foundation's free online art history course. ▶ tinyurl.com/43nchsrv
Art Explora Academy offers eleven original courses and a media library with a range of video and audio content to delve further into the key concepts of art history, leading to a certificate validated by Sorbonne University.

European Paintings: From Leonardo to Rembrandt to Goya. University of Carlos III of Madrid.
▶ tinyurl.com/3b8chm3e
Learn about the inspirational work of the leading European painters from approximately 1400 to 1800. Painters during this period were concerned with ideas such as the pursuit of beauty, the pleasures and pains associated with love, the demonstration of power and status, and the relationship of men and women to divinity and to nature.

REFERENCES

Bort Caruso, I. (n.d.). The pictures of health: Art's healing powers. tinyurl.com/2kb7xpxv

Brown, B. (2012). *Daring Greatly: How the Courage to Be Vulnerable Transforms the Way We Live, Love, Parent and Lead.* New York: Avery.

Cowan, B., R. Laird, and J. McKeown. (2021). *Museum Objects, Health and Healing: The Relationship between Exhibitions and Wellness.* Abingdon, UK: Routledge.

Ellena, E., and B. Huebner, dir. (2009). *I Remember When I Paint: Treating Alzheimer's through the Creative Arts,* 54 min. tinyurl.com/5yhb7r23

Gilbert, E. (2015). *Big Magic: Creative Living beyond Fear.* New York: Riverhead.

Honoré, C. (2004). *In Praise of Slow: How a Worldwide Movement Is Challenging the Cult of Speed.* London: Orion.

Idema, J. (2014). *How to Visit an Art Museum: Tips for a Truly Rewarding Visit.* London: Laurence King.

Malchiodi, C. (2013). *Art Therapy and Health Care.* New York: Guilford Press.

Palmer, A. (2014). *The Art of Asking: How I Learned to Stop Worrying and Let People Help.* New York: Grand Central.

Seidl-Fox, S., and F. Hobson. (2017). *The art of resilience: Creativity, courage and renewal.* Salzburg Global Seminar.

Tishman, S. (2017). *Slow Looking: The Art and Practice of Learning through Observation.* New York: Routledge.

Tucker, A. (2012, November). How does the brain process art? *Smithsonian Magazine.* tinyurl.com/awdyd4ej

ENDNOTES

1   Wikipedia. (n.d.). Art. en.wikipedia.org/wiki/Art

2   American Congress of Rehabilitation Medicine. (n.d.). How the brain is affected by art. tinyurl.com/yp56ae4m

3   J. Weissman. (2022, February 25). The power of pictures in presentation design. *Forbes.* tinyurl.com/5n7cmuhf

4   A. Tucker. (2012, November). How does the brain process art? *Smithsonian Magazine.* tinyurl.com/dejuhpda

5   Family Caregivers of British Columbia. (2022, February 15). Episode 14: Creativity as a form of self care: Caregivers out loud. tinyurl.com/57naa94k

6   Z. Wei and C. Zhong. (2022). Museums and art therapy: A bibliometric analysis of the potential of museum art therapy. *Frontiers in Psychology* 13: 1041950. tinyurl.com/v7958zr3

7   Tate. (n.d.). A guide to slow looking. tinyurl.com/2s34utz6

INTRODUCTION

> "Just being aware is a powerful response, one that changes everything and opens up new options for growth and for doing."
>
> —JON KABAT-ZINN

Personal Story

One of the most anxious periods I have known in my life was when one of my sons, who was only four years old at the time, was suspected of having a very serious genetic disorder, from which he would not only die prematurely but would most likely suffer greatly. And there was a chance that—if the suspicion were correct—his twin brother would have the same condition. Never have I felt so paralyzed with fear. In my mind I saw my beautiful children deteriorating and dying, one after the other. The fear was in my bones. On the outside there probably wasn't much to see about me—I was functioning reasonably—but inside I felt like I was constantly shaking. At the time, I had years of meditation and mindfulness practice behind me, and I remember well that at some point, I was walking up the stairs with that crippling fear on my shoulders, when I found myself silently saying, "And now just this foot on this step ... and now just this one ..." With all my attention, in that moment I inhabited every cell of my feet and I felt briefly liberated. There really was only the present moment recollection, free from all the stories about the possible future.

The worst thing in my life didn't happen. My sons are both now healthy, resilient, and wonderful people who are nearly twenty years old.

What is the worst thing that happened to you today or this week that didn't actually happen? What if you could really see that most of the worst things in your life are just thoughts and nothing more than that? How free would you be then?

Human life irrevocably involves pain, stress, and loss: physical, mental-emotional, social, and material. That's all in the game. We all get sick. We all face death. We have little to no control over it. What we can influence is how we deal with what we encounter in life and how we relate to it. In a sense, we could say it is more about learning to love the life we live rather than striving for a life we love. Herein lies the door to a happy and contented life.
But how do we open that door?

With mindfulness.

We can establish mindfulness at every moment. Even right now ... Just take a moment to become aware of the experiences present in your body. Does your body feel tense or relaxed or both at the same time? And where is tension located in your body? Where in your body do you experience relaxation? What exactly does that feel like? Maybe those experiences are accompanied by thoughts or feelings. Explore these too with open interest. You may notice judgmental thoughts or anxiousness, joyfulness, or frustration coming up. And what if *all* these experiences were allowed to be there for now? What if you could allow them completely and breathe with them exactly as they are now? What would that be like?

You may experience that, by being present with an inquisitive, open attitude, and by allowing experiences to come in, a certain space and relaxation is created. This is the result of mindfulness. Mindfulness allows you to consciously choose how you want to respond to experiences that are present.

That's mindfulness in a nutshell: the ability to enter into a conscious, intimate, nonjudgmental relationship with each experience from moment to moment, with open interest and without immediate judgment, allowing yourself the freedom to choose the response you want to give. Mindfulness is something we can establish throughout our lives. It helps us shape a mind capable of giving wise and compassionate responses to all life experiences. It also strengthens our ability to help others with the challenges they face in their lives.

Understanding and Cultivating Mindfulness

The word *mindfulness* is a free translation of the ancient Pali word *sati*. Literally, this word means something like *present moment recollection*. When we are not mindful, we forget that the only reality is just *this* moment in all its manifestations. In this forgetful state, we all too often confuse thoughts with reality, past experience with present reality, and true happiness with the satisfaction of temporary needs that we hope to obtain permanently in the future.

Mindfulness is the willingness and ability to be attentively present to our experience from moment to moment with curiosity, wise discernment, and care, so that we can respond skillfully and compassionately. Mindfulness is always relational—how we relate to internal and external experiences, and to ourselves and the world around us. The basis for mindfulness is conscious attention, but mindfulness is much more than that. Conscious attention is mindful only when it goes hand in hand with qualities of open interest, caring, and kindness.

> **"Mindfulness is only mindful when embedded in wisdom, compassion, and ethics."**

Dimensions of Mindfulness

Mindfulness is like a diamond with many facets.[1] Different experiences require different facets of mindfulness. The more we can awaken them specifically, the more we are able to respond wisely and compassionately to life. By practicing mindfulness, the following skills become part of our personal traits.

In the next section, I will explore the five primary dimensions of mindfulness featured in Figure 3.2.

Figure 3.2: The diamond of mindfulness

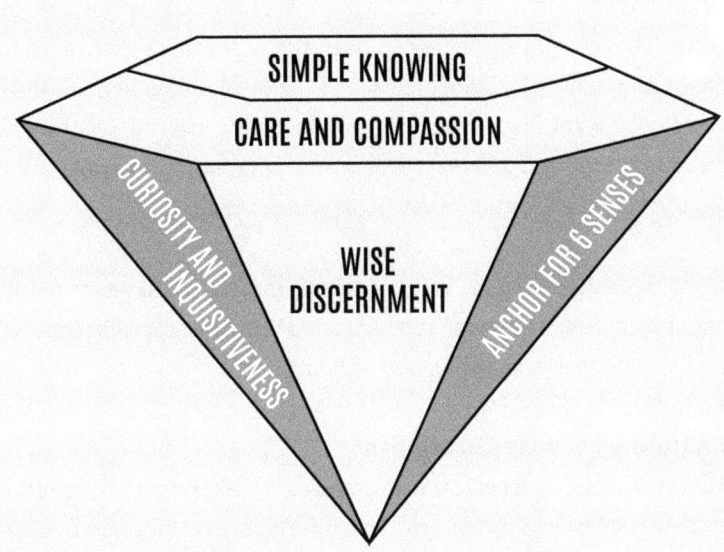

© 2024. Barbara Doeleman-van Veldhoven. The Best Version of Me.

1. **Mindfulness as the ability to really know (simple knowing).**
Mindfulness is like the sun. The sun has no pros and cons. The sunlight is not colored by moods, by assumptions, or by history. Not by fatigue or by hunger, not by desire or by envy. The sun has no agenda; it shines the same light on every experience and every situation from a distance and sees everything for what it is. So does mindfulness.

Mindfulness with its simple knowing recognizes:

- a feeling in the body as a feeling in the body
  (warm, cold, tense, sensation of clothing on the body, et cetera)

- a feeling tone for a feeling tone (pleasant, unpleasant, neutral)

- a mood or emotion as a mood or emotion
  (depressed, joyful, anxious, angry, et cetera)

- a thought as a thought (about anything)

That may sound simple, but it is not easy. Try it. Put this book down and look around. What do you see? What do you *really* see? Probably you notice the mind tends to label or link stories to what you perceive. For example: you see something lying around and you think, "I have to clean that up ... there is so much to clean up ... I have so much to do, I don't have time ... blahblahblahblah ..." And before you know it, you went from something you saw lying around to a story about not having enough time, and you feel restless and agitated. This happens to us all too often in everyday life and moves us away from reality.

Simple knowing is therefore the basis of mindfulness. It allows us to move from being immersed, overwhelmed, and identified with an experience into a more relational, inquisitive, and awake way of being.

2. Mindfulness as wise discernment.
Mindfulness is like a doorperson who assesses whether mentally emotional visitors have good or bad intentions. This differs from a doorperson who judges visitors based on their outward appearance.

Let's take *anger*. On the outside, the doorperson sees only anger. Judging from this appearance, a nonmindful doorperson would keep this guest from entering because the guest's appearance does not suit the doorperson. However, the mindful doorperson knows how to discern whether anger has good intentions to protect something—for example, an inclusive, psychologically safe workplace—or has bad intentions to destroy something—for example, to get even or to break a person down. Mindfulness has the wise discernment to keep toxic anger out while welcoming anger coming from a place of care so that a wise and compassionate response can be made to the situation.

Mindfulness unmasks negative thoughts that manifest themselves as thieves in the night, names them ("thoughts and nothing but thoughts"), and then consciously shifts attention to a sensory perception—for example, sounds, or the colors of an object, or the feeling of a foot touching the ground—as I did when I walked up the stairs and in my mind had already buried my sons. In that conscious moment, I recognized that these thoughts were totally unhelpful and instead brought the attention to my feet by being truly aware of the contact between the stairs and my feet with every step, thereby breaking the toxic cycle of a negative—catastrophizing—thought.

This discerning quality of mindfulness allows us to choose what we want to cultivate. As the Buddha taught: what we dwell upon becomes our state, becomes our trait, becomes our world.

3. **Mindfulness as an inquisitive and curious quality.**
Mindfulness is like a doctor examining a wound that has an arrow in it to see what the wound needs. A good doctor will never immediately pull out the arrow but will look at the wound with interest and care and will ask questions to find out how best to remove the arrow and treat the wound.

In this ancient description of the investigative quality of mindfulness, the arrow symbolizes an experience that we perceive as difficult, painful, or stressful. Mindfulness examines the wound—the situation or experience—and notices what is happening in the body, what thoughts and feelings arise, and what is needed to care for it.

The inquisitive quality of mindfulness teaches us to stay present and create space between what triggers us and our response to it. It helps us shift from jumping to conclusions and trying to fix the problem to investigating the situation and being curious. As a result, we can relate and respond more skillfully to what life presents us.

4. **Mindfulness as an anchor for the six senses.**
"We dance through life as puppets on the strings of our impulses," Marcus Aurelius claimed. Human nature has a strong tendency to move away from whatever we find unpleasant and toward whatever we find pleasant. This helps us survive. Think of the strong reflex to withdraw your hand from a hot stove or the impulse to put something tasty in your mouth when you're hungry. However, these tendencies—this hunger of our senses—are not always wise or helpful. They can cause us to have difficulty maintaining focus and even lead to avoidance or addictive behavior. Social media, for example, plays heavily into this tendency, causing many of us to spend more time on our phones than

is good for us. The anchoring quality of mindfulness is needed for focus and calm amid challenges and to be less prone to hyperarousal and stress.

5. **Mindfulness as a compassionate and caring friend.**
Mindfulness holds every experience in its arms with kindness, compassion, and care, without exception. It teaches us to take things less personally, even success and failure, gain and loss. The caring quality of mindfulness reduces the tendency to avoid potentially negative information—a common cognitive bias. Mindfulness not only aids in dealing with negative emotions but also facilitates more objective processing of unfavorable information.[2]

HOW DOES MINDFULNESS SUPPORT YOUR WELL-BEING?

Lost in Thought

Research shows that we spend about 47% (!) of our time lost in thought; in other words, our mind is somewhere else in place and time than our physical body.[3] This state of being lost in thought can be particularly triggered by fatigue, (imminent) danger, or low mood. Research also shows that people experience greater happiness and contentment when they are consciously present. This capacity for presence can be enhanced through cultivating mindfulness. It must be said that mindfulness is not the same as clearing your head—a persistent misconception about mindfulness. With mindfulness, we don't stop our thinking, but we learn to relate to our thoughts differently so that we are no longer trapped and ruled by them. With mindfulness we don't change the content of our thoughts; we learn to be unimpressed by their content and instead relate more skillfully to the process of thinking.

The Science of Mindfulness, Health, and Well-Being

The concept of mindfulness and the techniques used to establish mindfulness are millennia old and have their origins in both Eastern and Western traditions. Today's mindfulness programs are based on insights and knowledge from contemplative traditions, medicine, psychology, education, and scientific research.

The huge number of scientific studies on mindfulness shows that mindfulness appears to have a positive impact on:

1. **Stress reduction.** Mindfulness practices help people develop awareness of their thoughts, emotions, and bodily sensations in the present moment with a nonjudgmental attitude of acceptance and curiosity. This helps reduce stress and promotes a sense of calm and relaxation.[4]

2. **Emotional regulation.** Mindfulness enhances emotional regulation by increasing awareness of emotions as they arise and encouraging their observation without judgment. This cultivates emotional intelligence and helps people navigate difficult emotions more effectively.[5]

3. **Improved mental health.** Mindfulness has been shown to have positive effects on mental health conditions such as anxiety, depression, and substance abuse. Mindfulness develops self-awareness, self-compassion, and acceptance, all essential components of psychological well-being.[6]

4. **Enhanced cognitive functioning.** Mindfulness practices have been found to improve cognitive functions such as attention, memory, and decision-making. By training the mind to focus on the present moment and reduce distractions, mindfulness improves cognitive flexibility and enhances overall cognitive performance.[7]

5. **Increased resilience.** Mindfulness cultivates a mindset of resilience by encouraging people to approach challenges with an open and nonjudgmental attitude. It enhances our ability to rebound from setbacks, adapt to change, and find meaning and purpose in difficult circumstances.[8]

6. **Better relationships.** Mindfulness enhances interpersonal relationships by promoting active listening, empathy, and understanding. By being fully present in their interactions with others, people can improve communication, deepen connections, and foster more compassionate and supportive relationships.[9]

7. **Physical well-being.** Mindfulness practices have been associated with physical health benefits such as lowered blood pressure, reduced chronic pain, improved sleep quality, and a boosted immune system. Mindfulness reduces stress and contributes to overall physical well-being and slows down aging processes.[10]

Figure 3.3: The role of mindfulness in becoming "the best version of me"

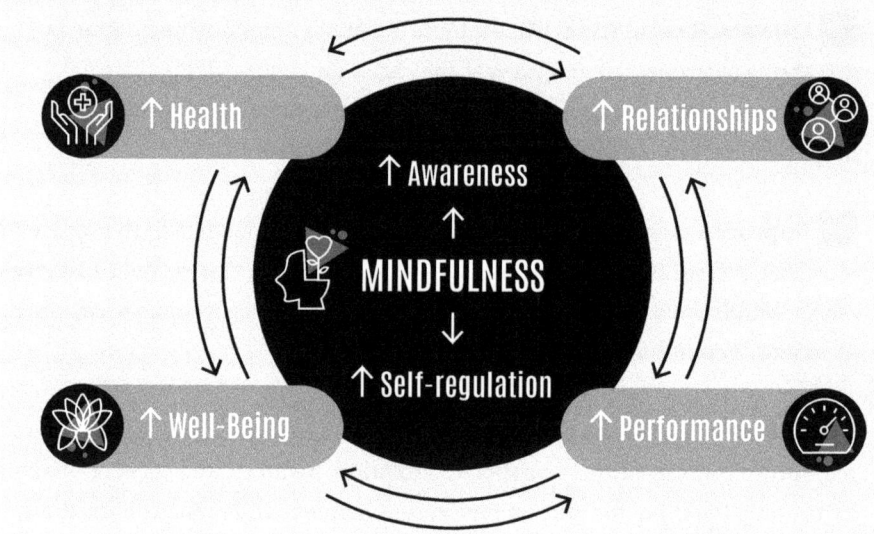

© 2024. Barbara Doeleman-van Veldhoven. The Best Version of Me.

BOOSTING YOUR WELL-BEING THROUGH MINDFULNESS

Mindfulness can be developed in many ways and can be practiced every moment of the day by bringing open and caring attention again and again to where you are and what you are doing, whether it is walking in nature, cooking, listening to music, or meeting another being. A particularly strong and proven method of cultivating mindfulness is by practicing meditation.

Meditation

Meditation practice involves techniques that train the mind to achieve a state of inner peace and heightened awareness. Meditation is relatively simple and can be done anywhere. It often involves sitting quietly, maintaining a specific posture, and directing attention to a specific object.

However, it is not always pleasant to be quietly and attentively present to the experiences that life presents to us. In meditative silence, we also encounter sadness, fatigue, fear, self-criticism, striving, and even trauma. Therefore, it is advisable to learn to meditate with a well-trained teacher who can provide guidance to properly develop your meditation technique so that you can reap the benefits.

You can find some recordings of guided meditations in the resources section at the end of this chapter.

Mindfulness Practice in Times of Stress

The next time you experience stress, pause for a moment and:
- **Observe** that stress is present, saying to yourself, "This is stressful."

- **Allow** the experience of stress, saying to yourself,
  "Stress is part of being human."

- **Inquire** how stress manifests:

  - **In the body:** You may feel your heart rate increase or your muscles tighten, your gaze narrow, your stomach retract, or something different. Be curious—like that doctor examining the arrow wound.
  - **In the mind:** What thoughts are at the forefront?
    What assumptions about yourself and the situation appear?
  - **In emotion:** Is there fear, sadness, anger, longing, loneliness, or some other emotion?

- **Touch yourself in a gentle way** by placing your hand on your heart area or by gently stroking your hand, and asking yourself, "What would I wish for myself in this situation?" In response, say, "I wish for myself (calm, ease, kindness, and so on) amid what is happening."[11]

Mindfulness is an innate human quality that can be cultivated and established in daily life and through mediation practices. It can have positive effects on various aspects of our lives, including health, well-being, relationships, and performance. By developing present-moment awareness and nonjudgmental attention, mindfulness offers a path toward greater self-awareness, understanding ourselves and the world around us more deeply, and living more fully. Last but not least, mindfulness is like a finger pointing at the moon, but it is important not to confuse the finger for the moon.

QUESTIONS FOR SELF-REFLECTION

- What is your understanding of mindfulness based on this chapter? How would you explain the concept of mindfulness to someone else?

- Why do you think mindfulness is important in today's fast-paced and often stressful world? How can practicing mindfulness benefit both individuals and society as a whole?

- How can you incorporate mindfulness into your daily life? What practical steps or strategies can you implement to cultivate mindfulness in your thoughts, actions, and interactions with others?

RESOURCES FOR EXPLORATION AND LEARNING

 TOP 3: ARTICLES

 Ackerman, C. E. (2017, March 6). **23 amazing health benefits of mindfulness for body and brain.** PositivePsychology.com.
▶ tinyurl.com/mt2m65fe
This article contains benefits of mindfulness training on health—both physical and mental—study, and the workplace.

 Bristow, J., R. Bell, and D. Nixon. (2020). **Mindfulness: Developing agency in urgent times.** The Mindfulness Initiative. ▶ tinyurl.com/yw7h3vyj
This paper opens a dialogue on the contribution of evidence-based mindfulness training to individual and collective agency.

Harvey, S. (2020, June 4). **A beginner's guide to starting a mindfulness practice.**
ShannonHarvey.com.
▶ tinyurl.com/3znxancp
Overwhelmed by insomnia and an incurable autoimmune disease, award-winning
health journalist Shannon Harvey needed to make a change. She dived into
mindfulness and wrote about what her research findings and her experiences
during her year of living mindfully.

TOP 3: BOOKS

Feldman, C., and W. Kuyken. (2019). **Mindfulness: Ancient Wisdom Meets Modern
Psychology.** New York: Guildford Press.
This book elaborates in exquisite detail what mindfulness is and where it comes from.

Gunaratana, B. (2011). **Mindfulness in Plain English.** Somerville, MA: Wisdom Publications.
This book is a classic source for understanding mindfulness.

Harris, S. (2015). **Waking Up: Search for Spirituality without Religion.**
St. Louis: Black Swan.
This book is a guide to meditation as a rational spiritual practice informed by
neuroscience and psychology.

TOP 3: ASSESSMENTS AND TESTS

Five Facet Mindfulness Questionnaire (FFMQ). Dr. Ruth Baer.
▶ tinyurl.com/3vz9crdj
The FFMQ is a self-report assessment to explore facets of mindfulness.

Mindful Attention Awareness Scale (MAAS).
▶ tinyurl.com/mppxj5c6
This MAAS scale is a 15-item (1–6 Likert scale) questionnaire to assess
dispositional (or trait) mindfulness.

Mindfulness Quiz. Greater Good Magazine.
▶ tinyurl.com/32bdr83u
This quiz draws on a mindfulness scale developed by researchers at La Salle
University and Drexel University, led by psychology professor Lee Ann Cardaciotto.

TOP 3: VIDEOS

 All It Takes Is 10 Mindful Minutes. Andy Puddicombe. TEDx, 2013.
▶ tinyurl.com/2eav4w44
Mindfulness expert Andy Puddicombe describes the transformative power
of being mindful and experiencing the present moment.

 **How Mindfulness Changes the Emotional Life of Our Brains.
Richard J. Davidson. TEDx, 2019.**
▶ tinyurl.com/4kube5cs
Neuroscientist Richard Davidson explains how mindfulness changes the
emotional life of our brain.

 How to Tame Your Wandering Mind. Amishi Jha. TEDx, 2018.
▶ tinyurl.com/nz4a9xyx
Neuroscientist Amishi Jha shows how some simple techniques can
boost attention and well-being.

 TOP 3: FREE ONLINE COURSES

Although I highly recommend learning to meditate and to train mindfulness
guided by an experienced and well-trained mindfulness teacher, you could also
explore these courses:

 Guided Meditations. Barbara van Doeleman-van Veldhoven.
▶ tinyurl.com/uwz3jewe
Guided meditations by Barbara Doeleman-van Veldhoven, an expert on
mindfulness, compassion, and leadership.

 Mindfulness and Well-Being Foundations. Rice University.
▶ tinyurl.com/yjrrm7dm
This course provides a broad overview of the fundamental concepts, principles,
and practices of mindfulness.

 **Mindfulness and Resilience to Stress at Work. University of California,
Berkeley.**
▶ tinyurl.com/22ue2rby
This course offers research-based strategies for building resilience to stress and
fortifying our well-being in the face of challenges.

TOP 3: PODCASTS

Ten Percent Happier. Rhonda Magee, Law Professor Using Mindfulness to Defeat Bias. Dan Harris.
▶ tinyurl.com/4x9ffe99
A law professor for twenty years and a mindfulness teacher for lawyers and law students, Rhonda Magee argues that mindfulness can be a solution to combatting bias and discrimination.

Unwinding Anxiety with Awareness. Tara Brach and Judson Brewer.
▶ tinyurl.com/ybxnxdth
Psychologist and Buddhist teacher Tara Brach and neuroscientist Judson Brewer explore the power of mindfulness-based strategies on how we can become disenchanted with the habit of anxiety.

Why Meditate? Joseph Goldstein and Sam Harris.
▶ tinyurl.com/56ujz5tc
Author and Buddhist teacher Joseph Goldstein and neuroscientist, philosopher, and *New York Times* best-selling author Sam Harris answer questions about the practice of mindfulness. They discuss the nature of negative emotions, the importance of ethics, and other topics.

Note: The highest-quality evidence for the importance of mindfulness is its effect on mental health conditions such as depression, anxiety, stress, eating disorders, and addiction, as well as for better coping with chronic conditions such as pain and cancer.[12]

Although scientific evidence in the field of mindfulness is acknowledged as being robust, there are ongoing debates about what is and is not "mindfulness." Because scientific precision is a precursor to shared meaning, these debates are stifling rigorous academic research. To enhance scientific progress in mindfulness research, further investigations of mindfulness classifications need to be developed.[13]

ENDNOTES

1   Much of what I know about mindfulness I learned from my beloved Buddhist teachers whom I deeply honor, including Christina Feldman, Akincano Weber, John Peacock, Martine Batchelor, Stephen Batchelor, Tara Brach, Jack Kornfield, Joseph Goldstein, Pema Chödrön, Jaya Rudgard, Martin Aylward, and others. Without them, I would not have the understanding of what mindfulness really is.

2   E. Ash, D. Sgroi, A. Tuckwell, and S. Zhuo. (2023). Mindfulness reduces information avoidance. *Economics Letters 224*, 110997. tinyurl.com/46ztyvw6

3   M. A. Killingsworth and D. T. Gilbert. (2010). A wandering mind is an unhappy mind. *Science 330* (6606), p. 932. tinyurl.com/cvw33kpc

4   R. Vonderlin, M. Biermann, M. Bohus, and L. Lyssenko. (2020). Mindfulness-based programs in the workplace: A meta-analysis of randomized controlled trials. *Mindfulness 11* (7), pp. 1579–98. tinyurl.com/mvcmj479

5   Y. Tang, B. Hölzel, and M. Posner. (2015). The neuroscience of mindfulness meditation. *Nature Reviews Neuroscience 16*, pp. 213–25. tinyurl.com/2kc45wcn

6   W. Kuyken, F. C. Warren, R. S. Taylor, B. Whalley, C. Crane, G. Bondolfi, R. Hayes, M. Huijbers, H. Ma, S. Schweizer, Z. Segal, A. Speckens, J. D. Teasdale, K. van Heeringen, M. Williams, S. Byford, R. Byng, and T. Dalgleish. (2016). Efficacy of mindfulness-based cognitive therapy in prevention of depressive relapse: An individual patient data meta-analysis from randomized trials. *JAMA Psychiatry 73* (6), pp. 565–74. tinyurl.com/ycka6fxe;
S. B. Goldberg, R. P. Tucker, P. A. Greene, R. J. Davidson, D. J. Kearney, and T. L. Simpson. (2019). Mindfulness-based cognitive therapy for the treatment of current depressive symptoms: A meta-analysis. *Cognitive Behaviour Therapy 48* (6), pp. 445–62. tinyurl.com/yc4r7jrh;
D. Querstret, L. Morison, S. Dickinson, M. Cropley, and M. John. (2020). Mindfulness-based stress reduction and mindfulness-based cognitive therapy for psychological health and well-being in nonclinical samples: A systematic review and meta-analysis. *International Journal of Stress Management 27* (4), pp. 394–411. tinyurl.com/muntw88w;
S. B. Goldberg, K. M. Riordan, S. Sun, and R. J. Davidson. (2022). The empirical status of mindfulness-based interventions: A systematic review of 44 meta-analyses of randomized controlled trials. *Perspectives on Psychological Science 17* (1), pp. 108–30. tinyurl.com/592crasc;
L.-N. Gill, R. Renault, E. Campbell, P. Rainville, and B. Khoury. (2020). Mindfulness induction and cognition: A systematic review and meta-analysis. *Consciousness and Cognition 84*, 102991. tinyurl.com/yck8enuy;
T. Whitfield, T. Barnhofer, R. Acabchuk, A. Cohen, M. Lee, M. Schlosser, E. M. Arenaza-Urquijo, A. Böttcher, W. Britton, N. Coll-Padros, F. Collette, G. Chételat, S. Dautricourt, H. Demnitz-King, T. Dumais, O. Klimecki, D. Meiberth, I. Moulinet, T. Müller, E. Parsons, L. Sager, L. Sannemann, J. Scharf, A.-K. Schild, E. Touron, M. Wirth, Z. Walker, E. Moitra, A. Lutz, S. W. Lazar, D. Vago, and N. L. Marchant. (2022). The effect of mindfulness-based programs on cognitive function in adults: A systematic review and meta-analysis. *Neuropsychology Review 32*, pp. 677–702. tinyurl.com/yc89f3zc

8   J. D. Creswell and E. K. Lindsay. (2014). How does mindfulness training affect health? A mindfulness stress buffering account. *Current Directions in Psychological Science 23* (6), pp. 401–7. tinyurl.com/52zfk6cz

9   J. N. Donald, B. K. Sahdra, B. van Zanden, J. J. Duineveld, P. W. B. Atkins, S. L. Marshall, and J. Ciarrochi. (2019). Does your mindfulness benefit others? A systematic review and meta-analysis of the link between mindfulness and prosocial behaviour. *British Journal of Psychology 110* (1), pp. 101–25. tinyurl.com/yjrznkt7;
D. R. Berry, J. P. Hoerr, S. Cesko, A. Alayoubi, K. Carpio, H. Zirzow, W. Walters, G. Scram, K. Rodriguez, and V. Beaver. (2020). Does mindfulness training without explicit ethics-based instruction promote prosocial behaviors? A meta-analysis. *Personality and Social Psychology Bulletin 46* (8), pp. 1247–69. tinyurl.com/mn7pjr9y; Vonderlin et al. 2020.

10 R. A. Heckenberg, P. Eddy, S. Kent, and B. J. Wright. (2018). Do workplace-based mindfulness meditation programs improve physiological indices of stress? A systematic review and meta-analysis. *Journal of Psychosomatic Research 114*, pp. 62–71. tinyurl.com/2p9kk79t;
L. A. J. Scott-Sheldon, E. C. Gathright, M. L. Donahue, B. Balletto, M. M. Feulner, J. DeCosta, D. G. Cruess, R. R. Wing, M. P. Carey, and E. Salmoirago-Blotcher. (2020). Mindfulness-based interventions for adults with cardiovascular disease: A systematic review and meta-analysis. *Annals of Behavioral Medicine 54* (1), pp. 67–73. tinyurl.com/6bka49f7;
N. S. Schutte, J. M. Malouff, and S.-L. Keng. (2020). Meditation and telomere length: A meta-analysis. *Psychology & Health 35* (8), pp. 901–15. tinyurl.com/59r9xb62

11 Inspired by the R.A.I.N. meditation by Tara Brach (tarabrach.com/rain) and the self-compassion mantra by Kristin Neff (self-compassion.org).

12 E. Khoo, R. Small, W. Cheng, T. Hatchard, B. Glynn, D. B. Rice, B. Skidmore, S. Kenny, B. Hutton, and P. A. Poulin. (2019). Comparative evaluation of group-based mindfulness-based stress reduction and cognitive behavioural therapy for the treatment and management of chronic pain: A systematic review and network meta-analysis. *BMJ Mental Health 22*, pp. 26–35. tinyurl.com/pf3fycpd;
L. E. Carlson. (2016). Mindfulness-based interventions for coping with cancer. *Annals of the New York Academy of Sciences 1373*, pp. 5–12. tinyurl.com/yxv32ejs

13 N. T. van Dam, M. K. van Vugt, D. R. Vago, L. Schmalzl, C. D. Saron, A. Olendzki, T. Meissner, S. W. Lazar, C. E. Kerr, J. Gorchov, K. C. R. Fox, B. A. Field, W. B. Britton, J. A. Brefczynski-Lewis, and D. E. Meyer. (2018). Mind the hype: A critical evaluation and prescriptive agenda for research on mindfulness and meditation. *Perspectives on Psychological Science 13* (1), pp. 36–61. tinyurl.com/3f5fn6dc;
N. T. Phan-Le, L. Brennan, and L. Parker. (2022). The search for scientific meaning in mindfulness research: Insights from a scoping review. *PLoS ONE 17* (5), e0264924. tinyurl.com/bdhhebhr

SELF-REGULATION

Written by Dr. Lucrecia Grandolini

"Anyone can become angry—that's easy. But to be angry with the right person, to the right degree, at the right time, for the right purpose, and in the right way— that is not within everyone's power, and that is not easy."

—ARISTOTLE, *THE NICOMACHEAN ETHICS*

INTRODUCTION

Self-regulation is the ability to use the awareness of our emotions and thoughts, in the present moment, to guide or adjust our behavior appropriately in alignment with our intentions or goals. Self-regulation is therefore crucial for success in many aspects of our lives, including both our well-being and the well-being of others. Failing to effectively self-regulate can lead to suffering and unhealthy behaviors, thereby impacting the quality of our personal and professional lives and those of the people around us. Self-regulation is not just an individual ability: it is both influenced by and influences the ability to regulate at a group or team level. Moreover, it is also shaped by the social, cultural, and environmental context. Most of the time, regulation of our emotions and thoughts is an automatic process that happens without us even noticing, yet research shows that we can improve self-regulation further with deliberate practice and attention.[1]

Personal Story

Marina was looking forward to having a conversation about her annual salary and bonus with her line manager with great excitement and anticipation. It had been an extraordinary year for the organization and for her professionally. The company had managed to successfully navigate the post-pandemic world, doubling its profits while aggressively expanding its global footprint. Professionally, Marina had achieved her long-desired promotion and worked extremely hard to turn her team into a high-performing one. Given the context, she was confident that her salary conversation was going to be very positive. Yet, to her absolute surprise, the outcome was not what she expected. As her line manager communicated the salary figures to her, Marina could feel her heart racing, her back tensing, and a range of intense negative thoughts and emotions flooding her mind. The familiar inner voice of not being good enough was loud and clear, taking immediate control of her thoughts. Feelings of confusion, anger, disappointment, sadness, and wanting to quit right on the spot rapidly bubbled up inside her. Marina took a deep breath, sat straight up in her seat, and attended to her body signals without reacting or racing for the exit. She sat with the discomfort of those feelings for a couple of seconds while she processed the range of emotions and thoughts that surfaced. Marina took another long, deep breath, soothed herself, and expressed her disappointment clearly and assertively to her line manager. After articulating the reasons why the figures did not match her expectations, her line manager listened attentively and proposed they reconvene later in the week to agree to a way forward.

Marina's response exemplifies an adaptive ability to self-regulate and effectively cope with intense negative emotions and thoughts instead of reacting to them impulsively. Marina's response did not happen by chance, however, but came as the result of deep inner work to accept her whole self and welcome the full range of inner experiences without judgment.

Like Marina, many of us grew up learning to accept and talk only about certain good or positive emotions and avoid the discomfort of feeling our own feelings. Over time, we mastered the art of suppressing our negative emotions by shoving them deep down inside to limit their expression, using humor to diffuse their impact, becoming cynical, or avoiding difficult conversations altogether.

In short, we have developed an array of creative, unconscious strategies to ignore, minimize, deflect, and disguise negative emotions so that we don't have to deal with them. From a psychodynamic perspective, these unconscious psychological processes have been referred to as *defense mechanisms* and have been the subject of study by numerous researchers for more than two centuries.[2] Examples of defense mechanisms include repression (i.e., unconscious forgetting), denial (i.e., refusing to acknowledge reality), and displacement (i.e., redirecting emotions to a safer target), to name a few.

It is important to understand that these defense mechanisms exist in all of us, even though most of the time we are completely unaware that we are utilizing them. Their primary function is to protect us from emotions and thoughts that would otherwise be too overwhelming and distressing to deal with. Their aim is therefore to reduce anxiety and create the illusion of certainty and safety for the self. However, not all defense mechanisms are equal; there is a hierarchical continuum from those that are more primitive to those that are more adaptive and mature. For instance, people with more mature defense mechanisms can distance themselves from threatening and overwhelming feelings without distorting reality. Utilizing humor, sublimation, or altruism can lead to a greater ability to effectively cope with reality. In contrast, more primitive or immature defense mechanisms (e.g., denial, projection, or somatization) are characterized by a significant distortion of the external reality, thereby impacting the ability to effectively function and cope with distressing emotions. Thus, when a defense mechanism becomes too rigid or inadequate, our ability to regulate our emotions and thoughts suffers and, over time, our well-being pays the price. Defense mechanisms therefore play a key role in how successfully and flexibly we can regulate our inner experiences (i.e., emotions and thoughts).

So, what can we do about this? As Carl Jung famously asserted, "Until you make the unconscious conscious, it will direct your life and you will call it fate." It is only when we explore our triggers and patterns of defense, and become aware of our hidden emotions and deep fears, that we can free ourselves from compulsive

repetition. Accepting these concealed and divided parts of ourselves—
what Jungian psychotherapists call our shadow—is critical in on path to our
wholeness and well-being.

But becoming aware of our triggers and defenses rarely happens by reading
a book or lying on a yoga mat. It usually happens when we are in the throes of
conflict—when we are "hooked"—and are angry, afraid, anxious, or frustrated.
It is only when we pay attention to our inner experiences and notice old patterns
that we realize we have a choice in how to respond. Through the act of radical
acceptance of all emotions and aspects of our self, including the shadow parts,
our lives are enriched; we can grow in compassion and deepen our connection
with ourselves and with others.

Understanding Self-Regulation

Various terms have been used to describe the ability to manage our thoughts
and emotions and enable goal-directed or deliberate behavior. In fact, as
Figure 2.4 illustrates, self-regulation can be understood as an umbrella term
that encompasses many different constructs that may be used to describe
similar skills, abilities, and internal psychological processes.

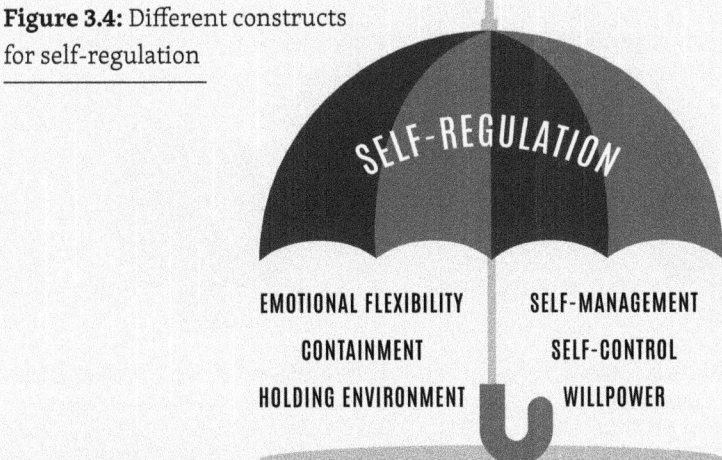

Figure 3.4: Different constructs
for self-regulation

SELF-REGULATION

EMOTIONAL FLEXIBILITY   SELF-MANAGEMENT

CONTAINMENT   SELF-CONTROL

HOLDING ENVIRONMENT   WILLPOWER

© 2024. Dr. Lucrecia Grandolini. The Best Version of Me.
Adapted from Murray, Rosenbalm, and Christopoulos.[3] Self-Regulation and Toxic Stress.

Self-regulation has been closely associated with self-management, which is one of the key components of emotional intelligence, in addition to self-awareness, social awareness, and relationship management.[4] Daniel Goleman and others explain that the better able we are to identify, understand, and address our own emotions and thoughts, the better we can make sense of and adapt to our environment, pursue goals, deal with stress, and understand the emotions and thoughts of others.

It is important to note that self-regulation and self-control are not the same, even though in everyday language they are sometimes used interchangeably. In fact, they are fundamentally different processes. Self-control is about inhibiting or obstructing emotions, thoughts, or behaviors. For example, we exert self-control to prevent the impulse of eating the leftover cake in the fridge if we want to lose some extra weight. On the contrary, self-regulation allows for the expression of emotions, thoughts, or actions but in a moderated, adaptive way. For instance, we allow ourselves to feel angry for being cut off by the driver next to us, but rather than yelling at them out of rage, we practice deep breathing and turn on our favorite song to self-soothe and calm down.

Figure 3.5: Differences between self-regulation and self-control

Self-regulation **allows** the expression of the emotion, thoughts, or actions but in a moderated and adaptive way.

Self-regulation enables us to identify and work with the entire range of emotions and thoughts, leading to a more sustainable way of coping with them.

Self-control **inhibits** the expression of emotions, behaviors, or impulses in service of a particular goal.

Self-control can be helpful in the short term but can limit the richness of emotional experiences and lead to negative implications in the long run (e.g., increasing stress).

How Self-Regulation Develops: Nature Needs Nurture

Even though self-regulation is a critical human ability, none of us is born with this capacity. In fact, how we regulate our emotions and thoughts as an adult has its roots in early childhood and is shaped by those initial years of our lives. Research shows that the development of this crucial ability is dependent on the quality of the *co-regulation* provided by parents or caregivers in the early years of a child's life.[5] In other words, infants need a primary caregiver able to adequately perceive, make sense of, and consistently respond to their needs through attuned and caring interactions, thereby establishing a sense of safety and stability for them.[6] This means that the parent or caregiver is primarily responsible for regulating the child's inner states (i.e., their emotions and thoughts) by the way they respond to them.

From a psychodynamic perspective, this process is called *containment*.[7] The theory of containment suggests that the infant projects onto their parent or primary caregiver feelings that are upsetting, painful, or even intolerable. The caregiver, in turn, feels the emotion themselves, and is able not to react to it but instead to *contain* it, and give it back to the infant in a moderated or "digested" way so that the infant can integrate it as their own emotion.

Another important notion from psychodynamic theory that plays a crucial role in the ability to regulate our emotions is the concept of a *holding environment*.[8] This entails not only a physical but, more importantly, psychological space where we feel safe enough to feel our feelings and think our thoughts. We can be open with our thoughts and emotions without becoming too distressed, overwhelmed, or fearful of being judged or rejected. A holding environment is characterized as a responsive, empathic, and repairing environment. For example, a coaching conversation or a walk with a close friend can be a holding environment where we can explore deep fears, anxieties, hopes, or dreams with trust and openness without fear of judgment. The metaphor of the holding environment is rooted in the experience of the infant who is being held by the parent—literally and figuratively—with care and attention, making them feel comforted and soothed.

Research highlights the importance of the quality of relationship (i.e., secure attachment) between the infant and the parent or caregiver in shaping the child's ability to balance their emotions, cope with stress, establish a sense of security for exploring the world, and make sense of and tell a coherent story about their lives.[9] These important attributes are all critical to meaningful interpersonal interactions with others.

Thus, it is through these repeated experiences of containment, holding, and effective co-regulation in our early childhood that we can develop our own ability to identify, understand, express, and modulate thoughts, emotions, and behaviors later in life. What parents or primary caregivers do (and how they do it) matters; this lays the foundations for healthy self-regulation, which is critical for thriving in life.

The role of context
Self-regulation does not develop in a vacuum. It is nested and influenced by multiple contexts, including the mesosystem (e.g., social environment, including family, peers, mentors, team, and others) and the macrosystem (e.g., societal norms, cultural values, and so on). It is important to note that this relationship is not deterministic but dynamic and reciprocal in nature.

Figure 3.6: Understanding self-regulation in multidimensional context

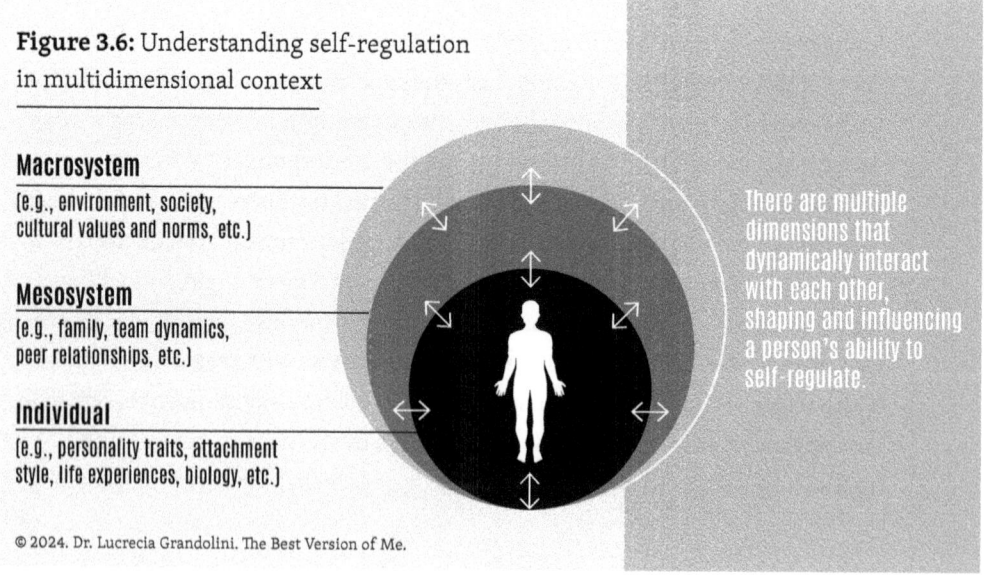

Macrosystem
(e.g., environment, society, cultural values and norms, etc.)

Mesosystem
(e.g., family, team dynamics, peer relationships, etc.)

Individual
(e.g., personality traits, attachment style, life experiences, biology, etc.)

There are multiple dimensions that dynamically interact with each other, shaping and influencing a person's ability to self-regulate.

The social context plays an important role in our ability to self-regulate. Research shows that prolonged stress that overwhelms the child's coping ability can produce long-term changes in their neurobiology and negatively impact their capacity for self-regulation.[10] At the same time, a greater ability to self-regulate can lead to increased resilience and ability to cope with intense stress and demands. Furthermore, evidence from research with adolescents shows that their ability to self-regulate is influenced by their social relationships (e.g., peers, friends, mentors, teachers) and, at the same time, their self-regulation ability contributes to the quality of those social relationships.[11] Finally, the societal and cultural macrocontext also influences the ability to self-regulate. According to social psychologist Geert Hofstede's studies on cultural dimensions across countries, societies that score high on collectivism tend to emphasize social harmony and conformity, which can lead to individuals regulating their emotions in a way that is consistent with the expectations and norms of the group.[12] Conversely, cultures that score high on individualism tend to value autonomy and self-expression, which can result in individuals regulating their emotions in line with their personal goals and desires. Thus, a multiplicity of factors come into play when understanding self-regulation in context.

Self-Regulation beyond the Individual: The Emotional Life of Groups

Our ability to self-regulate is a dynamic process that does not only take place at the level of the individual (i.e., inside of ourselves or at an intrapersonal level). Emotional regulation (or dysregulation) is also a phenomenon that happens at the level of a dyad (i.e., interpersonal level) and of a larger group. Wilfred Bion, a prominent psychoanalyst and proponent of psychodynamic theory, introduced the concept of the emotional life of groups, highlighting the dynamics and mechanisms through which groups manage their collective emotions.[13] Bion's theory revolves around the idea that groups, much like individuals, have the capacity to experience and process emotions—ranging from anxiety to excitement—and that this ability influences how a group functions and interacts. The group as a whole becomes an entity that is much greater than the sum of its parts and has a character of its own. Bion identified three *basic assumptions*, which are fundamental ways that groups unconsciously organize themselves to manage intense emotions or conflict: dependency, pairing, and fight-flight.

Left unattended, these basic assumptions can lead to emotional turbulence and derail the group from performing the task or goal it was set to do. Bion also introduced the concept of the *work group* as an ideal state in which a group effectively manages its emotions and focuses on the task at hand. In this state, the group remains aware of its emotions but doesn't allow them to dominate or derail its purpose. Instead, the group acknowledges and channels emotions constructively to enhance group cohesion and problem-solving capacity. In summary, Bion's theory emphasizes that the way in which an individual member within a group acts is the result of their own needs, history, personality, and traits as well as the group's own needs, history, and behavioral patterns. Thus, understanding and working with the various ways a group manages its collective emotions can lead to more effective group functioning and collaboration.

HOW DOES SELF-REGULATION SUPPORT YOUR WELL-BEING?

The ability to effectively identify and manage our emotions, thoughts, and behaviors in order to meet our goals is a key predictor of well-being—including our mental health, emotional well-being, physical health, academic achievement, and even socioeconomic success.[14] As a result, there is a powerful correlation between the effectiveness of our ability to self-regulate and our overall well-being.

Suppressing our emotions has a significant cost to our health: as a famous movie character played by Woody Allen says, "I never get angry. I grow a tumor instead." Research shows that inefficient self-regulation (e.g., ignoring or suppressing our emotions and needs, whether consciously or unconsciously) heightens our stress response, causing body inflammation, and thereby leading to physical illness such as cancer, diabetes, heart disease, irritable bowel syndrome, multiple sclerosis, and other autoimmune conditions and chronic diseases. As physician Gabor Maté explains, this is because emotions are physiologically electrical, chemical, and hormonal discharges from the nervous system. Emotions influence—and are influenced by—the functioning of our bodies, including our immune defenses and major organs that regulate our response to stress. However, when we repress our emotions (i.e., unconsciously block them from awareness), it disorganizes and confuses our physiological responses. In some people, this causes defenses to go awry and become the destroyers of health rather than protectors of it.[15]

Research shows that dysfunctional self-regulation is a primary contributor to the origins, development, and maintenance of several mental health illnesses including depression, borderline personality disorder, eating disorders, and a range of other psychopathological symptoms.[16] Emotional dysregulation occurs when a person interprets a situation or their own emotions in a way that makes them feel extremely overwhelmed, leading to negative or self-destructive behaviors such as struggling to control impulsive behavior or having unpredictable outbursts. However, even when the ability to self-regulate is not completely dysfunctional, research shows that difficulty with regulation may lead a person to experience longer or more severe negative affect (e.g., anger or anxiety), interpersonal difficulties, and behavioral and health problems, and to become less resilient to stressful events.[17] Consequently, an inefficient capacity for self-regulation can lead to a vicious cycle, severely impacting one's well-being.

Impact of Self-Regulation Goes beyond Oneself

Achieving increased levels of self-regulation is not only desirable but a key requirement for our well-being and the well-being of others. In fact, research demonstrates that improving self-regulation for one person or a group may have a generational impact over time. One such explanation is the phenomenon of *emotional contagion*, first described by social psychologist Elaine Hatfield.[18] Emotional contagion refers to an individual's tendency to mimic and synchronize with other people's facial expressions, postures, vocalizations, and movements. Several empirical studies have shown how emotions spread quickly and spontaneously between individuals, and between individuals and larger groups. This phenomenon can occur even through nonverbal communication, without a single word being spoken. For example, psychologists Howard Friedman and Ronald Riggio conducted an experiment in which three strangers sat facing one another in silence for a minute or two, and the most emotionally expressive of the three transmitted his or her mood to the other two without talking.[19]

Research has further demonstrated how a leader's mood and behaviors can drive the mood and behaviors of others, impacting overall performance.[20] The researchers concluded that if the leader's emotional state and accompanying behavior is a significant driver of business success, then the leader's primary task is emotional leadership. This does not mean that leaders should always be in a good mood or display their emotions in an uncontained or unmodulated way. Instead, it requires leaders to become aware of their inner emotional and psychological states and be able to self-regulate and moderate the impact they have on others. Research shows that a leader's emotional influence is greater than the influence of team members; thus, leaders are more emotionally contagious or resonant.[21] In other words, the extent to which we can effectively regulate our emotions, thoughts, and behaviors influences how other people feel, think, and behave, which leads to an impact on the overall well-being and productivity of a group.

BOOSTING YOUR WELL-BEING BY IMPROVING YOUR SELF-REGULATION

Self-regulation can be developed, yet it is not a straightforward undertaking. There is no magic formula when it comes to understanding our complex emotional and psychological inner landscape. And, in fact, it can be a difficult task to confront our emotional truths and accept the aspects of ourselves that are hidden, neglected, or denied, and which are holding us back. Yet in the difficulty of the practice lies its wisdom. By adopting a curious and open mindset, try the following practices to increase your ability for self-awareness and self-regulation.

- **Slow down.** Pause for thirty seconds. Take a deep breath. Give yourself time to stop and reflect instead of jumping into solution mode or responding immediately. By slowing down, we can notice a pattern in our reactions and defense mechanisms that are at play. In most cases, we have a choice about how to respond, and nothing is as urgent as we perceive it to be. As coaching and leadership development expert Jerry Colonna explains, we often use busyness as a mask, as a defense.[22] If we actually slow down, we might have to face whatever it is we are running from.
  Consider: What am I defending against with busyness? What other options do I have? In which ways are my defense mechanisms serving me? In which ways are they not?

- **Learn your triggers and take responsibility.** We all have emotional triggers (e.g., experiences, situations, memories) that spark an intense emotional reaction. Remember that what other people say or do may be the stimulus for our emotional reaction but never the cause. Our feelings and emotions are the result of how we choose to perceive what others have done or said. As Epictetus famously asserted, "People are disturbed not by things, but by the view they take of them."

  Consider: What happens when I get triggered? How do I react (e.g., shutting down, becoming passive-aggressive, going into fight mode, or becoming conflict-avoidant)? What do I believe about myself when this happens? What story do I tell myself?

- **Befriend all your emotions.** Emotions are not good or bad; they just are. They are powerful signals of what is important to us. Welcome the full range of emotions. Get curious about them. The practice of realizing that we are judging our emotional states is a step forward in accepting all aspects of ourselves and of others.

  Consider: What type of relationship do I have with my emotions? Is it a caring, open, and compassionate one? Or is it a judgmental and disapproving one? Do I have a different relationship with different types of emotions? What are the emotions that I avoid feeling? What are the emotions that I am comfortable with feeling?

- **Explore your attachment style.** Reflect on your attachment style and how it may influence your ability to self-regulate. Consider how your early relationships and experiences have shaped your patterns of seeking (or not seeking) support, managing stress, and relating to others. Research shows that people with higher levels of anxious attachment are more likely to up-regulate (i.e., amplify their emotional experience), leading to overreaction and high levels of negative emotion.[23] In contrast, avoidant attachment is linked to low levels of intimacy and emotional involvement in close relationships; suppression of painful thoughts, feelings, or memories; projection of negative self-traits onto others; and denial of fears.

  Consider: When reflecting on my way of relating to others, do I tend to display a more anxious or avoidant style of attachment? How does this relate to my childhood and early experiences with my parents or caregivers and family members? In which ways is my attachment style showing up in my relationships with myself, my family, or my team and organization?

- **Contain the container.** Emotions are contagious, and groups have an emotional life of their own. Many times, as leaders/parents/caregivers, we take responsibility for providing a "containing" space, or for being able to hold and tolerate a group or family emotional experience, even when it is intense or difficult to manage. However, in doing so, we may take on unprocessed emotional baggage that ends up draining us and impacting our own well-being. Thus, practices such as regular self-reflection, seeking support from others (e.g., friends, colleagues, or supervisors), and engaging in self-care activities such as exercise or meditation can help us regulate our emotions. *Consider: When I act as a container for others, where do I process my own emotions and projections I am holding on behalf of others? Which containing practices do I use in service of my own well-being?*

- **Take the "balcony" perspective.** Our day-to-day lives are on the busy "dance floor." We go through the day without taking time to step onto "the balcony" and observe the patterns and dynamics as they unfold in front of and within us. A healthy degree of self-distancing gives us the perspective we need to adjust our emotional reactions and respond to a situation more effectively. *Consider: How often do I step back physically (e.g., take a brisk walk before answering an email) or mentally (e.g., zoom out and pretend to be a fly on the wall) from an emotionally charged situation? Do I critically consider what data or information am I basing my assumptions on? What am I taking for granted? What are some alternative ways of thinking about this situation?*

- **Confront your mask and engage in shadow work.** We all have concealed aspects of ourselves that are hidden in order to protect us against the deep fear of not feeling accepted, loved, or safe in a relationship or environment. These denied, unprocessed, or unintegrated parts show up in ways that are not always helpful for us or others. For example, we may project rejected aspects of ourselves onto others and judge or criticize them rather than accepting them as our own. Shadow work is therefore the practice of understanding those parts of the self that are hidden or denied, so that we can integrate them and live a more meaningful and authentic life. Think about engaging in self-inquiry processes such as psychodynamic therapy or counseling in order to delve deeper into your shadow.

- *Consider: What did my family not talk about when I was growing up? What behaviors, attributes, or traits do I judge the most in others? What aspects of myself I would rather not think about? How do I reclaim those parts of me?*

- **Practice radical acceptance.** Focus your attention on the present moment and appreciate the transient nature of our thoughts and emotions in an open, welcoming, and nonjudgmental way. If we practice radical acceptance, we are not trying to actively change or modify emotion, thoughts, or reactions to a situation but rather accept and experience them fully. It is not about giving up or becoming self-complacent; it is actually the opposite. As psychologist Carl Rogers famously said, "The curious paradox is that when I accept myself just as I am, I can change." As a result, radical self-acceptance is the pathway to embodying the best version of ourselves and living a meaningful life. *Consider: How much time and effort have I spent trying to change myself to become smarter, fitter, more productive, or more likeable? What would it feel and look like to unconditionally love myself and strive for wholeness over perfection?*

CONCLUSION

Developing our ability to self-regulate is a never-ending task, a lifelong learning pursuit, one that must be approached with curiosity and openness. It takes courage and compassion to look deep inside and accept the ignored, neglected, and hidden aspects of our emotional lives. But there is no other path toward wholeness. As Buddhist nun and teacher Pema Chödrön puts it, "The most fundamental aggression to ourselves, the most fundamental harm we can do to ourselves, is to remain ignorant by not having the courage and the respect to look at ourselves honestly and gently."[24]

The benefits of achieving higher levels of self-regulation are multiple and compounding. By taking responsibility for our emotions and learning how to regulate them, we can create a deeper sense of connection to ourselves, others, and the environment. Moreover, we can enhance our own well-being and the well-being of those around us.

QUESTIONS FOR SELF-REFLECTION

- What is my relationship with my emotions and thoughts? Is it a caring, open, and compassionate one? Or is it a judgmental and disapproving one?

- Are there certain emotions or thoughts that I find more challenging to experience? How do these emotions or thoughts relate to my family experiences and early childhood?

- What do I need to let go of and embrace in myself to expand my capacity for self-regulation?

RESOURCES FOR EXPLORATION AND LEARNING

TOP 3: ARTICLES

Goleman, D., R. E. Boyatzis, and A. McKee. (2001). **Primal leadership: The hidden driver of great performance.** *Harvard Business Review.*
▶ tinyurl.com/fuhunkds
This article argues that effective leadership is not just about skills or competencies but also about emotional intelligence. The authors introduce the concept of "primal leadership," which refers to the emotional impact that leaders have on their followers. They argue that leaders who are able to manage their own emotions and connect with the emotions of their followers are more likely to achieve great performance.

Mind Tools. (n.d). **8 Ways to Improve Self-Regulation.**
▶ tinyurl.com/5hhjbstx
This article provides eight practical strategies and tips to enhance your emotional self-regulation ability.

Simply Psychology. (2023, June 15). **Defense mechanisms in psychology explained (+ examples).**
▶ tinyurl.com/3fyynvk6
This article explains some of the primary defense mechanisms from a psychodynamic perspective and provides practical examples of how they show up in everyday interactions.

TOP 3: BOOKS

Colonna, J. (2019). **Reboot: Leadership and the Art of Growing Up.** New York: Harper Business.
Written in a conversational and engaging style, Jerry Colonna explains the importance of embarking on a radical self-inquiry journey to address the emotional baggage holding you back in your professional and personal relationships. The book is structured around four key themes: self-awareness, self-acceptance, self-compassion, and self-forgiveness, and includes practical exercises for readers.

David, S. (2016). **Emotional Agility: Get Unstuck, Embrace Change, and Thrive in Work and Life.** New York: Avery.
Susan David provides a framework for developing emotional agility, which involves being able to recognize and manage our emotions while also being flexible and adaptive to changing circumstances. It also emphasizes the importance of aligning our actions with our values and being able to move toward our goals even when faced with difficult emotions.

Siegel, D. J. (2020). **The Developing Mind: How Relationships and the Brain Interact to Shape Who We Are.** New York: Guilford Press.
Drawing from a huge body of recent research from multiple disciplines, including neurobiology, neuroscience, and attachment theory, Daniel Siegel explains the ways in which neural processes are fundamentally shaped by interpersonal relationships throughout life.

 TOP 3: ASSESSMENTS AND TESTS

 Adult Attachment Questionnaire (AAQ).
▶ tinyurl.com/yc2eb6pk
This questionnaire will allow you to classify your attachment patterns based on two dimensions: anxiety and avoidance.

 Cognitive Emotion Regulation Questionnaire (CERQ).
▶ tinyurl.com/38srpwux
This widely used self-report questionnaire measures how individuals cognitively regulate their emotions in response to stressful and negative events.

 Emotional Agility. Susan David and Christina Congleton.
▶ tinyurl.com/4e96afpu
This assessment will help individuals understand how best to manage their emotions in the workplace using emotional agility.

TOP 3: VIDEOS

Atlas of the Heart. Brené Brown.
▶ tinyurl.com/2dm6adu8
Through interviews with experts and personal stories, this documentary series explores how complex emotions and experiences shape our lives and define us as humans. Each part focuses on a different emotion: love, heartbreak, vulnerability, and courage, and provides tools and strategies for navigating them in a healthy and productive way.

How We Can Decide How to Feel When Something or Someone Makes Us Feel Mad? Dr. Gabor Maté.
▶ tinyurl.com/29tmjfkm
In this nine-minute video, Dr. Gabor Maté discusses the importance of emotional regulation and self-awareness. He explains that our emotions are not just reactions to external events but are also shaped by our internal beliefs and past experiences. Maté argues that by becoming more aware of our emotional triggers and underlying beliefs, we can learn to regulate our emotions in a more productive way.

Why Emotions Are Important. Dan Siegel.
▶ tinyurl.com/yr73w4jf
In this one-minute, science-based explanation, Dr. Dan Siegel shares why emotions are a vital part of our mental and physical health. He discusses the important link between emotional regulation and social connection and argues that developing emotional intelligence can lead to greater empathy and understanding of others.

TOP 3: FREE ONLINE COURSES

For Enhancing Your Emotional Intelligence:
Cultivating Immensely Human Interactions. University of Michigan.
▶ tinyurl.com/5dptbm5p
This four-week course explores the intra- and interpersonal skills that form part of emotional intelligence, including self-awareness, self-management, social awareness, and relationship management.

For Finding Ground, Managing Fear. Reboot.
▶ tinyurl.com/2czp35uh
During this free, thirty-day self-guided course, you will explore what it means to find your ground and manage fear when feeling overwhelmed or uncertain to step more fully into the leaders we long to be. The course also includes a week of guided journaling to help you unpack, reflect on, and integrate what you learn about yourself.

For Shadow Work. Reboot.
▶ tinyurl.com/2h9f9ef6
In this free, five-day self-guided course, you will learn what shadow is, how to recognize it in your life and work, and the role that shadow plays in an organization. Each day contains readings about shadow, a guided journaling exercise, and additional materials for continued learning.

TOP 3: PODCASTS

Brené Brown Says You're Doing Feelings Wrong. Ten Percent Happier.
▶ tinyurl.com/2kvnpk2u
In this forty-eight-minute video, research professor and author Brené Brown discusses the importance of acknowledging and understanding the full spectrum of emotions. She explains that in her research, she has found that most people are only able to identify three emotions: happy, sad, and pissed off.

The Love that Heals: Welcoming in Our Shadow—
with Jerry Colonna and James Hollis. The Reboot Podcast.
▶ tinyurl.com/a6f22543
In this episode of the Reboot Podcast, CEO coach Jerry Colonna and Jungian analyst James Hollis discuss the concept of embracing our shadow selves in order to heal and grow. They explain that our shadow selves are the parts of ourselves that we try to hide or deny, but that these aspects can actually hold the key to our personal growth and transformation. Colonna and Hollis explore how we can learn to welcome and integrate our shadow selves, and how this process can help us to become more whole and authentic.

When The Body Says No: The Cost of Hidden Stress—
Dr. Gabor Maté. How To Academy Podcast.
▶ tinyurl.com/y4n5zfkb
In this episode, physician and author Gabor Maté explores the connection between emotions and illness and disease. Maté discusses the importance of metabolizing anger and processing trauma in order to heal and grow. He shares insights from his work with patients who have experienced addiction, chronic illness, and other challenges, and offers practical advice for cultivating self-awareness and finding the still voice within.

ENDNOTES

1 S. David. (2016). *Emotional Agility. Get Unstuck, Embrace Change, and Thrive in Work and Life.* New York: Avery.

2 S. Freud. (1957 [1894]). The neuro-psychoses of defence. In *The Standard Edition of the Complete Psychological Works of Sigmund Freud 3*, pp. 41–61. London: Hogarth Press; A. Freud. (1936). *The Ego and the Mechanisms of Defence.* London: Karnarc Books; G. Vaillant, M. Bond, and C. O. Vaillant. (1986). An empirically validated hierarchy of defense mechanisms. *Archives of General Psychiatry 43* (8), pp. 786–94.

3 D. W. Murray, K. Rosenbalm, C. Christopoulous, and A. Hamoudi. (2017). Self-regulation and toxic stress: Seven key principles of self-regulation in context. OPRE Report #2016-39. Washington, DC: Office of Planning, Research, and Evaluation, Administration for Children and Families, US Department of Health and Human Services.

4 D. Goleman, R. Boyatzis, and A. McKee. (2002a). The emotional reality of teams. *Journal of Organizational Excellence 21* (2), pp. 55-65. tinyurl.com/y9m2ds78

5 P. Fonagy, G. Gergely, E. Jurist, and M. Target. (2002). *Affect Regulation, Mentalizing, and the Development of the Self.* New York: Other Press.

6 What attachment theory pioneer John Bowlby called a "secure base." See J. Bowlby. (1988). *A Secure Base: Parent-Child Attachment and Healthy Human Development, vol. 12.* New York: Basicbooks.

7 W. R. Bion. (1970). *Attention and Interpretation.* London: Tavistock. Reprinted in: W. R. Bion. (1977). *Seven Servants: Four Works by Wilfred R. Bion.* New York: Aronson.

8 D. Winnicott. (1965). *The Maturational Processes and the Facilitating Environment.* London: Hogarth Press.

9 D. Siegel. (2020). *The Developing Mind: How Relationships and the Brain Interact to Shape Who We Are.* New York: Guilford Press.

10 J. P. Shonkoff, A. S. Garner, B. S. Siegel, M. I. Dobbins, M. F. Earls, L. McGuinn, J. Pascoe, and D. L. Wood. (2012). The lifelong effects of early childhood adversity and toxic stress. *Pediatrics 129* (1), pp. e232–46. tinyurl.com/tw34r6sb

11 J. P. Farley and J. Kim-Spoon. (2014). The development of adolescent self-regulation: Reviewing the role of parent, peer, friend, and romantic relationships. *Journal of Adolescence 37* (4), pp. 433–40. tinyurl.com/msj59r76

12 G. Hofstede. (1980). *Culture's Consequences: Comparing Values, Behaviors, Institutions, and Organizations across Nations.* Beverly Hills, CA: Sage.

13 W. R. Bion. (1955). Group dynamics: A review. *International Journal of Psycho-Analysis 33*, pp. 235–47; E. Jaques. (1955). Social systems as a defence against persecutory and depressive anxiety. In M. Klein, P. Heimann, and R. E. Money-Kyrle (Eds.), *New Directions in Psycho-Analysis*, pp. 478–98. London: Tavistock; I. E. P. Menzies. (1960). A case-study in the functioning of social systems as a defence against anxiety: A report on a study of the nursing service of a general hospital. *Human Relations 13* (2), pp. 95–121. tinyurl.com/2jawee3n

14 K. Drake, J. Belsky, and R. M. P. Fearon. (2014). From early attachment to engagement with learning in school: The role of self-regulation and persistence. *Developmental Psychology 50* (5), pp. 1350-61; M. Fenton-O'Creevy, E. Soane, N. Nicholson, and P. Willman. (2011). Thinking, feeling, and deciding: The influence of emotions on the decision making and performance of traders. *Journal of Organizational Behavior 32*, pp. 1044-61. tinyurl.com/2p92ewwj; R. F. Baumeister and T. F. Heatherton. (1996). Self-regulation failure: An overview. *Psychological Inquiry 7* (1), pp. 1-15. tinyurl.com/8725nrvt; M. Berking and P. Wupperman. (2012). Emotion regulation and mental health: Recent findings, current challenges, and future directions. *Current Opinion in Psychiatry 25* (2), pp. 128-34. tinyurl.com/yc4rtkx9; D. A. Robson, M. S. Allen, and S. J. Howard. (2020). Self-regulation in childhood as a predictor of future outcomes: A meta-analytic review. *Psychological Bulletin 146* (4), pp. 324-54.

15 G. Maté. (2003). *When the Body Says No: The Cost of Hidden Stress.* Toronto: Knopf.

16 J. F. Thayer and R. D. Lane. (2000). A model of neurovisceral integration in emotion regulation and dysregulation. *Journal of Affective Disorders 61* (3), pp. 201-16. tinyurl.com/5e2vf5bh; D. S. Mennin and D. M. Fresco. (2009). Emotion regulation as an integrative framework for understanding and treating psychopathology. In A. M. Kring and D. M. Sloan (Eds.), *Emotion Regulation in Psychopathology: A Transdiagnostic Approach to Etiology and Treatment*, pp. 356-79. New York: Guilford Press; L. Schulze, G. Domes, A. Kruger, C. Berger, M. Fleischer, K. Prehn, C. Schmahl, A. Grossmann, K. Hauenstein, and S. C. Herpertz. (2011). Neuronal correlates of cognitive reappraisal in borderline patients with affective instability. *Biological Psychiatry 69* (6), pp. 564-73. tinyurl.com/4td7k9nt

17 C. Verzeletti, V. L. Zammuner, C. Galli, and S. Agnoli. (2016). Emotion regulation strategies and psychosocial well-being in adolescence. *Cogent Psychology 3* (1), 1199294. tinyurl.com/y3spxh8e

18 E. Hatfield, J. L. Cacioppo, and R. L. Rapson. (1993). Emotional contagion. *Current Directions in Psychological Sciences 2* (3), pp. 96-99. tinyurl.com/bdeemvab

19 H. S. Friedman and R. E. Riggio. (1981). Effect of individual differences in nonverbal expressiveness on transmission of emotion. *Journal of Nonverbal Behavior 6*, pp. 96-104. tinyurl.com/ynpd7vmk

20 D. Goleman, R. Boyatzis, and A. McKee. (2002b). *Primal Leadership: Unleashing the Power of Emotional Intelligence.* Boston: Harvard Business Review Press.

21 R. E. Boyatzis and A. McKee. (2005). *Resonant Leadership: Renewing Yourself and Connecting with Others through Mindfulness, Hope, and Compassion.* Cambridge, MA: Harvard Business School Press.

22 J. Colonna. (2019). *Reboot: Leadership and the Art of Growing Up.* New York: Harper Business.

23 C. Liu and J. L. Ma. (2019). Adult attachment style, emotion regulation, and social networking sites addiction. *Frontiers in Psychology 10*, 2352. tinyurl.com/3vwzxd5p

24 P. Chödrön. (2002). *When Things Fall Apart: Heart Advice for Difficult Times.* Boston: Shambhala.

RESILIENCE AND ADAPTABILITY

Written by Dr. Jacqueline Brassey

INTRODUCTION

In this chapter, I will delve into the pivotal role of resilience and adaptability in personal growth. Though definitions of resilience abound, for our purposes I will define it not only as the ability to bounce back from challenges but also to bounce forward beyond them, which is why I have added adaptability in addition to resilience. Think of it as not merely enduring the rain but learning to dance joyfully in it. In our journey to become the best version of ourselves, it is imperative to harness both resilience and adaptability.[1]

> "If the rhythm of the drum beat changes, the dance step must adapt."
> —AFRICAN PROVERB

Personal Story

During one of my most recent holidays with my family, I found it very hard to relax. Having maintained a pace that felt like a thousand miles an hour for many months in a row, it was hard to change gears and focus on family and resting. It took me two weeks to feel like I could finally relax, which was just about the time we returned home.

This holiday made me reflect on my youth. I grew up in a Christian family where on Sundays we focused on church, Sunday school, family gatherings, and rest. We did not work or do any homework for school; we did not watch television. Instead, we focused on being together as a family, relaxing, reading a book, and having conversations. Back then, I did not always like it, but today I sometimes long for that time—having one full day off every week, without feeling guilty, was and is not a bad idea at all.

The secret ingredients for resilience and adaptability in many aspects of our life include rest, recovery, and relaxation. We must find ways to process new learning and insights in our whole brain and body. In today's world, this is harder and harder to accomplish. I know I am not alone in this struggle. In the work that I do, I often hear people say, "I can't afford to do nothing." We all sometimes feel that we are trapped in the myth of falling behind, not fully realizing that we fall behind if we don't choose to rest and are intentional about it.

Rest and recovery are often overlooked in the context of resilience and adaptability.[2] However, they offer both the recovery mechanism after hard work (to help us bounce back from hardship and effort) as well as the fertile ground for growth and development (to help us bounce forward).

I admire Edith Eger's work on being *intentional* and, above all, embracing the belief that we all have a *choice*, as she beautifully describes in one of her most famous books, *The Choice: Embrace the Possible*. A Holocaust survivor, Eger lived through the most inhumane circumstances that any human being can experience when she was deported and imprisoned in concentration camps during World War II. During this time, she found an inner strength and resilience that helped her survive. Her work focuses on the transformational power of choice as a core element of resilience and adaptability.

A related concept is that of taking radical accountability or full self-responsibility for your life. No matter the situation, you can take ownership for what you feel, say, and do in response. In both light and dark times, *being intentional with and being able to choose to move forward and toward what matters most* is resilience and adaptability in action.[3]

You need three main ingredients to make this happen:

(1) the ability of awareness and the courage to choose;

(2) the skills to follow up effectively on this choice, be it in the moment or over a period of time; and

(3) sufficient energy power or muscle to make it happen. This is about adopting a different lifestyle, and that needs a mindset to support it.

Resilience and adaptability are carried by (1) the mind and brain, (2) the body and your energy supply, and (3) the context in which you operate, and it all starts with awareness and choice.

To explain this concept, and to make it practical, I will explore resilience and adaptability in the context of four elements of overall or holistic health: mental, physical, social, and spiritual health, based on the modern understanding of the health framework by the McKinsey Health Institute.[4] I focus on health through a positive lens, taking a well-functioning perspective.

Figure 3.7: A modern understanding of health—four elements

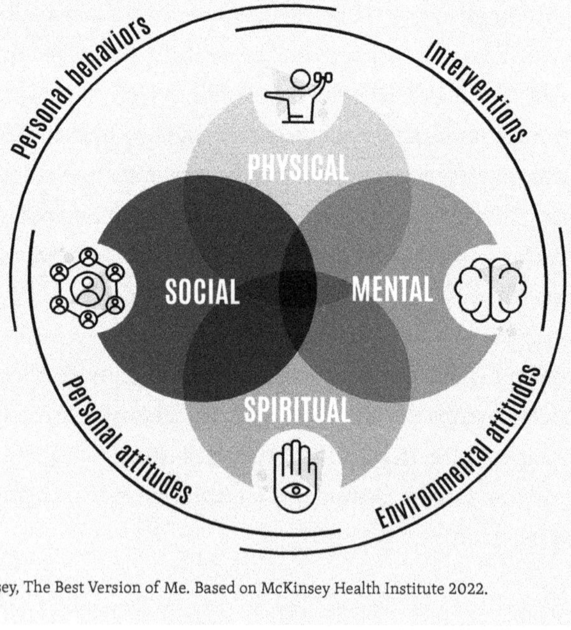

© 2024. Dr. Jacqueline Brassey, The Best Version of Me. Based on McKinsey Health Institute 2022.

Mental Health

"Mentally healthy individuals have the resilience to cope with normal stresses and adverse events while maintaining a positive and realistic sense of self."[5]

One important way to build mental resilience and adaptability in support of mental health is through the development of flexible mindsets and beliefs, or what you believe to be true.[6] Mindsets and beliefs matter, as research has shown, not only for supporting mental health but also facilitating the development of physical, social, and spiritual health. Stanford University professor Dr. Alia Crum has found that beliefs can impact even physical outcomes. In a study where she explained to hotel housekeepers that through their work they would get a lot of physical exercise, they improved on physiological parameters (including blood pressure and weight) after a few weeks in comparison to hotel housekeepers who had not received this explanation. The main difference between the two groups was the information they received through their participation in the study and the possible impact it had on their mindsets and beliefs.[7] In addition, Crum discovered that how we appraise stress impacts how we are impacted by stress.[8]

Physical Health

"Physical health is the extent to which an individual can competently perform physical tasks and activities without significant discomfort ..."[9]

Building physical resilience and adaptability, paradoxically enough, occurs when you put your body under stress (combined with space for recovery). Another word for stress is discomfort, and it is usually something we want to avoid. For example, going for a run means we put stress on our bodies; when first starting out, we will quickly run out of breath, which is uncomfortable. Our urge is then to stop, slow down, and walk instead. But when we push through the barrier of discomfort, our body develops physically and becomes stronger. If we follow a careful program, eventually our resilience will improve, and our body will adapt to the strain.[10] The same goes for weight training, and there are many more variations. One that has grown in popularity recent years is taking an icebath or even starting the day with a cold shower, for which there is scientific evidence for improving physical resilience, adaptability, and mental strength.[11]

Social Health

"Social health represents an individual's ability to build healthy, nurturing, genuine, and supportive relationships ..."[12]

Ongoing research at Harvard University has shown that having social connections and relationships and being part of a community helps us live longer and be happier. Social laughter is an important element of that: research has shown that it can even elevate the pain threshold.[13] Being able to build and nurture healthy social connections is one way to develop social resilience and adaptability. For some people, this happens naturally through family, school, work, and other social activities such as sports. For others, this doesn't happen naturally, and at different stages of life we may find ourselves more isolated than at others. The "how" is different for everyone. Those of us with more extroverted personalities may enjoy having many social events and a large network of friends and acquaintances, whereas those with more introverted personalities may prefer having fewer such events and friends. The key is to get to know yourself and your personal preferences and to reflect on how you can take care of your social resilience and adaptability in a sustainable way.

Spiritual Health

"Spiritual health enables people to integrate meaning in their lives ...
Spiritually healthy people have a strong sense of purpose ..." [14]

One of my all-time favorite books about spiritual health is Viktor Frankl's *Man's Search for Meaning*. Frankl, a Holocaust survivor and psychiatrist, developed the idea of "logotherapy" as a result of what he learned as a concentration camp prisoner. According to the McKinsey Health Institute, "'*Logos*' is the Greek word". Logotherapy is therefore healing (or therapy) through meaning. We have the freedom to search for, find and realize the meaning of our lives."[15] Frankl discovered that prisoners who found meaning and remained hopeful for survival despite experiencing inhumane circumstances were more likely to survive than those who did not. In addition, Columbia University professor Lisa Miller has studied spiritual health and highlighted increasing scientific evidence for the importance of meaning and its impact on resilience, adaptability, and spiritual health.[16]

HOW DO RESILIENCE AND ADAPTABILITY SUPPORT YOUR WELL-BEING?

Well, this of course depends on how we define well-being, given that there are multiple ways to measure it.[17] One way of looking at well-being is through the aforementioned concept of holistic health, or the sum of one's mental, social, spiritual, and physical abilities to function well. It's important to note that people can experience positive or well-functioning holistic health even in the presence of an illness or disability. By adopting this definition of well-being for this chapter, I will add a few more insights as evidence of how resilience and adaptability impact your well-being. For example, a recent employee study conducted across thirty countries found that 49% of the variance in holistic health (which refers to the change in the holistic health measure) was associated with experiences in the workplace. The researchers found that multiple factors in the workplace influence holistic health, from policies at the organization level to experiences at one's team or job level, to individually driven experiences supported by personal skills and abilities. Two key drivers for holistic health at the individual level were general self-efficacy and affective adaptability.[18] In other words, employees who had higher levels of self-efficacy and affective adaptability also reported higher levels of holistic health. In this study, a sample survey item used to measure self-efficacy was, "Thanks to my resourcefulness, I know how to handle unforeseen situations," and for affective adaptability, "If I have to change my plans, I stay relaxed."[19] Both survey items demonstrate how being resilient and adaptable impact well-being (holistic health).

BOOSTING YOUR WELL-BEING THROUGH RESILIENCE AND ADAPTABILITY

The journey to improving resilience and adaptability is worth taking. The great news is there are many tools to help you along the way, all of which support each other. The starting point for developing resilience and adaptability is first cultivating holistic awareness of what matters to you and what you value. When you learn these things, you can proactively and intentionally build your resilience and your adaptability (and when you need to, recover and replenish) but also respond in the moment when you experience immediate challenge (when you need to use your reserves and muscles). The following practices will help you on your journey. I have included one practice per element of holistic health: mental, spiritual, physical, and social.

Practice 1 (mental): Reframe mindsets with curiosity.
Our mindsets and beliefs influence how we experience the world around us and how we respond to a variety of situations. Our brain works through prediction; that is, leveraging what we have already learned until we need to add new viewpoints to our repertoire. To build mental resilience and adaptability, we can open our curious mind when we get stuck or feel stressed or tense. We can do this by asking a few simple questions: What can I learn from this? Tell me more? I wonder why?

In addition, you can use the mindset shifts tool mentioned in the resources to work your curiosity muscle even more.[20] Reflect on a challenging situation that you recently experienced where you were not at your best. Write down what happened and ask yourself whether you were aware of your thoughts in the moment. Which mindset prevailed, and how did you behave as a result? Do you think using different mindsets could have led to a different outcome? What can you learn from this reflection? What is the intention you can build for future challenging situations? Writing in a notebook for a few weeks to track your experiences and reflections can help you see a pattern, learn from it, and change your behavior where helpful. Explore how becoming more curious and pivoting mindsets can help you navigate challenging conversations and situations.

Practice 2 (spiritual): Summon your inner council or holding council.[21]
The following steps have been adapted from Lisa Miller's book *The Awakened Brain: The Psychology of Spirituality and Our Search for Meaning*.

- Sit down. Close your eyes.

- Place before you a table. To your table you may invite anyone, living or deceased, who truly has your best interests in mind.

- With all of your guests sitting there at your table, ask them if they love you.

- And now to your table, invite your higher self—the part of you that is much greater than anything you have or haven't done, anything you have or don't have.

- Ask your eternal, higher self if you love you.

- And now to your table invite your higher power, whoever or whatever it is to you. Ask if your higher power loves you.

- And now, with all of those people sitting there, ask,
  "What do I need to know right now? What do you need to tell me?"

- These people are your inner council (or holding council). Though different people may show up at your table at different times, your inner council is always there for you. You can ask them questions anytime, anywhere.

Practice 3 (physical): Develop comfort with discomfort.
Building resilience can also be done by doing something physically challenging such as taking a cold shower, walking up and down the stairs, or doing sit-ups. The secret lies in learning to become comfortable with the physical discomfort of doing so. Though uncomfortable, deliberate cold exposure, for example, can also positively impact the health of your brain and body. In fact, there is scientific support for the effects of cold exposure on health and performance as Stanford University professor Andrew Huberman has explained.[22] For various evidence-based protocols and tips for experimenting with cold showers, explore expert sources from the Huberman Lab or UCLA.[23]

Practice 4 (social): Become a mentor or coach.
There are many ways to both build meaningful relationships and cherish the ones you already have. But this does not come naturally to all of us, and some people don't have a strong support network of friends, family, or colleagues. The good news is that there is a lot you can do to improve your support network, and small steps matter! For example, you could find a way to volunteer by being a buddy or an ally to someone else, or you could find someone with whom to build a professional peer coaching relationship. This could be someone in the same profession as yours or even someone unrelated to work, perhaps from a sports club, university (such as a student mentor), eldercare community, nongovernmental organization, or animal shelter. There are many opportunities if you open yourself up to trying something new. Stepping out of your known environment and exploring new realities not only helps others but also helps you broaden your horizons!

CLOSING THOUGHTS

To close this chapter, I would love to honor my grandmother Jacoba, after whom I was named when baptized. My grandmother, born in 1903, was always full of stories; she was very authentic (she would just say things as she saw them without sugarcoating anything); she was serious and God-fearing, but I also remember her for her laughter and humor. She died at the respectable age of ninety-two after having lived through two world wars and losing four of her twelve children at very young ages. She must have known a thing or two about resilience and adaptability, for sure! I wish I could have another cup of coffee with her today to ask for her life lessons. I dedicate this chapter to my grandmother Jacoba with this last quote from another inspirational woman, Gladys McGarey, who recently published a book at the incredible age of 102! It is a quote about laughter, relevant to the topic of this chapter (especially laughter's role in social resilience), and which made me think of my grandmother:

> **"Laughter without love is cruel. It's mean [and] cold, but laughter with love is joy and happiness."**
> —Gladys McGarey, author of *The Well-Lived Life: A 102-Year-Old Doctor's Six Secrets to Health and Happiness at Every Age*

Apart from playing a central role in social health, perhaps humor, laughter, compassion, and love can also help to unlock broader resilience and adaptability, especially when the going gets tough!

RESOURCES FOR EXPLORATION AND LEARNING

TOP 3: ARTICLES

Brassey, J., A. De Smet, and M. Kruyt. (2023, January 19). **Developing dual awareness.** McKinsey Quarterly.
▶ tinyurl.com/4tbxnet6
A core part of becoming intentional about adaptability and resilience is a concept called "dual awareness." In this article, the authors explain dual awareness, what it means, and how to develop it, and provide examples from real life.

Brassey, J., and M. Kruyt. (2020, April 30). **How to demonstrate calm and optimism in a crisis.** McKinsey & Company.
▶ tinyurl.com/3xkzp8n9
In this article, the authors explain the importance of learning how to navigate uncertainty and remain calm (for which you need resilience and adaptability skills). They conclude with six additional practical tools that can be applied in day-to-day life.

Brassey, J., B. Herbig, B. Jeffery, and D. Ungerman. (2023, November 2). **Reframing employee health: Moving beyond burnout to holistic health.** McKinsey & Company.
▶ tinyurl.com/4sra5nxw
For a better understanding of how adaptability and resilience drive employee holistic health and are beneficial to reducing burnout symptoms, please explore this latest global study—the first of its kind—to examine this topic across thirty countries.

TOP 3: BOOKS

Brassey, J., N. van Dam, and A. van Witteloostuijn. (2022). **Authentic Confidence: Advancing Authentic Confidence through Emotional Flexibility: An Evidence-Based Playbook of Insights, Practices, and Tools to Shape Your Future.** 2nd ed. Zeist: VMN Media.
Authentic Confidence is a detailed book for leadership and development practitioners, human resources leaders, coaches, and anyone who wants to develop authentic confidence. The book combines detailed science with a practical toolkit that includes thirty-two tools to start building authentic confidence (and resilience!) right away.

Brassey, J., A. De Smet, and M. Kruyt. (2022). **Deliberate Calm: How to Learn and Lead in a Volatile World.** New York: Harper Business.
A core book about the concept of leadership adaptability, *Deliberate Calm* addresses how to learn and lead in a world that becomes more complex and unpredictable day by day.

Frankl, V. (2006). **Man's Search for Meaning.** Boston: Beacon Press.[†]
An absolute must read!

ASSESSMENTS AND TESTS

How Resilient Are You? Mind Tools.
▶ tinyurl.com/m4cn8dhu
An easy and practical test about resilience and adaptability.

Reaching Your Potential.
▶ tinyurl.com/3ysffzpb
As addressed in the book *Authentic Confidence* (listed above), developing emotional flexibility is central to resilience and adaptability. The authors offer a free online assessment based on validated scales of emotional flexibility.

Resources from Professor Ralf Schwarzer.
▶ tinyurl.com/2p9h2ke9
General self-efficacy is an indicator of resilience and adaptability. A good test on this is the scale developed by Professor Ralf Schwarzer. On his website you can find this instrument and many other open access resources.

VIDEOS

Authentic Confidence through Emotional Flexibility. Jacqueline Brassey.
▶ tinyurl.com/3rywm679
This was my first TEDxINSEAD talk after my own personal confidence crisis. This journey led me to study and write about resilience and adaptability in the years that followed.

How to Be a More Adaptable Leader Using Deliberate Calm. Aaron De Smet.
▶ tinyurl.com/yzfza9k4
A great explanation by my co-author and senior partner at McKinsey & Company, Aaron De Smet, about the key concepts in one of my latest books on adaptability, called *Deliberate Calm* (listed above).

---

† There are multiple editions of this book, and I have listed a more recent one here. The original first edition, published in 1959, was under the title *From Death Camp to Existentialism: A Psychiatrist's Path to a New Therapy.* The first editions of *Man's Search for Meaning* were published in 1962.

Zoning In and Out of Stress. Jacqueline Brassey.

▶ tinyurl.com/mt3rvjy6

In my second TEDxWassenaar talk, I explain how we navigate different zones of stress every day, how we can become aware of it, and how to start being more intentional in our responses to it.

PODCASTS

The Gift and Power of Emotional Courage. Susan David.

▶ tinyurl.com/yc3rwjun

One of the best TED talks ever about emotional agility.

Huberman Lab Podcast.

▶ tinyurl.com/bdz28hkk

I have been a huge fan of Andrew Huberman's work from day one. His podcasts are practical, evidence based, and hugely entertaining— great to listen to when on a walk or a run.

New Female Leaders Podcast. Jacqueline Brassey, in conversation with Caroline Glasbergen.

▶ tinyurl.com/hamjj795

In this podcast with Caroline Glasbergen, I explain a bit more about my personal journey and why authentic confidence is relevant for leadership today.

OTHER REFERENCES

Eger, E. E. (2017). *The Choice: Embrace the Possible.* New York: Scribner.

McGarey, G. (2023). *The Well-Lived Life: A 102-Year-Old Doctor's Six Secrets to Health and Happiness at Every Age.* New York: Atria.

ENDNOTES

1 S. Epstein. (2022, September 19). How adaptability helps you "bounce forwards" at work. BBC. tinyurl.com/hrn5e32b

2 J. Brassey and A. De Smet. (2023, September 19). Burnout is attacking our brains and making it harder to excel at work. "Deliberate calm" can help us adapt. *Fortune.* tinyurl.com/bdeezuc9

3 See also: J. Brassey, N. van Dam, and A. van Witteloostuijn. (2022). *Authentic Confidence: Advancing Authentic Confidence through Emotional Flexibility: An Evidence-Based Playbook of Insights, Practices, and Tools to Shape Your Future.* 2nd ed. Zeist: VMN Media.

4 The health framework of the McKinsey Health Institute can be found at tinyurl.com/8awm235t

5 For the complete definition, see tinyurl.com/8awm235t

6 This is also part of two of my own books that I co-authored: *Authentic Confidence* (with Nick van Dam and Arjen van Witteloostuijn) and *Deliberate Calm* (with Michiel Kruyt and Aaron de Smet); both can be found in the resources list.

7 A. J. Crum and E. J. Langer. (2007). Mind-set matters: Exercise and the placebo effect. *Psychological Science 18* (2), pp. 165–71. tinyurl.com/2euz2x87

8 M. Abrahams. (2021, September 16). Mindset matters: How to embrace the benefits of stress. Insights by Stanford Business. tinyurl.com/5n96afna

9 For the complete definition, see: tinyurl.com/8awm235t

10 In all of these examples, I recommend you seek professional advice from a fitness trainer, for example.

11 See, for example, Huberman Lab. (2022, May 1). The science and use of cold exposure for health and performance. tinyurl.com/y6ecrwe3

12 For the complete definition, see: tinyurl.com/8awm235t

13 Harvard Second Generation Study. (n.d.). adultdevelopmentstudy.org and R. I. M. Dunbar, R. Baron, A. Frangou, E. Pearce, E. J. C. van Leeuwen, J. Stow, G. Partridge, I. MacDonald, V. Barra, and M. van Vugt. (2011). Social laughter is correlated with an elevated pain threshold. *Proceedings of the Royal Society B 279* (1731), pp. 1161–67. tinyurl.com/3mn7d7bd

14 For the complete definition, see: tinyurl.com/8awm235t

15 For the complete definition, see: tinyurl.com/8awm235t

16 L. Miller. (2021). *The Awakened Brain: The Psychology of Spirituality and Our Search for Meaning.* New York: Random House.

17 See, for example: I. Wijngaards. (2018). *Measuring Worker Well-being: An Evaluation of Closed and Open-Ended Survey Questions.* Rotterdam: Erasmus University. repub.eur.nl/pub/136992. See also World Wellbeing Movement. (n.d.). worldwellbeingmovement.org

18 See J. Brassey, B. Herbig, B. Jeffery, and D. Ungerman. (2023, November 2). Reframing employee health: Moving beyond burnout to holistic health. McKinsey & Company. tinyurl.com/4sra5nxw

19 See The general self-efficacy scale (GSE). (n.d.). tinyurl.com/2hm445xw; and K. van Dam and M. Meulders. (2020). The adaptability scale: Development, internal consistency, and initial validity evidence. *European Journal of Psychological Assessment 37* (2), pp. 123–34. tinyurl.com/ytdr23wh

20 J. Brassey, A. De Smet, A. Kothari, J. Lavoie, M. Mugayar-Baldocchi, and S. Zolley. (2021, August 2). Future proof: Solving the "adaptability paradox" for the long term. McKinsey & Company. tinyurl.com/yt9t3b3s

21 Adapted from Miller 2021, p. 203. Reproduced with permission. Dr. Miller would like to bring this visualization through "a legacy of teachers, with its origin by the late Dr Gary Weaver, who helped to renew awakened awareness in traumatized youth who had felt cut off."

22 A. Huberman. (2022, May 1). The science & use of cold exposure for health & performance. Huberman Lab Neural Network Newsletter. tinyurl.com/mpzrtf5n

23 See the Huberman Lab website: hubermanlab.com and UCLA Health. (2023, January 25). 6 cold shower benefits to consider. tinyurl.com/39kth65f

LEARNING

Written by Jan Rijken

INTRODUCTION

Learning is essential for each of us; it is a key driver for our personal, social, and individual development. We have a huge individual potential and opportunities to continue learning throughout our lives. If we do not avail ourselves of learning opportunities, we run the risk of stagnation in career growth as well as missed chances for personal fulfillment and well-being.[1]

> "Live as if you were to die tomorrow.
> Learn as if you were to live forever."
> —MAHATMA GANDHI

Personal Story

I first realized the essence of learning for myself and my well-being at the age of eleven. At the end of primary school, while living in the Netherlands, my father announced that he had accepted a new job in England, which meant that our family would move to Coventry in a few months' time. My parents strongly advised me to take English lessons to prepare myself for life in England, but I did not feel the urgency to comply. When we moved to our new country, I suddenly became aware of the need to learn English to survive on a personal level and to understand the classes when my new secondary school term started. In addition, I needed to build relationships with new friends and understand local habits and values while slowly trying to contend with puberty and all its physical, biological, and emotional changes. With support from family, friends, and teachers, and by keeping a dictionary close at hand (there was no Google Translate!), I took advantage of formal and informal learning opportunities and developed a better version of myself, one who had a new sense of well-being, who was better equipped to handle all challenges in my new English environment, and who was more confident in (sometimes painful) learning experiences.

Key Characteristics of Learning

In order to assess how we can boost our own well-being through learning, it is important to understand the concept of learning: what it is, how it actually works, where it happens in our lives, and how each and every person can embrace it. It can be helpful to think of personal examples to make this understanding come alive.

Learning is a process that never ends. It extends beyond formal education to a continuous journey of acquiring new knowledge and skills throughout one's life. Lifelong learning means that individuals have the capacity to grow, develop, and expand their knowledge and abilities at any age or stage of life.

> **"Learning is influenced by individual differences, interests, and preferences. We all have a unique learning style, and our own strengths and challenges that need to be considered in order for learning to be effective learning."**

Such individualized and personalized learning approaches provide tailored experiences that align with our abilities, motivations, and goals.

Learning involves the acquisition and assimilation of new knowledge, concepts, information, and skills, and requires engagement from you as the learner. Activities such as reading, listening, observing, practicing, reflecting, and problem-solving are necessary for effective learning outcomes. The most effective method for learning occurs when it is contextualized within real-life situations where we can make connections between what we are learning with the practical scenarios we encounter daily. This type of connection helps us understand the relevance and significance for what motivates us to learn.

Learning relates to metacognitive processes—in other words, thinking about our own thinking. It includes reflection, self-assessment, and monitoring of our learning progress. Metacognition helps learners develop self-awareness, self-regulation, and the ability to evaluate their understanding and performance.

Learning often occurs in social contexts through collaboration with others. Social interactions such as discussions or group work provide opportunities for sharing perspectives, exchanging ideas, and constructing knowledge collectively. Collaborative learning fosters communication skills that are essential in today's workplace and in one's own personal life.

Transfer of learning occurs when people apply the information, strategies, and skills they have learned to a new situation or context. This transfer is not a discrete activity but is instead an integral part of the learning process. One's learning transfer can be accelerated by linking learning to the transfer context (work and personal) and learning together with others. Your learning transfer can also increase when such learning is practical, relevant, and meaningful to you.

HOW DOES LEARNING SUPPORT YOUR WELL-BEING?

Learning has an essential impact on well-being, but learning in relation to well-being is not a one-way street. Of course, learning can impact personal health in a positive way. Likewise, if people are feeling healthy and energetic, this can further enable their ability to learn.

Furthermore, learning can provide a sense of purpose and meaning in life. When we engage in learning activities that are aligned with our values and interests, we can experience a deeper sense of fulfillment and satisfaction. Moreover, learning allows us to pursue our passions, contribute to society, and find meaning in our endeavors, which positively impacts our well-being.[2]

Figure 3.8: The impact of learning on well-being

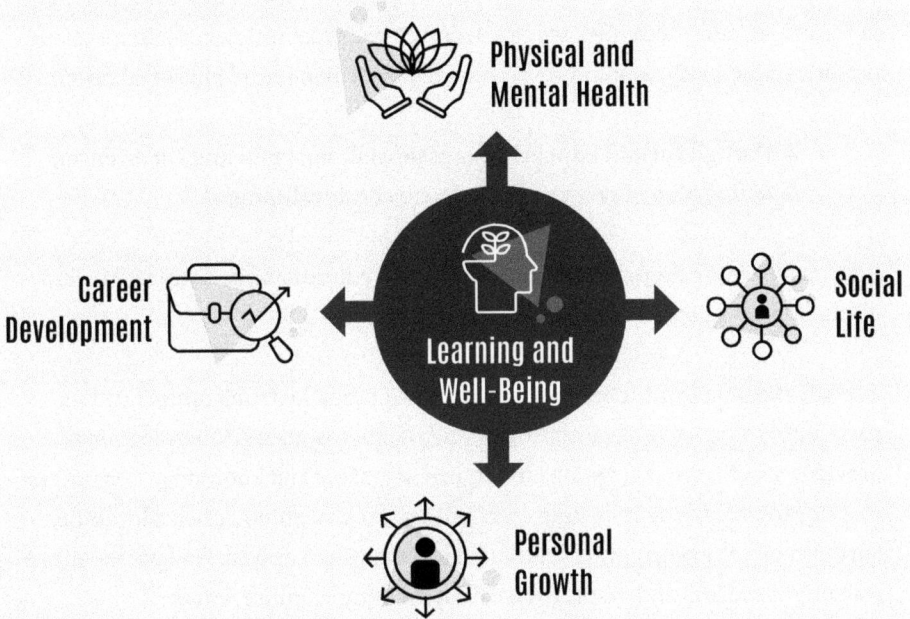

©2024. Jan Rijken. The Best Version of Me.

Research over the last twenty-five years shows that learning impacts well-being in **four dimensions:**

1. **Career development.**

First, learning has a profound impact on **career development**, empowering us to adapt to changing work environments, improve job performance, and seize new opportunities.[3] As a result, embracing lifelong learning is essential to navigating the complexities of the modern professional landscape. Whether through formal education, continuous professional development, informal learning, or online platforms, those of us who prioritize learning are more likely to achieve long-term career success. Such career success can in turn influence financial well-being, thus enabling a higher degree of financial empowerment.

Formal education has long been recognized as a significant factor in career advancement. Higher levels of education are associated with higher income, better job prospects, and increased opportunities for promotion. By engaging in formal learning activities, we can acquire new capabilities, contribute to our professional growth, and improve both job performance and job satisfaction.

> **"Although formal education is essential, *informal and experiential learning* also play a vital role in career development."**

Informal learning occurs outside of traditional educational settings and includes on-the-job experiences, mentoring, and self-study.

The advancement of technology has revolutionized learning opportunities, particularly through online platforms and digital resources. *Online learning* provides us with flexible options to acquire new skills and knowledge, regardless of geographical location or time constraints, and also enhances employability. Furthermore, the recent AI revolution in learning enables us to find personalized learning resources and inspiration through a simple online search.

2. Personal growth.

Second, learning serves as a catalyst for **personal growth** by helping individuals acquire new knowledge and skills and challenge their assumptions. It broadens our horizons, deepens our understanding, and encourages us to explore different perspectives. As we engage in learning experiences, we expand our cognitive abilities, develop critical thinking skills, and enhance our problem-solving capabilities. This intellectual growth fuels personal development and empowers us to face new challenges with confidence.[4]

Learning fosters self-reflection and self-awareness, crucial elements of personal growth. By engaging in introspection and reflecting on our experiences, we gain insight into our strengths, weaknesses, values, and aspirations. The process of learning equips us with adaptability and resilience, essential qualities for personal growth in an ever-changing world. Learning encourages us to consider new ideas, embrace change, and adapt to evolving circumstances. Through learning, we develop the capacity to navigate uncertainty, overcome setbacks, and bounce back from failures, fostering personal resilience and growth. Personal growth is not a one-time event but an ongoing journey. Lifelong learning is a key driver of continuous personal growth and empowers us to adapt to societal changes, pursue new passions, and unlock our full potential.

3. Physical and mental health.

Third, research consistently demonstrates the profound impact of learning on health outcomes, especially **physical and mental health**. Learning and education have long been recognized as a significant determinant of *physical health* outcomes. One study example found that individuals with higher levels of education tend to have lower rates of chronic diseases such as diabetes, cardiovascular disease, and obesity. This relationship can be attributed to several factors, including improved health literacy, access to better health care resources, and adoption of healthier behaviors.

Learning also impacts *mental health* in a crucial way. Research has consistently shown that engaging in lifelong learning activities such as reading, taking courses, or acquiring new skills can have a protective effect against cognitive decline and neurodegenerative diseases. A study by Stueder-Luthi revealed that older adults who participated in cognitive training programs experienced improvements in memory and attention, leading to enhanced overall cognitive function and reduced risk of dementia.[5]

4. Social life.

Fourth, learning has a huge impact on our **social life** and helps us foster social integration and inclusion. Learning can bring people together and provide opportunities for social connection and engagement. It can also help us develop key skills such as empathy and social awareness, and can improve our ability to negotiate and resolve conflicts, all of which can enhance our relationships and social support networks.

Learning experiences such as attending workshops, taking classes, or participating in community-based programs can enhance *interpersonal relationships*. Similarly, learning can promote *social integration and inclusion* by bridging gaps between different social groups. Moreover, intercultural education programs, which focus on fostering cultural awareness and understanding, can improve intergroup attitudes and reduce prejudice among individuals from diverse backgrounds.

Furthermore, educational opportunities for marginalized groups such as adult literacy programs or vocational training can reduce social inequality, improve employment prospects, and facilitate integration into society.

BOOSTING YOUR WELL-BEING THROUGH LEARNING

Now that we have reviewed both the concept of learning and how learning can impact well-being, what follows are evidence-based and practical strategies for boosting your well-being through learning, both what you can you do now and in the future.[6]

Understand the concept of learning. Familiarize yourself with the concept of a growth mindset. Recognize that abilities and intelligence can be developed with effort, practice, and a positive attitude. Embrace the belief that your abilities are not limited but can be improved over time.

Embrace challenges. View challenges as opportunities for growth rather than obstacles. Instead of shying away from difficult tasks, approach them with enthusiasm and a willingness to learn. Embrace the idea that mistakes and setbacks are part of the learning process and celebrate effort and progress.

Cultivate a positive attitude. Maintain a positive and optimistic outlook—glass half-full rather than half-empty. Replace negative self-talk and self-doubt with positive affirmations and a belief in your ability to learn and grow. Surround yourself with positive influences and supportive individuals who encourage your growth.

Embrace learning as a lifelong process. Recognize that learning is not confined to formal education but is a continuous process throughout life. Seek out new knowledge, skills, and experiences, sometimes simply because you need it. Explore subjects outside your comfort zone and be open to new perspectives.

Value feedback. Embrace feedback as a valuable tool for growth rather than as criticism. Listen to constructive feedback, reflect on it, and use it to guide your learning and development. Surround yourself with "disagreeable givers" who provide you with feedback on which of your skills may need to be unlearned.

Develop resilience. Accept that setbacks and failures are part of the learning process. Instead of giving up when faced with challenges, develop resilience and bounce back stronger. Learn from your mistakes, adapt your strategies, and keep moving forward. For more information, see the chapter on Resilience.

Cultivate curiosity. Nurture a sense of curiosity and a love for learning. Ask questions, seek answers, and explore new ideas. Approach learning with an open mind and a genuine interest in discovering new knowledge and perspectives.

Set realistic goals. Set specific, achievable goals that motivate and challenge you. Break larger goals into smaller, manageable tasks. Monitor your progress and adjust your goals as needed. Celebrate your accomplishments along the way.

Embrace technology. Leverage technology to enhance your learning experiences. Use online platforms, educational apps, podcasts, and webinars to access a wealth of educational content. Engage in online forums and communities to connect with like-minded individuals and expand your knowledge. Use AI to cocreate personalized learning opportunities and generate learning experience ideas.

Seek mentorship and networking. Connect with individuals who have expertise in areas you wish to learn more about. Seek mentorship from professionals in your field of interest or join professional networks and organizations. Engage with mentors and network with peers to gain valuable insights and opportunities to learn more.

Reflect and evaluate. Regularly reflect on your challenges, achievements, and personal learning journey. Evaluate what you've learned, identify areas for improvement, and set new learning goals. Engage in self-reflection to track your progress, make adjustments, and continue growing.

In conclusion, learning has a profound impact on well-being, and there are practical steps you can take to boost your well-being through learning. Start by understanding the concept of learning and adopting a growth mindset. Embrace challenges as opportunities for growth and cultivate a positive attitude.

Recognize that learning is a lifelong process, and seek out new knowledge and experiences. Value feedback as a tool for improvement and develop resilience to navigate setbacks. Cultivate curiosity and set realistic goals that keep you motivated. By implementing these strategies, you can continue learning and enhance your well-being in the process.

QUESTIONS FOR SELF-REFLECTION

Consider the following questions for self-reflection that you can ask yourself before or during a learning experience:

- How can I actively apply and integrate what I learn in my life?
- How do I handle setbacks or challenges in my learning process?
- When was the last time I got out of my comfort zone (and what did I learn)?

RESOURCES FOR EXPLORATION AND LEARNING

TOP 3: ARTICLES

Tupper, H., and S. Ellis. (2022, December 21). **What's holding back your career development?** *Harvard Business Review.*
▶ tinyurl.com/2p9es256
The authors, who train over 100,000 people a year in career development, have identified four common challenges that get in the way of people's growth. They categorize them as when, who, what, and where challenges.

Rains, A. (2020, December 21). **How to develop a personal growth mindset that fuels business success.** *Forbes.*
▶ tinyurl.com/za8v4f39
While personal growth and professional growth may seem like two separate concepts, they're more intertwined than you may think. For a leader, it's crucial to learn how to develop a personal growth mindset not only in yourself, but also throughout your entire company.

Watson, D., O. Tregaskis, C. Gekdili, O. Vaughn, and A. Semkina. (2018). **Well-being through learning: A systematic review of learning interventions in the workplace and their impact on well-being.** *European Journal of Work and Organizational Psychology 27* (2), pp. 247–68.
▶ tinyurl.com/yckax24w
This journal article features a systematic review of the effectiveness of learning interventions with regard to their impact on well-being.

 TOP 3: BOOKS

Elliott-Moskwa, E., and C. S. Dweck. (2022). **The Growth Mindset Workbook: CBT Skills to Help You Build Resilience, Increase Confidence, and Thrive through Life's Challenges.** Oakland, CA: New Harbinger.
This workbook offers essential skills grounded in cognitive behavioral therapy (CBT) to change the way you think about your own talents and abilities.

Peterson, K., and D. A. Kolb. (2017). **How You Learn Is How You Live: Using Nine Ways of Learning to Transform Your Life.** Oakland, CA: Berrett-Koehler.
This book describes deep, research-based insights into the ideal process of learning to guide you in identifying your dominant learning style.

Van Hooydonk, S. (2022). **The Workplace Curiosity Manifesto: How Curiosity Helps Individuals and Workspaces Thrive in Transformational Times.**
Washington, DC: New Degree Press. This book combines real learning stories and case studies to reveal opportunities and challenges for success through curiosity.

TOP 3: ASSESSMENTS AND TESTS

123test.
▶ tinyurl.com/54pz5fa5
A free assessment resource for skills assessment. Assessing your strengths and measuring the 16 most common and work-related competencies.

LinkedIn skills assessment.
▶ tinyurl.com/5n8h3yhe
A video explaining how you can do skill assessments on Linkedin.

Quizlet.
▶ tinyurl.com/4nfmsmkk
A free study resource that enables people to improve their grades and reach their learning goals through assessments, science-backed flashcards, practice tests, and expert-written solutions.

TOP 3: VIDEOS

Developing a Growth Mindset. Carol Dweck.
▶ tinyurl.com/2uer39fk
This video explores whether it's beneficial to tell children that they are smart or talented. Professor Carol Dweck delves into this topic, discussing her pioneering research on growth mindsets.

How to Improve Your Well-Being. The Clifton Strengths Podcast.
Jaclynn Robinson.
▶ tinyurl.com/2s4kjemh
In this video you'll learn how well-being practices can be used to support others, and how it looks when someone is thriving versus struggling.

TED Talks for Education beyond the Classroom.
The Love of Lifelong Learning Playlist.
▶ tinyurl.com/y3kj4jd8
Learning doesn't end when you throw your graduation cap in the air. These Ted talks celebrate education beyond the classroom.

TOP 3: PODCASTS

Can We Unlearn Something that We Have Already Learned?
The Naked Scientists Podcast. Laura Ford.
▶ tinyurl.com/bdfyannk
It is not only learning that can appear to be quite hard; it's unlearning that we struggle with. How do we unlearn? Is there any technique for unlearning things?

Learning a New Skill Works Best to Keep Your Brain Sharp. NPR.
▶ tinyurl.com/mtzs65y7
Presents study results from the University of Texas on learning. Brain training is big business, with computerized brain games touted as a way to help prevent memory loss. But new research shows you might be better off picking up a challenging new hobby.

Personal Development Podcasts. DevelopGoodHabits.com.
▶ tinyurl.com/y7cpzyy8
Fifteen personal development podcasts for your self-growth through learning. A curated list of the best podcasts that inspire and motivate you to walk in the direction of self-growth and personal development.

TOP 3: FREE ONLINE COURSES

Duolingo.
▶ duolingo.com
A free language-learning platform that offers courses in dozens of languages.

Khan Academy.
▶ tinyurl.com/468f72rh
A free educational resource that includes courses and instructional videos on a variety of topics, including math, science, and the humanities.

TED-Ed.
▶ ed.ted.com
A free educational platform that includes animated videos and lessons on a variety of topics from science to literature.

ENDNOTES

1   Jarvis, P. (2010). *Adult Education and Lifelong Learning: Theory and Practice*, 4th ed. Abingdon, UK: Routledge.

2   German Institute of Adult Education & European Commission. (2014). BELL—Benefits of Lifelong Learning.

3   World Economic Forum. (2023, January 16). Davos 2023: What you need to know about jobs and skills. tinyurl.com/3yt4jn72

4   Dweck, C. S. S. (2007). *Mindset: The New Psychology of Success: How We Can Learn to Our Full Potential.* New York: Random House.

5   Stueder-Luthi, B., V. Boesch, S. Lusti, and B. Meier. (2022, August 1). Fostering cognitive performance in older adults with a process- and a strategy-based cognitive training. *Neuropsychology, Development, and Cognition. Section B, Aging, Neuropsychology, and Cognition.* pp. 1-23. tinyurl.com/36asm4np

6   Watson, D., O. Tregaskis, C. Gekdili, O. Vaughn, and A. Semkina. (2018). Well-being through learning: A systematic review of learning interventions in the workplace and their impact on well-being. *European Journal of Work and Organizational Psychology 27* (2), pp. 247-68. tinyurl.com/32xh6an5

"Learning is the beginning
of wealth. Learning is the
beginning of health.
Learning is the beginning of
spirituality. Searching and
learning is where the miracle
process all begins."

—Jim Rohn

04
PURPOSE

FINANCIAL EMPOWERMENT
RELATIONSHIPS
CONTRIBUTION
SPIRITUALITY
VALUES, BELIEFS, AND ATTITUDES

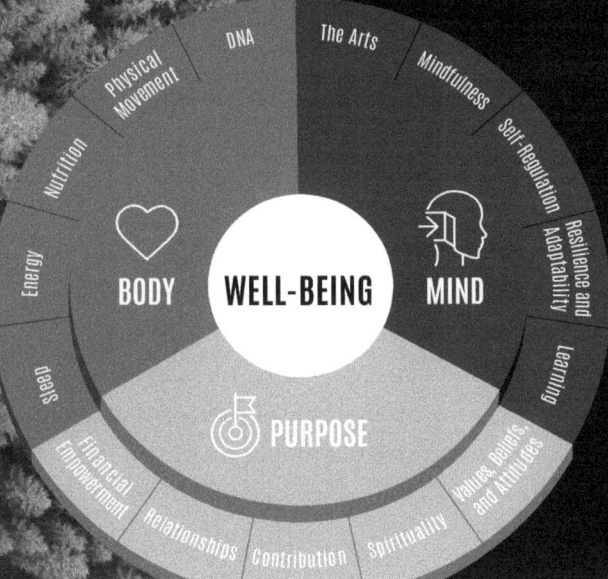

Nature
Environment

Social
Environment

Work
Environment

Climate
Environment

INTRODUCTION

Written by Dr. Nick van Dam

> "Life is never made unbearable by circumstances,
> but only by lack of meaning and purpose."
>
> —VIKTOR E. FRANKL

In the third section of *The Best Version of Me*, we venture beyond the realms of body and mind to explore integral aspects of our lives that collectively shape our personal fulfillment and societal contributions. This section, composed of five transformative chapters that offer a holistic approach to personal development, enables readers to build a life that is not only successful on the outside but also rich and fulfilling on the inside.

Financial Empowerment

In this chapter, we dive into understanding what it means to be financially empowered. This goes beyond basic financial literacy, exploring the profound role money plays in our lives, not just as a means of transaction but as a significant influence on our choices, opportunities, and sense of security. We examine the concept of financial empowerment as a critical component of personal autonomy and self-efficacy, demonstrating how having control over our finances directly impacts our overall well-being.

Relationships

We investigate relationships as the essence of being human. This chapter explores the varied forms of relationships, from intimate bonds and friendships to community involvement and reciprocal interactions, highlighting their vital role in our lives. We examine the significant benefits of fostering positive relationships such as enhanced emotional health and a deeper sense of belonging. The chapter also provides practical strategies for nurturing healthy relationships. These insights are designed to help you build and maintain meaningful connections, which are crucial for personal growth and well-being. By understanding and valuing the power of relationships, this chapter guides you toward enriching your life and becoming the best version of yourself through the art of human connection.

Contribution

The act of contribution profoundly shapes our psychological well-being by understanding its key characteristics and the fulfilling role it plays in our lives. We categorize contribution into five distinct types: individual, collective, professional, societal, and humanitarian. Additionally, we provide actionable steps for advancing your contribution in meaningful ways. Whether through small, everyday acts or larger, community-focused initiatives, this chapter offers guidance on how to effectively make a difference.

Spirituality

We embark on a journey to understand the diverse interpretations of spirituality. This chapter presents spirituality not as a one-dimensional concept but as a multifaceted experience, explored through the lens of the knowledge-continuum model. We consider the transformative power of spirituality in various aspects of life such as finding purpose and meaning beyond our daily existence, fostering a sense of interconnectedness with the larger universe, cultivating inner peace and resilience in the face of life's challenges, and harmoniously integrating rationality with intuition. Each of these elements offers a unique pathway to deepen our spiritual understanding and experience. Finally, the chapter provides practical strategies for infusing spirituality into your daily life.

Values, Beliefs, and Attitudes

In this chapter, we investigate the core components that fundamentally shape our perception of the world and guide our actions. We will take a closer look into the nature of our values, beliefs, and attitudes, exploring how these internal compasses are formed and how they influence every aspect of our lives, from daily decisions to long-term goals. We also examine the power that comes from aligning our values and beliefs with our actions. In addition, the chapter provides practices and strategies to help reinforce and advance your values, beliefs, and attitudes.

> "The best thing money can buy is financial freedom."
> —ROB BERGER

INTRODUCTION

What do people say about money? That it is the root of all evil—the thing some people love to hate, whereas others argue it is something we can't live without. Our society has deemed material wealth as the ultimate goal in life, a sign to others that you are better than they are. However, could it be that money provides us with a distorted perception of the meaning of life? A distortion of what true wealth, health, and joy are all about? Now I ask you: is money all that it is believed to be?

Let's be clear, money is an absolute necessity in today's world. Even if you fight the system and are antagonistic toward money and its associations, money is crucial to our survival. Be it for food, security, or pleasure, money (fortunately or unfortunately) is part of life. But what is it about money that we love so much, and why have we given it such power over us? Why have we allowed it to define who we are and, most important, why have we used money to define our self-worth?

Personal Story

Susan, an individual whom one would deem suitably successful, was asked to be the custodian and administrator of a large nonprofit fund. As she ventured down the path of the project and learned the operational requirements, she was suddenly overwhelmed with anxiety about managing the project finances. Her personal relationship with money was problematic—not that she had a bad credit record—but purely because thinking about money left her feeling stressed and overwhelmed.

It became apparent that Susan's deep-rooted life experiences as both a child and an adult had framed her perspective about money. Though she had a fair amount of financial acumen, it was tainted by her past personal experiences. After acknowledging her feelings about money, Susan considered why her reaction was always so negative.

Susan finally had a poignant realization—she had created a negative perception about money for herself. She now knew what she needed to do. To change her future relationship with money, she had to reframe her way of thinking about it.

Our Relationship with Money

Our relationship with money can be a difficult one. It reflects our upbringing, life experiences, and innermost beliefs.[1] On the surface, money is a tool for financial transactions. It can provide for the food on our table and the roof over our heads. It can serve as a sign of power and freedom. It can epitomize glorious material goods. It can showcase stupidity and egotistical and self-interested behavior. It can help cure disease and enhance beauty. And it is what society uses to define status and self-worth. Let's look at why empowerment around money is so important.

> **"People consistently use money to measure themselves against others, leading to persistent dissatisfaction."**

There exists a fascinating psychological dynamic about money: people consistently use it to measure themselves against others. As a result, regardless of their financial status, people may perpetually perceive themselves as coming up short, leading to persistent dissatisfaction.[2] To combat this dissatisfaction, let us unpack the essence of financial empowerment.

Financial Empowerment

There are various definitions of financial empowerment, including "the ability and confidence of individuals and communities to make positive financial decisions that promote their long-term financial stability and financial well-being."[3] Financial empowerment is characterized by an individual's sense of control over their finances. Individuals who are financially empowered typically possess a stronger sense of agency in their financial dealings. This empowerment enables them to make proactive decisions such as saving regularly, budgeting effectively, and planning ahead, which are essential traits of financial resilience.[4] Being financially empowered also means having the knowledge and confidence to navigate financial systems, access resources, and avoid pitfalls such as fraud and excessive debt, which enhances one's resilience in the face of financial challenges.

Moreover, financial empowerment can directly influence one's ability to build and maintain a financial cushion, a critical aspect of financial resilience. This cushion allows individuals to cope better with unexpected financial crises without derailing their long-term financial health. In essence, financial empowerment equips individuals with the tools, knowledge, and confidence to not only manage their current financial situation but also to effectively plan for and navigate future financial challenges, thereby bolstering their financial resilience.

However, studies and data[5] from various countries indicate a widespread lack of financial empowerment, leading to several concerning trends, which hold true across both developed and developing nations, even though the specifics may vary significantly from one country to another:

- Financial stress is a common issue, with a considerable number of people citing income challenges or insufficient funds as a primary source of stress;

- A substantial segment of the global population lacks sufficient savings or accessible credit to manage unexpected financial crises;

- Only a minority of individuals express a sense of preparedness and confidence regarding their retirement plans;

- Many people are caught in a continuous cycle of debt, often living from one paycheck to the next;

- A notable percentage of women continue to depend financially on their partners.

These findings have significant implications for both individuals and societies at large. For example, the prevalence of financial stress highlights a critical need for enhanced financial education and support systems. If left unchecked, such stress can lead to detrimental effects on mental and physical health, reducing overall quality of life and productivity. The fact that a substantial portion of the global population lacks enough savings or access to credit to handle financial emergencies points to a vulnerability that exacerbates poverty and inequality during personal emergencies.

Additionally, the lack of preparedness and confidence in retirement planning for most individuals suggests potential future burdens on social welfare systems and an increase in poverty rates among the elderly. This lack of foresight and planning could result in significant economic and social challenges, including increased reliance on support from family members and a reduction in the overall standard of living for the aging population.

Furthermore, the widespread issue of people being trapped in a cycle of debt underscores systemic problems in wage distribution and financial systems that fail to promote saving and wealth accumulation for the broader population. This cycle not only hinders individual financial growth but also reduces economic progress as consumers limit their spending.

Last, the continued financial dependency of a considerable percentage of women on their partners raises concerns about economic gender inequality. This dependency not only limits women's financial autonomy and increases their vulnerability in cases of relationship breakdowns but also hinders progress toward gender equality in economic participation and opportunity.

Overall, these trends underscore the need for comprehensive policy interventions, financial literacy programs, and economic reforms aimed at enhancing financial empowerment and resilience across all demographics. Addressing these issues is crucial for promoting equitable economic growth, reducing poverty, and improving overall societal well-being.

HOW DOES FINANCIAL EMPOWERMENT SUPPORT YOUR WELL-BEING?

We all have different lives. No two are the same and, as a result, each and every one of us has a different frame of reference for money. Because understanding ourselves and our feelings about money is critical for recognizing our financial-related actions, creating a positive relationship with money can contribute to financial empowerment in the following ways:

Reduced stress. A primary source of stress for many people is financial insecurity. By achieving financial empowerment, one can significantly reduce worries about paying bills, covering unexpected expenses, and preparing for the future. Financial empowerment thus leads to reduced stress and overall better mental health.

Freedom of choice. Financially empowered people have the freedom to make choices that can enhance their quality of life. Whether it's choosing to invest in higher education, taking a much-needed vacation, or pursuing a passion project, having the financial means provides the autonomy to make these choices.

Improved physical health. Reduced financial stress can lead to better physical health. Stress can manifest physically in various ways such as headaches, heart issues, and sleep disturbances. Being financially stable can reduce these stress-related ailments.

Increased opportunities. Financial empowerment can open doors to better education, housing, and employment opportunities, all of which can lead to an increased sense of well-being and contentment.

Planning for the future. Being financially empowered means being able to plan for the future, be it for retirement, children's education, or other long-term goals. This foresight and preparation can bring peace of mind and a sense of security.

Personal growth and development. With a stable financial foundation, people can often invest in opportunities for personal growth such as courses, workshops, or therapy, which can lead to improved well-being.

Positive role modeling. Parents who are financially empowered can set positive examples for their children, teaching them the importance of financial literacy, saving, and investing. This can create a positive ripple effect for future generations.

Community involvement. Financially empowered people often have the means and time to give back to their communities through monetary donations, volunteering, or supporting local businesses. Being involved in the community and contributing positively can provide a sense of purpose and connection.

> **"Financial freedom presents women with many options
> and the opportunity for a life of fiscal independence."**

Reduced debt. Financial empowerment typically means reduced debt, which can be a significant drain on well-being when it spirals out of control. Without constant worry about debt, people can focus on other enriching aspects of life.

Enhanced self-esteem. Achieving financial empowerment can also lead to enhanced self-esteem and self-confidence. When people feel in control of their finances, they often feel more in control of their lives in general, leading to increased feelings of self-worth.

Impact on women. Financial empowerment can be a catalyst for changing the traditional role of women in society. Financial freedom presents women with many options and the opportunity for a life of fiscal independence. However, many women still face career challenges that hinder their professional and financial advancement.[6]

In summary, research suggests that financial empowerment can be considered one of the most important factors in enabling people to take greater control of their health and well-being.[7]

Can Money Buy Happiness?

Interestingly enough, some research says that it may. According to psychologist and well-being expert Gethin Nadin, "Money contributes to happiness when it helps us make basic needs, but the research tells us that above a certain level more money doesn't actually yield more happiness."[8] Speaker and author Matt Phelan writes that "the research [Nadin] refers to here is a 2010 study out of Princeton [University]. The data suggests that happiness increased with salary until participants earned $75,000 per annum. Beyond this point, the correlation between salary and happiness decreased."[9]

It is important to consider that this amount may differ from country to country and even within regions in the US, requiring adjustments based on the cost of living, inflation, and other local economic factors.

BOOSTING YOUR WELL-BEING THROUGH FINANCIAL EMPOWERMENT

In the critical journey toward enhancing overall well-being, financial empowerment plays a pivotal role. Next, I'll introduce a strategic, three-step process designed to transform your financial health and, in turn, improve your quality of life.

Figure 4.1: Strategic steps for transforming your financial health

1.
Gain foundational knowledge

2.
Take action

3.
Take control

©2024. Ursula Fear. The Best Version of Me.

1. Gain foundational knowledge.

The first step includes understanding your financial situation, recognizing the impact of your financial decisions, and staying informed about financial opportunities and risks. Individuals seeking to enhance their financial empowerment can take several specific actions to raise their awareness of and ability to manage their personal finances. First, actively seeking out educational resources such as books, online courses, and financial literacy blogs or podcasts is crucial for building foundational knowledge. Second, participating in financial workshops or webinars, often offered for free by community centers, banks, or online platforms, can provide deeper insights into budgeting, saving, investing, and debt management. Third, regularly reviewing and tracking personal finances by using budgeting apps or spreadsheets to understand spending habits and identify areas for improvement can be beneficial.

2. Take action.

Gaining foundational knowledge sets the stage for taking action. Here, we delve into practical measures such as budgeting, saving, investing, and debt management, providing actionable advice to help you make informed financial choices.

First, creating a monthly budget provides a clear picture of your income, expenses, and potential savings, ensuring that you live within your means. By allocating funds to different categories, you can prioritize essential expenses and reduce frivolous spending. Moreover, establishing a monthly budget is a proactive step toward achieving financial goals, managing unforeseen expenses, and building a safety net. In essence, it is a blueprint for financial stability and long-term prosperity.

Second, understanding the importance of savings is crucial for securing financial stability and achieving long-term goals. Savings act as a safety net, providing security in times of unexpected expenses or financial emergencies, and are the foundation upon which wealth is built. The first step in effective saving is to consistently set aside a portion of your income, treating savings like any other essential expense. It's important to have a clear purpose for your savings, whether it's for retirement, buying a home, education, or an emergency fund. This purpose-driven approach not only motivates saving but also guides how much you should save.

However, merely saving money is not enough; investing your savings is key to ensuring that your money grows over time. Investing can seem intimidating, but it allows your savings to outpace inflation and increase in value. It's essential to choose investment options that align with your risk tolerance and financial goals. This could range from low-risk options such as bonds and fixed deposits to higher-risk options such as stocks or mutual funds. Diversifying your investments is also critical for minimizing risk and maximizing return. Remember, the goal of investing is not just to save what you have but to multiply it wisely. By combining disciplined saving with smart investing, you can significantly enhance your financial health and work toward realizing your long-term aspirations.

Third, effectively managing debt involves a multifaceted approach: start by thoroughly assessing your debt and creating a realistic budget to control spending. Prioritize repaying high-interest debt first, or start with smaller debt for quick wins. Consider debt consolidation for simplification and potential interest reduction, and don't hesitate to negotiate with creditors for better repayment terms. Boost income through additional work, and avoid incurring new debt during repayment. Simultaneously, build a modest emergency fund to prevent future debt. Staying committed to your plan and continually educating yourself about financial management are key to achieving and maintaining financial stability.

3. Take control.

The final step empowers you to take charge of your financial destiny. It involves setting long-term financial goals, creating a sustainable plan to achieve them, and adapting to changing life circumstances.

First, set long-term financial goals by identifying what you want to achieve. These goals could include buying a home, saving for retirement, funding education, or building an investment portfolio. Be specific about what each goal means to you and set a timeline for each.

Second, develop a budget that accommodates your regular expenses and leaves room for savings and debt repayment. An understanding of compound interest can be beneficial for both minimizing long-term debt and maximizing wealth. Utilize budgeting tools or apps to track your spending, and stay on course.

Third, build an emergency fund with the aim of saving enough to cover three to six months' worth of living expenses. This fund will help you stay on track with your long-term goals even when unexpected expenses arise.

CONCLUSION

We are the creators of our own lives, and it's up to us to take control of our finances. Don't be intimidated by the way others showcase their wealth, because true prosperity is not always observable. Create a new relationship with money, and welcome money into your life to aid you in your journey toward wealth, health, and joy.

TOP 10 TIPS

Consider these insights as you begin to reshape your relationship with finances. These pivotal points will undoubtedly guide you on your path.

1. **There is no right or wrong.** Your personal experience with and perception of money are real. Good financial advice for one person is not necessarily the best advice for another.

2. **The definition of wealth is not the same for everyone.** For some people, being wealthy may mean walking into a supermarket and buying whatever they wish. For others, it may come from owning a sports car. For others still, it may mean having no debt. And for some, wealth does not necessarily need to be displayed.

3. **Control your money.** Understand what it means for you to control your money. Be mindful of your spending. What bad habits need to change? How can you become debt free?

4. **Start talking about money.** We have been taught not to talk about money openly; such conversations are often considered taboo. Challenge yourself and others to talk about money without feeling any shame or guilt.

5. **Have patience.** Time is everything with investing. Average returns come after an above average period of time.

6. **Share your abundance.** Give generously by supporting charitable causes, helping those less fortunate, and spreading kindness wherever you go. Whether it's donating to a local food bank, volunteering your time to mentor someone, or simply offering a listening ear to a friend in need, your actions can make a meaningful difference in the lives of others. Embrace the idea that your abundance, whether material or emotional, can be a force for positive change in the world.

7. **Mindset is key.** Train your brain to look at money differently. Move from a mindset of scarcity to a mindset of more than enough. What you sow is what you reap.

8. **Start young.** Encourage your children to build a healthy relationship with
money as soon as possible. Teach them about saving, budgeting, and spending wisely.

9. **Learn and unlearn.** Consider new perspectives about money, and leave behind those that no longer serve you. Make financial management a good friend. Even if you don't deal with finances in your profession, gain a basic understanding of financial success in your field.

10. **Remember: you can't change yesterday's newspaper.**
The past is the past. Move on, and focus on tomorrow.

QUESTIONS FOR SELF-REFLECTION

- What is your relationship with money?

- How will you achieve six months of financial savings as a safety net?

- How will you (re)define success in your life?

RESOURCES FOR EXPLORATION AND LEARNING

 TOP 3: BOOKS

Hill, N., B. Franklin, J. Allen, W. D. Wattles, E. Holmes, F. S. Shinn, et al. (2007).
The Prosperity Bible: The Greatest Writings of All Time on the Secrets to Wealth and Prosperity. New York: TarcherPerigee.
From Amazon's description of the book: "*The Prosperity Bible* is a one-of-a-kind resource that collects the greatest moneymaking secrets of authors from every field—religion, finance, philosophy, and self-help—and makes them available in a single, handy volume."

Hounsel, M. (2020). **The Psychology of Money: Timeless Lessons on Wealth, Greed, and Happiness.** Petersfield, UK: Harriman House.
From Amazon's description of the book: "In *The Psychology of Money*, award-winning author Morgan Housel shares 19 short stories exploring the strange ways people think about money and teaches you how to make better sense of one of life's most important topics."

Julian, L. S. (2001). **God Is My CEO: Following God's Principles in a Bottom-Line World.** Avon, MA: Adams Media.
From Amazon's description of the book: "Many business leaders struggle with the dilemma of being successful and living a life with purpose. *God Is My CEO* offers a practical and inspirational source of guidance for achieving a balanced and accomplished life."

TOP 3: ARTICLES

Berger, M. W. (2023, March 6). **Does more money correlate with greater happiness?** PennToday.com.

▶ tinyurl.com/mtm7xwkt

From the article: "Reconciling previously contradictory results, researchers from Penn and Princeton find a steady association between larger incomes and greater happiness for most people but a rise and plateau for an unhappy minority."

Phelan, M. (2022, November 22). **Does money make you happy?** TheHappinessIndex.com.

▶ tinyurl.com/vzpc89db

From the article: "One of the big questions when it comes to happiness, particularly in a work context, is whether money can make you happier. If you keep chasing the next job with a larger salary, will you be happier? Does paying your team more make them happier?"

Suliman, A. (2023, March 8). **Can money buy happiness? Scientists say it can.** *Washington Post.*

▶ tinyurl.com/5n8zpdne

It's a question that philosophers, economists and social scientists have grappled with for decades: can money buy happiness? This article provides insights on this topic based on research from Daniel Kahneman and Matthew Killingsworth.

TOP 3: VIDEOS

After I Read 40 Books on Money—Here's What Will Make You Rich. Mark Tilbury.

▶ tinyurl.com/37s72ae9

In this comprehensive YouTube video, British businessman Mark Tilbury distills key insights gleaned from reading 40 diverse books on finance and wealth creation. The video offers wisdom on effective strategies and habits that can significantly enhance one's financial success, aiming to guide viewers on the path to riches based on extensive research and literature.

I Got Rich When I Understood This. Warren Buffett.

▶ tinyurl.com/39d7wmpf

In this enlightening YouTube video, billionaire investor Warren Buffett shares the pivotal principle that significantly contributed to his immense success in accumulating wealth. Buffett imparts valuable financial wisdom and insights, condensed from his extensive experience in investing, in an effort to educate and inspire viewers on the key strategies for building lasting wealth.

What Financial Experts Won't Tell You about Money.
Erika Kullberg and Morgan Housel.
▶ tinyurl.com/4v45c794
From the video description: "Author of the *New York Times* bestseller *The Psychology of Money* Morgan Housel shares ... his realistic tips and strategies for saving, investing, and achieving financial freedom. Learn how to have a better relationship with your money without compromising happiness along the way."

TOP 3: PODCASTS

Boosting Your Financial IQ. Steve Coughran.
▶ tinyurl.com/5dxmbnnr
From the podcast description: "The Boosting Your Financial IQ podcast deconstructs accounting and financial concepts to provide listeners with a holistic understanding of how money works and how to create more value."

How Your Childhood Can Predict Your Future. Financial Education.
▶ tinyurl.com/4kzaapsk
From the podcast description: On the Interesting Ideas on This Podcast, the speakers "talk about money, lifestyle, investing, how to make money online, e-commerce and so much more."

Financial Literacy, Spiritual Learning and Finding Your Mission.
Achieve Your Goals Podcast. Robert Kiyosaki.
▶ tinyurl.com/498mu8th
From the podcast description: Businessman and author Robert Kiyosaki "shares his top tips on financial literacy [and] spiritual learning and helps you find your mission, so you can live an abundant and fulfilling life."

ENDNOTES

1   B. Klontz, S. L. Britt, J. Mentzer, and T. Klontz. (2011). Money beliefs and financial behaviors: Development of the Klontz Money Script Inventory. *Journal of Financial Therapy* 2 (1) 1. tinyurl.com/5n6nf25x

2   National Disability Institute. (n.d.). Financial empowerment. tinyurl.com/6ac6frur

3   National Disability Institute n.d.

4   OECD. (2020). OECD/INFE 2020 international survey of adult financial literacy. tinyurl.com/m58x9dhp

5   International Labour Organization. (2000, April 28). Ninety per cent of world excluded from old age pension schemes. Many schemes badly managed. Problems foreseen in coping with ageing populations and diversifying risk. tinyurl.com/3548hw4b;
M. R. Despard, T. Friedline, and S. Martin-West. (2020). Why do households lack emergency savings? The role of financial capability. *Journal of Family and Economic Issues* 41 (3), pp. 542–557. tinyurl.com/mr2nphpy
R. Hodson, R. Dwyer, and L. Neilson. (2014). Credit card blues: The middle class and the hidden costs of easy credit. *Sociological Quarterly* 55 (2), pp. 315–340. tinyurl.com/3uxt4zbv;
Holland Times. (2023, January 9). Many women are financially dependent on their partners. tinyurl.com/4k42scw3;
K. Ng. (2022, April 25). Less than half of women consider themselves financially independent. *Independent*. tinyurl.com/mpve658r;
S. Estep. (2023, August 17). Women's financial well-being in 2022. AmericanProgess.org. tinyurl.com/2s45eejd

6   E. Field, A. Krivkovich, S. Krugele, N. Robinson, and L. Yee. (2023, October 5). Women in the workplace 2023. McKinsey & Company. tinyurl.com/27v77vnf

7   A. R. Quisumbing, ed. (2003). Power and resources within the household: Overview. *In Household Decisions, Gender, and Development: A Synthesis of Recent Research*, pp. 19–22. Washington, DC: International Food Policy Research Institute.

8   M. Phelan. (2022, November 22). Does money make you happy? TheHappinessIndex.com. tinyurl.com/5yxs3tvj

9   Phelan 2022.

"To live is to choose.
But to choose well,
you must know who you are
and what you stand for,
where you want to go and
why you want to get there."

—Kofi Annan

RELATIONSHIPS

Written by Carla Szemzo

"Our greatest joy and our greatest pain come in our relationships with others."
—STEVEN R. COVEY

INTRODUCTION

Relationships are the core of being human.
"[R]elationships with other humans are both the foundation and the theme of the human condition: We are born into relationships, we live our lives in relationships with others, and when we die, the effects of our relationships survive in the lives of the living, reverberating throughout the tissue of their relationships."[1]

Personal Story

In 2020, I lost my favorite person in the world: my grandma. Simultaneously, my aunt, who was only sixty years old, passed away from COVID-19. Two months later, my mother was diagnosed with an advanced breast cancer. I felt that my life was falling apart and that I didn't have control over these situations. To navigate these negative waves, I realized that the only thing that I could control was my well-being.

I started reading more about positive habits, neuroscience, and meditation. I also improved my physical habits (playing sports, spending time outdoors, getting better sleep) and reinforced my spirituality. But most importantly, I relied on my closest relationships. I am used to being the supportive rock for my friends, family members, coworkers, and students. But for the first time, I allowed myself to receive all the love and help that I have given to my dear ones for years.

Eight months later, my mother was fully recovered, my first nephew was born, and I received a promotion, obtaining my dream job that was fully aligned with my life purpose. Looking back, the support that I had from family and friends during this storm allowed me to conquer adversity and flourish. I was able to identify my unconditional relationships: the ones that not only accompany us in triumph but also provide hope during difficult times. To those of you that supported me during that time, thank you!

The impact of these relationships on well-being is undeniable. They transform lives and prove that when hearts come together, they create a harmonious symphony of joy and fulfillment.

Let's begin this chapter by defining what relationships are and situating their relevance within well-being practices. The American Psychological Association defines a relationship as "a continuing and often committed association between two or more people, as in a family, friendship, marriage, partnership, or other interpersonal link in which the participants have some degree of influence on each other's thoughts, feelings, and actions."[2]

Types of Relationships

When reflecting on relationships, the common tendency is to focus on our immediate family members or romantic partners. However, it is essential to emphasize the significance of nurturing a wide array of connections that can profoundly influence our daily well-being. These relationships extend beyond our closest circle and encompass various social connections that play a crucial role in shaping our overall happiness. Let me focus on some of the most relevant types as illustrated in Figure 4.2.

Figure 4.2: Types of relationships

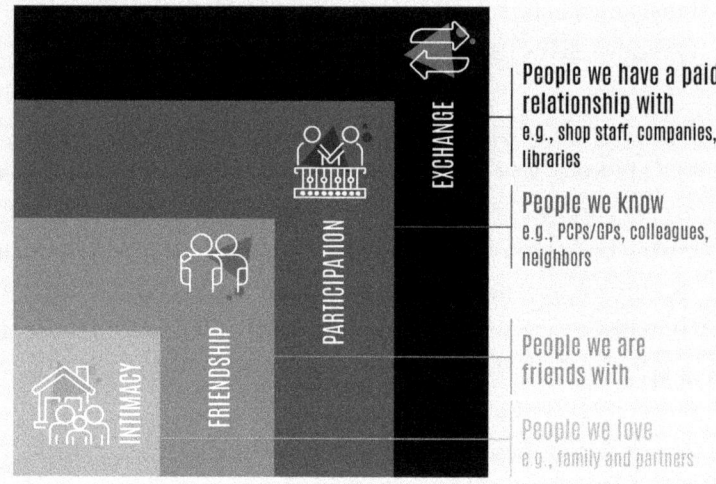

People we have a paid
relationship with
e.g., shop staff, companies,
libraries

People we know
e.g., PCPs/GPs, colleagues,
neighbors

People we are
friends with

People we love
e.g., family and partners

EXCHANGE

PARTICIPATION

FRIENDSHIP

INTIMACY

Table 4.1: Types of relationships

With yourself	The relationship you have with yourself forms the basis for all other relationships in your life. By investing in self-love, self-acceptance, and self-compassion, you enhance your capacity to build and maintain healthy, fulfilling connections with others. Developing your relationship with yourself is a fundamental step for your personal growth.
With friends	Friends are those with whom we establish deep connections based on shared interests, experiences, and values. They provide emotional support and companionship, and often play a vital role in our well-being. According to Aristotle, there are three kinds of friendships: **1. Utility.** Friendships of utility are based on what the two people involved can do for one another. **2. Pleasure.** Friendships of pleasure are based on enjoyment of a shared activity and the pursuit of fleeting pleasures and emotions. **3. Virtue.** Friendships of virtue are with people you like for themselves and who push you to be a better person—the "real" friends that will provide life-long relationships.
With romantic partners	Relationships with romantic partners involve both a deep emotional and physical connection. These relationships include love, trust, intimacy, and mutual support. A strong romantic relationship can provide emotional fulfillment, companionship, and happiness.

With family members	One's relationship with family members—children, parents, siblings, extended family members—is the most fundamental relationship in one's life. These relationships provide love, support, and a sense of belonging.
With mentors	Mentors are experienced individuals who provide guidance, advice, and support based on their expertise and wisdom. They can help in both personal and professional development, offering valuable insights and helping navigate challenges. I wasn't aware of the relevance of a relationship with a mentor until I met Nick van Dam, who subsequently became the most committed and caring mentor I've ever had.
With work colleagues	Establishing a professional network is crucial for career development. These relationships provide opportunities for collaboration, learning, and advancement in the workplace. These connections are particularly important to our well-being because of the number of hours we invest in them.
With a community	Engaging with a community—whether local, regional, or global— fosters a sense of belonging and social connection. Such relationships can include a membership in a club or religious group, volunteering with others, and relationships with neighbors and fellow community members, among others.
With pets	Those of us who have had pets know how they offer unconditional love and companionship. Pets also provide emotional support and can help alleviate feelings of stress, anxiety, and loneliness. Interacting with pets can promote the release of oxytocin—a hormone in your body that promotes positive feelings—reduce symptoms of depression, and improve overall well-being. In addition, the responsibility of caring for a pet can provide purpose and a sense of meaning.

"The most relevant relationships in your life are those that bring you peace, joy, support, and a sense of belonging and purpose."

The significance of relationships can vary for each of us. Some may prioritize certain relationships more than others based on values, goals, and personal circumstances. However, it is important to keep in mind that the most relevant relationships in your life are those that bring you peace, joy, support, and a sense of belonging and purpose.

HOW DO RELATIONSHIPS SUPPORT YOUR WELL-BEING?

To determine what makes us happy, in 1938 researchers at Harvard University began following 724 participants as part of the longest-running study on human development. This research explored every part of who we are, from physical and psychological traits to social life and IQ, to learn how we can flourish. The detailed lessons from this study, published in *The Good Life: Lessons from the World's Longest Scientific Study of Happiness,* show that happiness and health do not result from wealth, fame, or working hard but instead mainly come from the strength of our **relationships.**[4]

It is key to cultivate and nurture healthy and positive relationships to maximize our happiness levels. What are the main benefits of building positive bonds?

1. **Longer life.** An article from Northwestern Medicine notes that "research suggests having social ties can increase longevity."[5] Moreover, in *The Blue Zones: Lessons on Living Longer from the People Who've Lived the Longest,* researcher Dan Buettner paints a compelling picture of the influence of positive relationships and social connections on the aging process. Buettner explores lifestyles and habits of people residing in specific regions across the globe known as blue zones, where individuals have longer and healthier lives. His findings underscore the significance of nurturing meaningful relationships as a fundamental component of a prolonged and satisfying life. Though longevity is shaped by various factors such as a healthy diet, active lifestyle, and engagement in intellectual activities, residents of blue zones attribute much of their extended lifespans to their strong sense of community and the significant investment they make in fostering personal relationships.[6]

2. **Less stress and better physical well-being.** Northwestern Medicine also found that "being in a committed relationship is linked to less production of cortisol, a stress hormone."[7] Positive relationships can provide emotional support during challenging times and help individuals cope with stress. This research indicates that strong social connections create better physical health outcomes such as helping to reduce rates of cardiovascular disease, recover faster from illness, and decrease anxiety.

3. **Boosted mental health.** Personal connections trigger the release of certain neurotransmitters, such as dopamine, oxytocin, and serotonin, which play crucial roles in regulating emotions, pleasure, and social bonding. According to the National Institutes of Health, social support and positive relationships can lead to enhanced brain function and improve the attention span.

4. **Greater sense of community and purpose.** Northwestern Medicine found that sharing experiences, thoughts, and emotions with others can contribute to a sense of belonging and purpose.[8]

5. **Increased self-esteem.** Positive relationships with supportive individuals can encourage healthy habits, personal growth, and positive self-acceptance.

> "... [H]appiness and health do not result from wealth, fame, or working hard, but instead mainly come from the strength of our relationships."

BOOSTING YOUR WELL-BEING THROUGH RELATIONSHIPS

Managing and leveraging healthy relationships is essential for personal and professional growth. Here are some final thoughts and recommendations to improve your human interactions. Think about those connections that you want to work on. Maybe it is the communication with your mother, the patience that you want to develop with your romantic partner, or the time that you would like to dedicate to your kids. The following strategies have helped me leverage human interactions while going through my own transformational journey.

Effective communication. Effective communication is key for building and maintaining relationships. Actively listen to others, express your thoughts and feelings clearly, and be attentive to nonverbal signs. Regularly check in with people and show genuine interest in their lives and experiences.

Empathy and compassion. Develop empathy to understand others' perspectives and emotions. Put yourself in their shoes, acknowledge their feelings, and respond with compassion. Be open to different viewpoints, and show understanding even when you disagree.

Reciprocity. Relationships thrive when there is a give-and-take dynamic. Offer support to others when needed. Be willing to receive help and express gratitude for the contributions others make to your life.

Trust and respect. Trust and respect are the foundation of strong relationships. Be trustworthy by keeping your commitments, being honest and fair, and being loyal to your words. Respect others' opinions, boundaries, and time.

Healthy boundaries. Establish healthy boundaries to ensure mutual respect. Communicate your needs and expectations. Be mindful of others' boundaries, time, and dedication. Respect when others say no, and learn how to say no yourself when your intuition tells you to do so.

Problem-solving. Conflicts are inevitable in relationships. Learn about problem-solving skills and negotiation, find common ground, and seek win-win solutions. Address conflicts honestly and respectfully to preserve the relationship and promote growth.

Appreciation and recognition. Express gratitude for the people in your life. Appreciate their contributions, celebrate their successes, and offer genuine compliments. Small gestures of kindness and recognition help to strengthen relationships.

Continued learning and growth. Relationships evolve over time, and it's important to continue investing in their growth. Learn about the people in your life and their interests, aspirations, and challenges. Seek feedback and be open to personal growth and self-improvement.

Authenticity. Be authentic and true to yourself when interacting with others. Genuine connections are built on honesty and openness.

Quality time. Invest quality time in your relationships. Schedule regular activities or conversations with friends, family, or colleagues to nurture meaningful connections.

Forgiveness. Be willing to apologize when you make mistakes and to forgive others when they do the same. A willingness to repair and move past conflicts is essential for maintaining strong relationships.

Remember, building and maintaining relationships requires time, effort, and commitment. By actively investing energy in your relationships, you can create a supportive network, foster meaningful connections, and achieve mutual success. In order to nurture healthy relationships, you should first be able to enjoy the most important relationship in life—the one that you have with yourself. How can you do this? By prioritizing your well-being above all else: make time for self-reflection to build self-awareness and heal past wounds to avoid hurting people in the future.

Finally, educators have noted that the emotional and social skills listed above can indeed be learned and should therefore be introduced early in children's lives. I would like to share my commitment to disrupt the current global education system by teaching younger generations how to manage relationships, emotional intelligence, and positive behaviors. Let's work together on giving back all the love that we have received from our closest relationships to the people that need this the most: children without families, teenagers that feel lonely, senior citizens, and so on. Think about the impact that this could have on well-being within our society on a large scale. As Dr. Barbara Fredrickson, one of the founders of positive psychology, has mentioned, "Love, and its absence, fundamentally alters the biochemicals in which your body is steeped."[9]

QUESTIONS FOR SELF-REFLECTION

In the steps below, I will help you navigate your primary relationships to determine the quality of these relationships. My goal is to help you identify how much energy and time you allocate to each in order to make them flourish. We will not only focus on the special bond that you have with your romantic partner or spouse but also navigate the connections you have built with your family, friends, pets, work colleagues, and so on.

We will learn together if you are dedicating the right amount of energy, time, focus, and real connection to the relationships that matter to you the most. Sometimes we are aware that we want to change our focus on a particular person, but we just don't know how to do so. Why? Because we might not have the right emotional tools, or we haven't healed the way that we connect with others in the subconscious version of ourselves due to past trauma, or we just don't know how to communicate effectively.

1. **Let's start by making list of the main tasks, activities, and people to which you allocate most of your time in a normal week. For example:**

- Children: 20 hours

- Partner or spouse: 15 hours

- Friends: 5 hours

- Work: 45 hours

- Social media: 9 hours

- Sports: 7 hours

- Sleep: 56 hours

- Other tasks: 11 hours

2. **Choose or add the people/relationships/activities from the list that are most meaningful in your life.**

3. Ask yourself the following questions:

- Am I investing most of my valuable time in the activities, projects, and people that I care about the most?

- Am I fully present when I am having lunch with my parents, partner, or friends, or am I constantly looking at my phone or thinking about my to-do list?

- Am I an active listener? When someone is talking to me, do I listen with 100% of my attention, or am I already thinking about what to say next?

- Do I feel that I am giving back the same love, time, and attention that I receive from others?

- If a doctor told me today that I have a terminal disease, and that I only have one month left to live, would I spend my time differently? If so, how?

RESOURCES FOR EXPLORATION AND LEARNING

TOP 3: ARTICLES

Luscombe, B. (2017, September 6). **A guy read 50 years worth of relationship studies.** He came up with 17 strategies. *Time.*
▶ tinyurl.com/yudxz8ut
This article provides a summarized practical list of recommendations to foster personal relationships, including dos and don'ts.

Mental Health Foundation. (n.d). **Relationships in the 21st century: The forgotten foundation of mental health and wellbeing.**
▶ tinyurl.com/4ahkmjve
This article explains with extensive evidence how, by having good-quality relationships, people can live longer and happier lives with fewer mental health problems.

Pearson, C., and J. Dunn. (2023). **The best relationship advice we've gotten so far this year.** *New York Times.*
▶ tinyurl.com/43fkxbdh
This article gives practical recommendations on how to navigate the main relationship challenges like fights, misunderstandings, and unhealed wounds.

TOP 3: BOOKS

García, H., and F. Miralles. (2016). **Ikigai: The Japanese Secret to a Long and Happy Life.**
London: Penguin.
This book share the Japanese philosophy that can be loosely translated as "the reason for being."
The book delves into the practices and principles behind the long and fulfilling lives of the people
of Okinawa, Japan, who are known for their longevity. The authors introduce the idea of *ikigai* as
the intersection of what you love, what you are good at, what the world needs, and what you can
be paid for. Finding your ikigai is believed to bring purpose, satisfaction, and a long, happy life.

Ricard, M. (2006). **Happiness: A Guide to Developing Life's Most Important Skill.**
Boston: Little, Brown.
This book provides practical guidance on how to cultivate happiness in one's life. Matthieu Ricard
is a Tibetan Buddhist monk and scientist who argues that happiness is not a fleeting emotion
but rather a skill that can be developed and enhanced through conscious effort and practice.
He provides a set of practical recommendations and habits on how to develop this skill.

Waldinger, R., and M. Schulz. (2023). **The Good Life: Lessons from the World's Longest
Scientific Study of Happiness.** New York: Simon & Schuster.
The directors of the Harvard Study of Adult Development, the longest scientific study of
happiness ever conducted, ask, what makes a life fulfilling and meaningful? The simple but
surprising answer is: relationships. *The Good Life* shows us that it's never too late to strengthen
the relationships you already have, and never too late to build new ones. The book provides
examples of how to do this.

 TOP 3: ASSESSMENTS AND TESTS

 Best Friend Quiz: Are You Really Best Friends? ProProfsQuizzes.
▶ tinyurl.com/yrux9bkm
From ProProfsQuizzes: "Take the ultimate Best Friend Quiz to discover if you and
your BFF truly shares an unbreakable bond! This fun and insightful quiz will put
your friendship to the test and determine if you're truly inseparable."

 Relationship Attachment Style Test. Psychology Today.
▶ tinyurl.com/re9uynyx
From Psychology Today: "From early on in life, we develop an attachment to our
primary caregivers that tends to remain constant. This attachment style has a
profound effect not only on our emotional development, but also upon the health
of our relationships. The main attachment styles covered in this test are Secure,
Anxious-Ambivalent, Dismissive-Avoidant, Fearful-Avoidant, Dependent, and
Codependent. Find out what your style is and how it affects your relationships
by taking this test."

Relationship Quiz: How Well Do You Know Your Partner? Gottman.com.

▶ tinyurl.com/24rr52za

From Gottman: "After doing extensive research for over four decades with thousands of couples, we've found that one of the most important components of a successful relationship is the quality of friendship between partners. And that requires knowing your partner's likes, dislikes, needs, desires, beliefs, fears, and life dreams. So, how well do you really know your partner? Take our quiz below to find out."

TOP 3: VIDEOS

4 Habits of All Successful Relationships.
Dr. Andrea and Jonathan Taylor-Cummings.

▶ tinyurl.com/4rh3hhky

From the video description: "ALL relationships face a similar set of hurdles. We all need to be equipped to get over the hurdles, so that our relationships don't just survive, but thrive. Based on over 20+ years' experience of working with countless couples, Dr. Andrea and Jon Taylor-Cummings share their observations of the 4 fundamental habits that all successful relationships exhibit."

How Compassion Could Save Your Strained Relationships. Betty Hart.

▶ tinyurl.com/dnfkauz7

From the video description: "When personal relationships and ideological differences crash, the result can lead to strained relations—or even years of silence and distance. In this video, Actor Betty Hart offers an alternative to cold shoulders through compassion, and a chance for growth and change instead of losing important time with our loved ones."

The Power of Vulnerability. Brené Brown.

▶ tinyurl.com/ypu4eh5v

In her "Power of Vulnerability" talk, Brené Brown shares personal stories and discusses the significance of vulnerability in human connection and personal growth. She emphasizes that vulnerability is not a sign of weakness but rather a source of strength. She mentions that vulnerability is the birthplace of love, belonging, joy, and creativity.

ENDNOTES

1   E. Berscheid. (1999). The greening of relationship science. *American Psychologist 54* (4), pp. 260-66. ww; quote from pp. 261-62.

2   American Psychological Association. (n.d.). Relationship. tinyurl.com/22dmsj5c

3   D. Robinson. (2019, February 19). Relationships. Shift. tinyurl.com/3jbuy777

4   R. Waldinger and M. Schulz. (2023). *The Good Life: Lessons from the World's Longest Scientific Study of Happiness.* New York: Simon & Schuster.

5   Northwestern Medicine. (2021, September). 5 benefits of healthy relationships: Why healthy relationships are so important. tinyurl.com/35d59bah; L. F. Berkman and S. L. Syme. (1979). Social networks, host resistance, and mortality: A nine-year follow-up study of Alameda County residents. *American Journal of Epidemiology 109* (2), pp. 186-204. tinyurl.com/pw2zuk38

6   D. Buettner. (2012). *Blue Zones: Lessons on Living Longer from the People Who've Lived the Longest.* Washington, DC: National Geographic.

7   Northwestern Medicine 2021.

8   Northwestern Medicine 2021.

9   B. Fredrickson. (2013, March 15). The science of love. Aeon. tinyurl.com/nhh5r8sf

"Happiness is not based on possessions, power or prestige, but on relationships with people you love and respect."

—H. Jackson Brown Jr.

CONTRIBUTION

Written by Emily Ricci

INTRODUCTION

Meaningful contribution profoundly shapes our overall psychological well-being and is one of the most powerful catalysts for feeling fulfillment and purpose in life. Most of us "contribute" when it's convenient or when we're asked. However, intentional effort to make a positive impact on others connects us to something greater than ourselves, more purposefully links us to the shared human experience, and improves every facet of our lives.

> **"We make a living by what we get;
> we make a life by what we give."**
> —WINSTON CHURCHILL

Personal Story

It had already been a long, lonely holiday season when my partner informed me that he would have to work on Christmas Eve. We had recently moved across the country to San Francisco for his career, and I had begun working from home, using a converted closet in our one-bedroom apartment for my "office," while he put in a grueling 100 hours a week at his new job. I was mostly alone and had to find ways to distract myself from overwhelming isolation and boredom. I poured myself into work, walked countless miles of the city, took classes at a local yoga studio, and cooked elaborate meals, but the solitude was crushing. As December marched on, I realized that with just a single friend in the city and my family thousands of miles away, I would be alone for the holidays, too.

One night after crying into another single-serving meal, I thought, you're *not* totally alone; you're just alone right now. Then another thought occurred to me: maybe if I helped someone else, it would not only make me feel better but also give my alone time some meaning. I found my way to the Positive Resource Center (PRC), a San Francisco nonprofit providing support and services to people affected by HIV/AIDS, substance abuse, and mental health issues.

On Christmas Eve, I stacked plates, folded napkins, and prepared tables for PRC's hugely popular holiday dinner at the historic War Memorial Opera House. A gentle awareness bloomed inside me as I surveyed the smiling faces, soft chatter, and smooth coordination across the sea of volunteers. Surrounded by dozens of bustling people, it was true that I felt less alone. But in the humble act of polishing a fork for someone less fortunate than myself, I felt a twinge of something greater than what had brought me there. It was an undeniable sensation of being bound to our common humanity—a feeling that I later learned was contribution.

Key Characteristics of Contribution

Contribution is taking deliberate action with a goal of positively impacting individuals (including the self), a community, society—even humanity as a whole. It's a fundamental human behavior that enriches lives, creates positive connections, and inspires a more compassionate and supportive world. Contributions can vary greatly depending on the contributor, ranging from small and simple acts of kindness to long-term commitments and large initiatives. Contributions may also vary in terms of time, effort, resources, expertise, and creativity.

Contributions can be identified by their six distinctive qualities: aligned, intentional, selfless, voluntary, impactful, and lasting.

Table 4.2: Six distinctive qualities of contribution

QUALITY	DESCRIPTION
Aligned	Calibrated with the needs and context of recipients.
Intentional	Deliberate effort driven by a genuine desire to help, support, or boost the well-being of others.
Selfless	Having no expectation of immediate or direct reciprocity.
Voluntary	Not driven by obligation but by empathy, compassion, and a goal of making a difference.
Impactful	Creating beneficial outcomes such as improving someone's life, solving a problem, addressing a need, or making a positive change.
Lasting	Generating impact beyond the immediate moment and potentially inspiring others to participate in and strengthen a positive cycle of change.

We might think that giving to others benefits only recipients, but contributions empower both givers *and* receivers. Recipients receive support, resources, and positive change, whereas givers gain a deep sense of fulfillment and purpose, in turn creating **meaning** and the powerful motivation to continue contributing.

As shown in Figure 4.3, contributions typically fall into one of five main types.

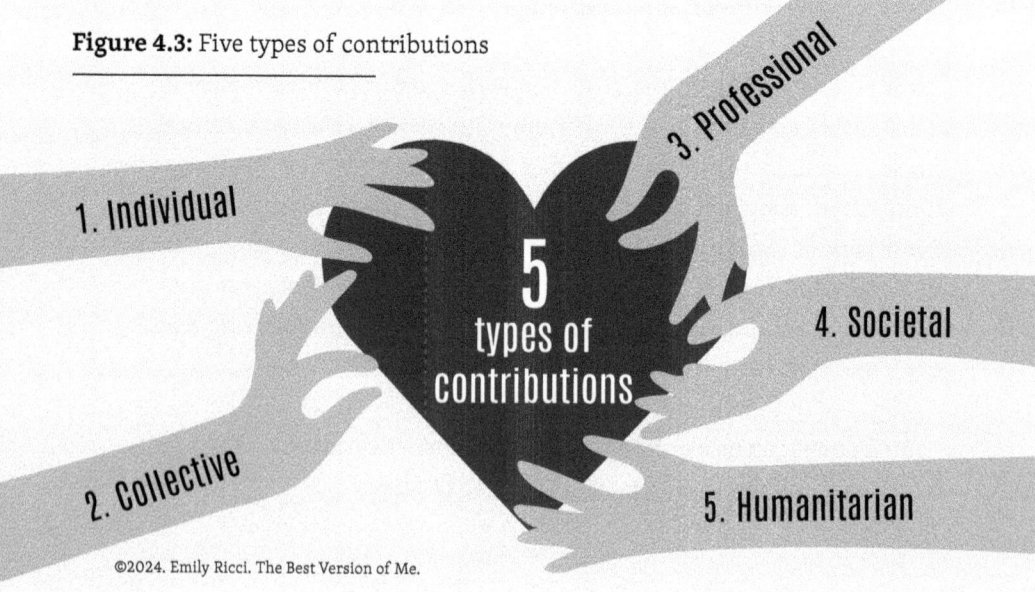

Figure 4.3: Five types of contributions

1. Individual
2. Collective
3. Professional
4. Societal
5. Humanitarian

5 types of contributions

©2024. Emily Ricci. The Best Version of Me.

1. **Individual.** Contributions don't need to have a direct recipient to be impactful if their ultimate goal is to inspire and help others. Activities that spur personal growth and well-being can be beneficial to our overall happiness and fulfillment, as well as create a broad positive ripple effect. Individual contribution may look like:

- Improving physical and mental well-being, including reducing stress through activities such as meditation and mindfulness, and enhancing energy through exercise, adequate sleep, and healthy eating.

- Pursuing new knowledge and skills, or setting and achieving personal goals, with a long-term aim of helping others.

- Developing self-awareness and emotional regulation by journaling feelings, thoughts, and behaviors.

- Nurturing healthy relationships with friends, family, and community members.

- Cultivating a growth mindset and practicing positive thinking to enhance resilience, optimism, and the ability to overcome challenges.

- Making charitable donations, volunteering, or participating in a community service project.

2. **Collective.** Taking selfless action to enhance the well-being of family, friends, and smaller groups can have positive effects on individuals and their immediate communities. Collective contributions could include:

- Offering emotional support and active listening to promote understanding and encouragement and to cultivate an empathetic environment.

- Recognizing and celebrating milestones, achievements, and special events to deepen bonds and show gratitude for others' contributions and presence.

- Participating in communal activities such as social outings and hobbies to reinforce relationships and create shared memories.

- Constructively addressing conflicts and disagreements to prevent negative escalation and develop communication and mutual understanding.

- Working together to solve problems, complete tasks, and exchange knowledge for heightened teamwork, creative thinking, and mutual respect.

3. **Professional.** Making professionally conscious contributions can benefit both your career and your personal growth, as well as help others flourish in your work environment. Contributing professionally is also a key driver for feeling a sense of purpose both inside and outside of work. Employers who support professional contributions help to create positive cultures where mutual support, growth, and collaboration can thrive. Professional contributions may be activities like:

- Sharing expertise through mentoring, coaching, and cooperative problem-solving to encourage organizational growth and continuous learning.

- Taking part in an organization's volunteer opportunities, or leading an initiative to have such opportunities instituted.

- Promoting diversity and inclusion to engender belonging and opportunities for all while bringing varied and valuable perspectives to the table.

- Assuming leadership roles and proactively identifying opportunities for process improvements, efficiency gains, and cost-saving measures.

- Contributing thought leadership through articles, blog posts, and presentations.

- Providing assistance or support to colleagues facing personal challenges and heavy workloads.

4. **Societal.** Societal contributions may range from social interactions to institutional, environmental, or cultural pursuits. Whether on a micro or macro level, contributing to organized groups with common cultural values, norms, and customs can have a profound positive impact on both givers and receivers and can enhance feelings of connection and belonging. Societal contributions may include:

- Participating in eco-friendly initiatives such as tree planting, clean-up campaigns, or recycling efforts.

- Giving to health-related campaigns, blood drives, or medical missions to improve access to health care for underserved populations.

- Advocating for and empowering marginalized and underrepresented groups.

- Contributing to art and cultural activities to preserve heritage, promote creativity, and enrich society.

- Assisting during natural disasters to help communities recover and rebuild.

- Advocating for mental health awareness, offering support to those in need, and challenging the stigma surrounding mental health.

5. **Humanitarian.** Humanitarian contributions emphasize shared human characteristics and experiences while spanning geographic, cultural, and societal boundaries. They are often focused on intrinsic human qualities such as empathy and creativity and create a sense of global solidarity. Humanitarian contributions may look like:

- Championing advancements in medical research, treatments, and health care access for longer, healthier lives on a global scale.

- Providing essential aid through humanitarian missions to address global crises and conflicts or assisting countries facing poverty, hunger, and lack of access to clean water to improve overall quality of life.

- Combating climate change, conserving natural resources, and promoting sustainable practices for a healthier planet and better living conditions for current and future generations.

- Ensuring access to quality education and promoting innovations in science and technology to support intellectual growth, economic empowerment, and social mobility.

- Advocating for the protection of human and equal rights for a more just and inclusive world.

HOW DOES CONTRIBUTION SUPPORT YOUR WELL-BEING?

Significant evidence supports contribution's ability to make us feel more connected to others and the world. Along with cultivating greater empathy, a deeper sense of purpose, and greater life happiness, contribution positively impacts our well-being in four important dimensions, as shown in Figure 4.4.[1]

Figure 4.4: Impact of contribution on well-being

1. Connection. Numerous studies reveal that prosocial behavior increases feelings of being connected to a greater whole such as a community or even all of humanity. These types of positive social interactions trigger our brains to release oxytocin and dopamine, making us feel the love and empathy that can bond us more deeply with others.[2]

Contribution also provides a natural path for forming new social networks. By increasing the diversity of our social ties, we grow our communities and perhaps even change the composition of our existing social groups. We may experience the phenomenon of "bridging," or forming relationships with people very different from ourselves, which gives us more diverse points of community and a rich social tapestry. When we contribute alongside others who, despite outward differences, share similar values, goals, and purpose, we satisfy our fundamental human need for connection.

2. Empathy. Research strongly suggests that acts of contribution expand our ability to understand and connect with the needs and emotions of others. As our networks blossom, we're likely to interact with people of different backgrounds, heightening our ability to find new perspective. A strong neurological link between contributing and empathy is also a factor; when acts of kindness trigger the release of feel-good neurochemicals in our brains, we're better able to relate to the experiences of others.[3]

Observing the positive impact of actions also inspires a positive feedback loop: good deeds generate positive feelings, positive feelings build confidence, and confidence makes us more motivated to continue helping. This virtuous cycle keeps us looking outward and remaining focused on the needs of others, positively impacting our mental and emotional health.

5. **Purpose.** Engaging in activities that benefit others is strongly linked to more positive emotions, including a sense of purpose. Feeling a sense of purpose helps us sustain motivation through life's ups and downs, and purposeful people tend to live longer and be more satisfied with their lives.[4] As many as 70% of us claim our sense of purpose is defined by our work, which is problematic if our employers haven't played a role in helping us find and support that purpose.[5] The good news is that a sense of purpose can be gained easily and through more diverse channels via social contribution.

Though contributions at any time in life enhance our health, they are especially potent during adolescence.[6] The brain's network of areas that activate in social interactions matures rapidly during the adolescent years, deepening an understanding of the complex feelings, perspectives, and needs of other people. Adolescents become better able to determine who needs their help and what kind of help they might need. By tapping into this understanding and aligning their abilities with helping, adolescents later become adults who are more wired to recognize the feeling of purpose.[7] Because many outlets for contribution are filled with people we likely admire, we may earn appreciation from our peers by emulating them. Making contributions not only influences how others see us but heightens our own feelings of self-respect as well as an overall sense of purpose.

4. **Happiness.** Aristotle extolled that helping others was *the* way to develop greater individual well-being, but modern perspectives challenge that notion. Fortunately, these rival views have been studied empirically, and the evidence is overwhelming: people who contribute feel more satisfied and happy with their lives than those who don't. In fact, one study showed that people who engaged in contribution activities for periods of several days experienced a measurable improvement in their mood, with the effects being more positive on days when they self-reported acts of kindness. What's more, they reported a persistent elevated mood for two days following the event.[8]

By stimulating the brain's mesolimbic pathway, contributing releases endorphins that create a "helper's high," boosting self-esteem, guarding against certain mood disorders and depression, and supporting us in the development of psychological resources such as effective stress management.[9] All of these things work in concert to make us happier over time.

BOOSTING YOUR WELL-BEING THROUGH CONTRIBUTION

We may believe we need to do something radical like joining the Peace Corps to make a positive difference in the world, but there are simpler steps we can take to start impacting our communities today.

Determine where you're needed. Remember that contributions can occur in the different contexts of our lives: we can provide *emotional support* to peers; *service* through chores or helping family members; *leadership* by taking on roles in local government, clubs, sports teams, and charities, and so on. We can also use our unique life perspectives and challenges to relate to and help others. For example, powerful activism and civic engagement are often motivated by issues of race, ethnicity, gender, sexual orientation, and religion.

Align with your values. We know the dread that comes from being cajoled into giving; when this happens, we are more likely to give to avoid humiliation rather than from generosity or true concern. However, this type of giving doesn't yield the typical positive benefits but instead leads to resentment. Aligning our contributions with our values not only feels better but increases the likelihood of greater commitment to a cause over time, benefiting both the individual and the cause itself.

Give to organizations with transparent aims and results. According to Harvard scientist Michael Norton, "Giving to a cause that specifies what they're going to *do* with your money leads to more happiness than giving to an umbrella cause where you're not so sure where your money is going."[10] The same goes for nonmonetary contributions. Look for organizations where you can trace your efforts back to the source: the people you wish to help.

Draw healthy boundaries. Perhaps surprisingly, there isn't a linear relationship between time spent on volunteering and overall well-being. Benefits emerge from even small amounts of conscious contribution, whereas heavy volunteering commitments may have adverse outcomes. Says Wharton professor Adam Grant, "Selfless giving, in the absence of self-preservation instincts, easily becomes overwhelming. It is important to be 'otherish,' defined as 'being willing to give more than you receive, but still keeping your own interests in sight.'" [11]

SUMMARY

Living a meaningful life comes down to three key things:
(1) believing that your life makes sense (coherence),
(2) knowing you are pursuing fulfilling activities (goal orientation), and
(3) feeling that your contributions make a difference (mattering).

In terms of overall life happiness, mattering borne of our **contributions to others** delivers incredible return on investment. Even simple acts such as helping a stranger, providing social support to a loved one, or being a reliable friend can create lasting positive effects and provide us with hope, optimism, belonging, and perspective. Though we don't all have the same resources, interests, or talents, we do all have at least some time to devote to helping others. Whether we're driven by our values, our concern for community, or our deeper personal development, we can identify ways to give, and in doing so, further enhance our lives and our world.

QUESTIONS FOR SELF-REFLECTION

Even when we know we want to help, we may not know where to begin.
Ask yourself these questions to get started:

- What causes do I care about? What naturally moves me to want to contribute?

- What skills can I offer others/community/society/humanity?

- Where can I most easily begin contributing (work, home, city, government)?

- In which areas can I further develop myself so that I can better give to others?

RESOURCES FOR EXPLORATION AND LEARNING

TOP 3: ARTICLES

Dhingra, N., A. Samo, B. Schaninger, and M. Schrimper, M. (2021, April 5).
Help your employees find purpose or watch them leave. *McKinsey Quarterly.*
▶ tinyurl.com/5buumnnx
Today's employees expect their jobs to bring a significant sense of purpose to their lives. Employers that do not help them meet this need must be prepared to lose talent to employers that will.

Hicks, J. A., and L. A. King. (2021, November 2). **Three ways to see meaning in your life.** *Greater Good Magazine.*
▶ tinyurl.com/yrkjd543
Feeling that your life has meaning is fundamental to the experience of being human, and people who feel this way tend to be healthier and happier. If meaning is so important, how can we cultivate the feeling that life is truly meaningful?

Reilly, C. (2023, February 21). **Do you want to know the best-kept secret to improving wellbeing?** *Forbes.*
▶ tinyurl.com/yxbk95fm
Volunteering is proven to be beneficial for our mental, physical, and emotional health, yet it is on the decline. Simple actions can help get us started on the path of contributing and thus positively influence our overall outlook on life.

TOP 3: BOOKS

Grant, A. (2013). **Give and Take: Why Helping Others Drives Our Success.** New York: Penguin. From Amazon's description: "For generations, we have focused on the individual drivers of success: passion, hard work, talent, and luck. But in today's dramatically reconfigured world, success is increasingly dependent on how we interact with others. In Give and Take, Adam Grant, an award-winning researcher and Wharton's highest-rated professor, examines the surprising forces that shape why some people rise to the top of the success ladder while others sink to the bottom."

MacAskill, W. (2015). **Doing Good Better: How Effective Altruism Can Help You Help Others, Do Work that Matters, and Make Smarter Choices about Giving Back.** New York: Avery. From Amazon's description: "An up-and-coming visionary in the world of philanthropy and a cofounder of the effective altruism movement explains why most of our ideas about how to make a difference are wrong and presents a counterintuitive way for each of us to do the most good possible."

Rath, T. (2020). **Life's Great Question: Discover How You Contribute to the World.** San Francisco: Silicon Guild. From Amazon's description: "Life's Great Question will show you how to make your work and life more meaningful, and greatly boost your wellbeing. In this remarkably quick read, author Tom Rath describes how finding your greatest contribution is far more effective than following talent or passion alone."

 TOP 3: ASSESSMENTS AND TESTS

 How You Contribute to the World Quiz. Contribify.com.
▶ contribify.com
Discover what matters most and how you best contribute to the world by completing this quiz, part of the book How You Contribute to the World by Tom Rath.

 Purpose in Life Quiz. Greater Good Magazine.
▶ tinyurl.com/yj8cu96j
Having true purpose is personally meaningful and makes a positive impact on the lives of other people. This quiz, primarily based on the Claremont Purpose Scale, helps you identify your purpose and strengthen it.

 Volunteer Personality Quiz. Get Connect by Galaxy Digital.
▶ tinyurl.com/28c6xzf2
If you want to contribute but don't know where to start, this short quiz will help you discover your "volunteer personality," along with opportunities you're best suited for.

TOP 3: VIDEOS

 The Business Benefits of Doing Good. Wendy Woods.
▶ tinyurl.com/mr3k9b4a
From TED: "'The only way we're going to make substantial progress on the challenging problems of our time is for business to drive the solutions,' says social impact strategist Wendy Woods. In a data-packed talk, Woods shares a fresh way to assess the impact all parts of business can have on all parts of society, and then adjust them to not only do less harm but actually improve things. Learn more about how executives can move beyond corporate social responsibility to 'total societal impact'—for the benefit of both a company's bottom line and society at large."

 Helping Others Makes Us Happier—But It Matters How We Do It. Elizabeth Dunn.
▶ tinyurl.com/4v9h3nkn
From TED: "Research shows that helping others makes us happier. But in her groundbreaking work on generosity and joy, social psychologist Elizabeth Dunn found that there is a catch: it matters how we help. Learn how we can make a greater impact—and boost our own happiness along the way—if we make one key shift in how we help others."

 How to Motivate People to Do Good for Others. Erez Yoeli.
▶ tinyurl.com/mtbf5chc
From TED: "How can we get people to do more good: to go to the polls, give to charity, conserve resources or just generally act better towards others? MIT research scientist Erez Yoeli shares a simple checklist for harnessing the power of reputations—or our collective desire to be seen as generous and kind instead of selfish—to motivate people to act in the interest of others. Learn more about how small changes to your approach to getting people to do good could yield surprising results."

 ## TOP 3: APPS

There are numerous apps designed to help match an individual's skills and interests with local and global ways to contribute. The three below are a great place to start.

Golden.
Whether you're a volunteer looking to discover a new adventure or an organizer looking to elevate your program, Golden can match you to a cause. Golden also offers the opportunity to track volunteer hours and earn rewards.

Impactive.
An all-in-one hub for organizing online, whether it's volunteering for your favorite campaign, advocacy organization, or nonprofits.

Volunteer Match.
Search and match with causes you're passionate about and find opportunities to volunteer locally, or recruit highly qualified volunteers for your nonprofit.

 TOP 3: FREE ONLINE COURSES

 Managing Happiness. Harvard University.
▶ tinyurl.com/2kkjx88h
This course encourages you to explore the science of happiness, allowing you to find your truest self.

 Purpose at Work. University of Michigan.
▶ tinyurl.com/33b7t232
This course helps you first examine what purpose is, the benefits of having a purpose, and how to find your purpose. Next, you'll examine the idea of purposeful work, including ways of finding it in the process of leading a more engaged and fulfilling life.

 The Science of Happiness. UC Berkeley's Greater Good Science Center.
▶ tinyurl.com/mwwjx67s
This course teaches the science of positive psychology and explores the roots of a happy and meaningful life. The course zeroes in on a fundamental finding from positive psychology: that happiness is inextricably linked to having strong social connections and contributing to something bigger than yourself.

ENDNOTES

1   J. Yeung, Z. Zhang, and T. Y. Kim. (2018). Volunteering and health benefits in general adults: Cumulative effects and forms. *BMC Public Health 18* (8). tinyurl.com/7n735p4c

2   Cleveland Clinic. (2022, December 7). Why giving is good for your mental health. tinyurl.com/4dmcrhf8

3   J. Santi. (n.d.). The secret to happiness is helping others. *Time.* tinyurl.com/32wsdv7e

4   B. Nichol, R. Wilson, A. Rodrigues, and C. Haighton. (2023). Exploring the effects of volunteering on the social, mental, and physical health and well-being of volunteers: An umbrella review. *Voluntas.* tinyurl.com/5cnaa6kf

5   N. Dhingra and B. Schaninger. (2021, June 3). The search for purpose at work. McKinsey & Company. tinyurl.com/bdzn4hac

6   UCLA Center for the Developing Adolescent. (n.d.). Meaning and purpose through contribution. tinyurl.com/3kbkekat

7   P. J. Ballard, S. S. Daniel, G. Anderson, L. Nicolotti, E. Caballero Quinones, M. Lee, and A. N. Koehler. (2021). Incorporating volunteering into treatment for depression among adolescents: Developmental and clinical considerations. *Frontiers in Psychology 5* (12), 642910. tinyurl.com/mwrfhb8e

8   K. Otake, S. Shimai, J. Tanaka-Matsumi, K. Otsui, and B. Fredrickson. (2006). Happy people become happier through kindness: A counting kindness intervention. *Journal of Happiness Studies 7* (3), pp. 361-75. tinyurl.com/mvu582p2

9   N. Lin, X. Ye, and W. Ensel. (1999). Social support and depressed mood: A structural analysis. *Journal of Health and Social Behavior 40* (4), pp. 344-59. tinyurl.com/ystk4vnw

10 Santi n.d.

11 M. Weber. (2018, November 21). The secret to happiness is compassion. Medium.com. tinyurl.com/38wt5ke9

"You are not here merely
to make a living. You are here
in order to enable the world to
live more amply, with greater
vision, with a finer spirit of
hope and achievement. You are
here to enrich the world, and
you impoverish yourself if you
forget the errand."

—Woodrow Wilson, 28th President of the United States

"Just as the ocean remains undisturbed by the incessant flow of waters from rivers merging into it, likewise the person who is unmoved despite the flow of desirable objects all around oneself attains peace [because one is anchored within], and not the person who strives to satisfy desires [because one is anchored externally]."

—INSPIRED BY THE BHAGAVAD GITA VERSE 2.70[1]

INTRODUCTION

Personal Story

In the highly volatile, uncertain, complex, and ambiguous world of health care entrepreneurship, William was a pioneer, charting a course in an intricately regulated market. His innovative spirit brought success in the early years, adorned with awards and accolades. But as his business soared, competitors turned hostile, and even his own supervisory board raised eyebrows at his methods.

Uncertainty crept in, eroding William's trust in those around him. The relentless pressure began taking a toll on his health, culminating in a heart attack. Suddenly, the indomitable entrepreneur found himself a patient, searching for solace within. After practicing meditation and deep introspection, he began to fathom the essence of spirituality. The notion of an internal anchor became his guiding light, a connection to something beyond the material world. William realized that his success hinged not on appeasing external stakeholders but on nurturing his inner self.

Months of reflection, contemplation, and self-discovery led William to trust the unknown realm within. He embraced the uncertainties, turning toward them for guidance. Gradually, he rekindled his lost trust in himself.

Emerging from this transformation, his business thrived with newfound harmony. He faced competition with equanimity, fostering deeper connections. The once-skeptical board marveled at their transformed leader. William's journey home to himself reshaped not only his business but his entire being—mentally, physically, and spiritually.

William's story underscores the profound link between spirituality and well-being—a testament to the transformative power within us all. This tale beckons you to explore further, where the wisdom of spirituality awaits, poised to illuminate your path.

Meeting the best version of myself means that *I am at home wherever I am.* In this chapter, I want to explain how the feeling of being at home wherever you are can be realized by anchoring one's life into spirituality. But what is spirituality? To describe spirituality, authors use terms such as something beyond explanation, a force beyond, awareness, belongingness, a sense of (inter)connectedness, essence, connecting to the life force, existence beyond physical life, consciousness, sacredness or divinity, trust or faith in or connection with divinity, inner experience, process or journey of awakening, ultimate purpose, desire or search for the ultimate, and a sense of meaning.[2]

The term spirituality has gained popularity as a result of people's use of spiritual techniques.[3] Although spirituality and spiritual techniques are not the same, people often perceive them as interchangeable. To learn more about the differences, one can find online a wide range of meditation guidance, talks, and explanations on spirituality from different traditions, covering various manifestations of spirituality in authentic, Indigenous, and modern ways.[4] The COVID-19 pandemic, in particular, accelerated exposure to such spiritual techniques.[5]

Individual professionals navigate their way to well-being through various spiritual practices, both inside and outside their organizations.[6] For example, some may visit spiritual retreats, whereas company leaders or corporate celebrities may introduce spirituality under the banner of workplace spirituality or spirit at work.[7] This may involve providing facilities such as meditation halls, breathwork sessions, or inspirational talks by monks, gurus, or priests.

In the light of spirituality, we come to realize that *our true home is not a physical location but a state of consciousness*. It is a state of being that transcends time, space, and circumstances.[8] Wherever we are, whether in the midst of chaos or tranquility, we can find solace and a profound sense of being at home by connecting to our spiritual essence, our anchor. To connect to this essence, we need to develop a particular quality. Therefore, I define spirituality as any entity's quality of becoming aware of the connectedness of one's existence beyond its perceived existence.[9] Other descriptions of this existence beyond perceived existence could be the unknown or the ocean of your Self. In other words, spirituality is any entity's quality (on its path) of becoming aware of the (inter)connectedness with its existence beyond its perceived existence (such as God, Love, Nature, Supreme, Consciousness, Self, Sacredness).[10] The notion of being at home wherever you are invites us to find a sense of belonging and contentment in every moment and in any situation. It encourages us to cultivate deep inner peace and harmony that transcends external circumstances. Similarly, spirituality teaches us to recognize our true nature and the interconnectedness of all things. When we understand that our true essence is not limited to the physical body or the transient aspects of life, we realize that our real home is not confined to a specific place or condition. Instead, our true home is the divine essence within us, the eternal aspect of our being that is connected to the larger composition of existence.

The essence of this view can be found in the K-continuum model (Figure 4.5), which explains the ontological base of spirituality (what it is) and the epistemological base of knowing spirituality (ways of understanding it).[11] This model may help you better connect beyond your ordinary perception of reality and realize a better version of you.

Figure 4.5: K-continuum of Knowledge

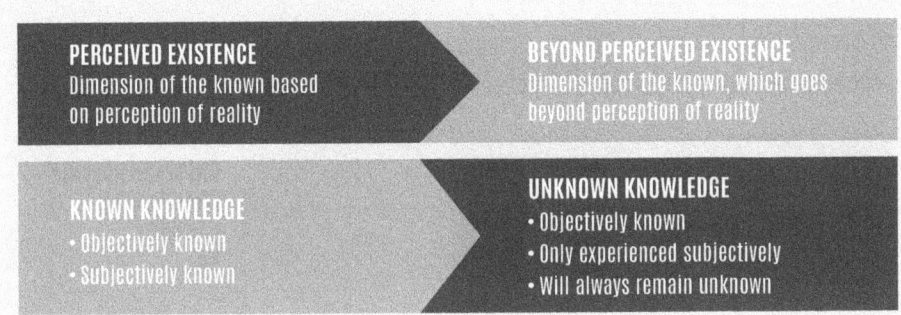

The K-continuum model consists of the known and the unknown positioned at opposite ends. Understanding this model requires a different mindset and a new framework to grasp its concepts. In the realm of science, our driving force is the pursuit of the unknown. The legitimacy of science lies in the curiosity to study things that are not yet known. What I am proposing is to delve into the nuances of the unknown.

Within the K-continuum model, I further distinguish the unknown into one part that can be known and two parts that are unknowable. One of these unknowable parts can be experienced, whereas the other is beyond our capacity for experience. The model explains that both the perceived reality and the reality beyond should be considered within the realm of spirituality. Both have an impact on our well-being.

In Figure 4.6, the realms of reality are divided into four categories of knowledge: the knowable known (K1), the knowable unknown (K2), the unknowable experienceable unknown (K3), and the unknowable unexperienceable unknown (K4). The K1 and K2 realms pertain to our sensory experiences, whereas K3 encompasses the realm of our mental senses. The abstract, conceptual, generative, and creative aspects of spirituality are likely to manifest from K3 and K4. These aspects of the unknowable can be explained in two groups associated with K3 and K4.

Figure 4.6: K-continuum of Knowledge

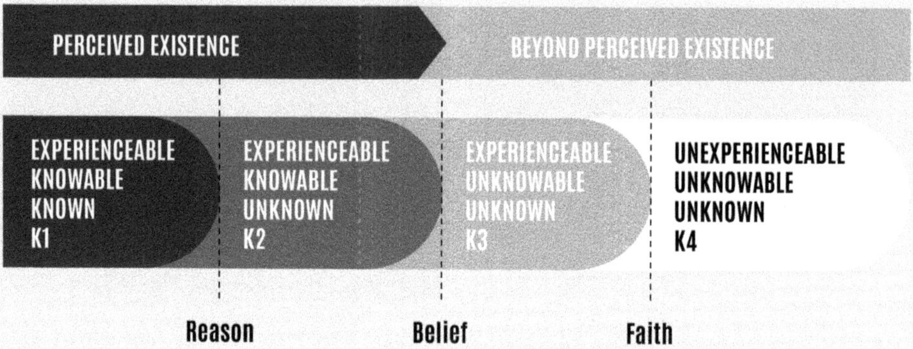

PERCEIVED EXISTENCE			BEYOND PERCEIVED EXISTENCE
EXPERIENCEABLE KNOWABLE KNOWN K1	EXPERIENCEABLE KNOWABLE UNKNOWN K2	EXPERIENCEABLE UNKNOWABLE UNKNOWN K3	UNEXPERIENCEABLE UNKNOWABLE UNKNOWN K4
Reason	Belief	Faith	

©2024. Dr. Sharda S. Nandram. The Best Version of Me. Adapted from Nandram (2022).

K1 and K2 represent realms of doing, whereas K3 and K4 take us from doing to being. The mode of doing is driven by reason, whereas the mode of being is driven by beliefs and faith, allowing us to accept unexpected events and find meaning in them. Doing, being, and the unfolding of events become an integrated and a holistic process.

HOW DOES SPIRITUALITY SUPPORT YOUR WELL-BEING?

Spirituality and well-being are intricately linked, offering profound benefits in the realm of management. Research on spirituality reveals that spirituality and health behaviors positively impact psychological well-being, with spirituality's influence partially mediated by healthy behaviors.[12] To meet the better version of ourselves, we need to be aware of the K-continuum and ensure that we do not confine ourselves to only one part of the continuum. Instead, we should move along the continuum, back and forth linearly or even nonlinearly, to tap into our infinite potential and establish a foundation for our well-being.

Here is how you can delve into the transformative power of spirituality, unraveling the ways it bolsters your well-being.

Find purpose and meaning. Spirituality provides a compass for navigating the labyrinth of life's challenges. It ignites a sense of purpose and meaning that transcends the routine of work. By connecting with your inner selves by mapping your activities in the known and unknown realms of reality, you discover that your true home lies not in the external world but in the realm within. This newfound purpose infuses your work with deeper significance, enhancing your overall well-being.

Foster interconnectedness. At the heart of spirituality is the recognition of our interconnectedness with the four abovementioned realms of existence of the K-continuum of Knowledge model. This awareness sparks empathy and compassion, essential qualities for effective leadership and harmonious team dynamics. When you acknowledge the intricate web of connections that bind you and others, whether these are in the known or the unknown realities, you and others become more inclined to collaborate harmoniously, thereby creating a positive work environment that nurtures your well-being and that of your colleagues.

Cultivate inner peace and resilience. Spiritual techniques can equip us with invaluable tools for managing stress, anxiety, and uncertainty—common companions in the corporate world—subsequently enhancing our well-being. By learning to trust your inner guidance and tapping into your spiritual essence, you cultivate inner peace and emotional resilience. This inner strength becomes a steadfast ally in times of adversity, bolstering your overall well-being. It serves as an internal anchor in your life.

Integrate rationality and intuition. Spirituality in management is not a departure from rationality but a harmonious integration of both rational and intuitive faculties. It empowers you to make holistic decisions that consider not only the bottom line but also the welfare of employees, the broader community, and the environment. As a leader guided by spirituality, you must navigate ethically and responsibly, recognizing the profound impact of your choices on all stakeholders.

BOOSTING YOUR WELL-BEING THROUGH SPIRITUALITY

Spirituality can be seen as a path toward achieving oneness with or connecting with a reality beyond one's perceived existence, ultimately enhancing well-being. Various spiritual techniques and strategies exist to aid in this journey. There are no universally right or wrong approaches; they are all deeply personal and contingent on each person's own context and stage of life.

In the realm of spirituality, *critical events in one's life often serve as catalysts for seeking the best version of oneself.* However, intentional application of various techniques, beliefs, scriptures, rituals, immersion in Indigenous traditions, and symbols can also aid in this endeavor. Here, I offer some strategies to infuse spirituality into your life based on the K-continuum of Knowledge. These spiritual strategies are not mutually exclusive. The underlying message in both assessments is to *strive for utilizing the entire continuum.*

K1 infused by spirituality.
Engage in actions with selflessness and dedicate them to a higher purpose.
Try to act in alignment with moral and ethical values in all your daily activities.

K2 infused by spirituality.
Gain knowledge and deepen your understanding of things that are new to you. This can involve any subject. Enlarge the scope by listening to spiritual teachings, and reflect deeply on them to understand and get new insights. In addition, engage in practices such as visiting sacred places, meditation retreats, self-discipline, chanting, study of sacred texts, austerity, and charity.

K3 infused by spirituality.
Visualize a form of the unknown that resonates with you, and cultivate a deep sense of love, devotion, and trust in your chosen form. Engage this form in daily practice as well as in prayers, chanting, and rituals, and introspect on the layers of your experiences that it generates. Connect with like-minded people with whom you can share your experiences in psychologically safe surroundings.

K4 infused by spirituality.
This journey involves recognizing the habitual patterns of your mind and, through meditation, moving beyond identification with the body-mind-intellect complex to find repose in the boundless sea of consciousness—the unknown—that encompasses every aspect of existence. Cultivate ethical behavior, and practice purity, contentment, self-discipline, and self-study as the foundation for your inner growth. Combine physical postures and breathing practices to calm the mind and provide vital energy to prepare you for meditation. Subsequently withdraw attention from external distractions and meditate on a chosen object, and ultimately experience spiritual union and inner realization.

Remember, *spirituality is a deeply personal journey,* and the ways in which you explore and integrate its principles will be unique to you. Embrace the practices, beliefs, and techniques that resonate with your inner truth and foster a deeper connection with yourself, your Self, and the world around you.

QUESTIONS FOR SELF-REFLECTION

The following self-reflection questions encourage you to explore your personal experiences and beliefs in the context of spirituality and well-being, helping you deepen your understanding of yourself and your spiritual journey.

- In the realm of self-inquiry, delve into the question, "Who am I?" What insights have you gained from this inquiry regarding your true self and its connection to well-being?

- What is the importance of self-examination in understanding what the mind essentially is?

- Reflect on your understanding of "selfless action." How have selfless actions contributed to your well-being and sense of purpose?

- Reflect on moments when your mind has become silent or still. What circumstances or practices led to these moments of mental quietude, and how did they affect your well-being?

- Consider your experiences with inner transformation and self-realization. How has self-knowledge and reflection impacted your spiritual journey and overall well-being?

- What spiritual practices or techniques have you personally found most effective in enhancing your well-being?

- For how long does one have to do self-inquiry to enhance their well-being?

- Think about meditation and the quest for spiritual union. How have meditation or mindfulness practices contributed to your mental and emotional well-being?

- Visualize the best version of yourself. How can aligning with this ideal self positively impact your well-being, and what steps can you take to move closer to this vision?

- How does the best version of you boost your well-being?

RESOURCES FOR EXPLORATION AND LEARNING

TOP 3: ARTICLES
The following three articles from peer-reviewed journals provide further reading on spirituality. The first article addresses spirituality's link to well-being, the second gives an example of spirituality in an organizational context, and the third examines the various ways in which spirituality has been conceptualized in the literature to facilitate the definition used in this chapter.

Bożek, A., P. F. Nowak, and M. Blukacz. (2020). **The relationship between spirituality, health-related behavior, and psychological well-being.** *Frontiers in Psychology 11*, 1997.
▶ tinyurl.com/5bhv9v63

Nandram, S. S. (2021). **Humane organizing in a post-COVID-19 world: Learning from Buurtzorg's trust-based decentralization.** *Journal of Management, Spirituality & Religion 18* (5), pp. 375–99.
▶ tinyurl.com/5n73nev2

Nandram S. S., and P. K. Bindlish. (2023). **Conceptualizing spirituality for management.** *International Journal of Indian Culture and Business Management 1* (1).
▶ tinyurl.com/mrnnmux8

TOP 3: BOOKS

The books listed below provide greater insights into spirituality. The first book is based on extensive neuroscientific research. You can use the second book as a guide for your own introspection. The third book is one of a kind and a must read if you wish to understand the power of spirituality in your personal life.

Miller, L. (2021). **The Awakened Brain: The New Science of Spirituality and Our Quest for an Inspired Life.** New York: Random House.

Tolle, E. (2004). **The Power of Now: A Guide to Spiritual Enlightenment.** Novato, CA: New World Library.

Yogananda, P. (2005). **Autobiography of a Yogi: The Original 1946 Edition plus Bonus Material.** Commerce, CA: Crystal Clarity Publishers.

TOP 3: ASSESSMENTS

Spirituality cannot be fully captured by measurements and assessment tools, but these three are some attempts by scholars to measure spirituality from different concepts. The first assessment is used at the workplace, the second uses the concept of spiritual well-being, and the third focuses on the concept of meaning.

Ashmos, D. P., and D. Duchon. (2000). **Spirituality at work: A conceptualization and measure.** *Journal of Management Inquiry* 9 (2), pp. 134–45.
▶ tinyurl.com/s9ryvvmb

Ellison, C. W. (1983). **Spiritual well-being: Conceptualization and measurement.** *Journal of Psychology and Theology* 11 (4), pp. 330–38.
▶ tinyurl.com/36vbfxtk

Steger, M. F., P. Frazier, S. Oishi, and M. Kaler. (2006). **The meaning in life questionnaire: Assessing the presence of and search for meaning in life.** *Journal of Counseling Psychology* 53 (1), pp. 80–93.
▶ tinyurl.com/2pvvm5kz

TOP 3: VIDEOS

If you felt inspired by this chapter, in the following videos I further explain spirituality and how it can be positioned in a business context. These videos will help you in your contemplations of what spirituality is.

Integrative Spirituality in the Fourth Industrial Revolution: From How We Do Things to Why We Exist. With Prof. Dr. Sharda Nandram. Vrije University Amsterdam. ▶ tinyurl.com/36xwv4fj

 Radical Thinkers Webinar #5: Spirituality & Business with Prof. Dr. Sharda Nandram. ▶ tinyurl.com/yswf4cmp

 Spirituality: Discipline for Doing Business with the Unknown. Inaugural address with Prof. Dr. Sharda Nandram. Nyenrode Business University. ▶ tinyurl.com/3z6c3x9y

---

TOP 3: PODCASTS

The following podcasts help you with deeper reflections on spirituality. Robert Kuhn's series addresses existential questions. Oprah Winfrey discusses what meditation is and what potential it has. Sri M invites you to learn about the yogic view of your mind.

 Asking the Ultimate Questions about Reality. Robert Lawrence Kuhn. ▶ tinyurl.com/bdhbr5vk

 Oprah's Super Soul: Deepak Chopra: Meditation 101. ▶ tinyurl.com/mr3mcw9a

 Sri M: The Yogi Mindset and True Success NOW. The Philosophy of Now Podcast. ▶ tinyurl.com/smsd65kc

---

TOP 3: FREE ONLINE COURSES

The following online courses will orient you to some aspects of spirituality.

 Chinese Thought: Ancient Wisdom Meets Modern Science—Part 1. University of British Columbia. ▶ tinyurl.com/mwsu6jmc

 Positive Psychology: Resilience Skills. ▶ tinyurl.com/48sm4ryr

 The Science of Well-Being. Yale University. ▶ tinyurl.com/bpuutftv

ENDNOTES

1   S. Mukundananda. (2013). Bhagavad Gita: The song of god. Jagadguru Kripaluji Yog.
    tinyurl.com/mr2zphrh

2   C. T. Tackney, S. F. Chappell, and T. Sato. (2017). MSR founders narrative and content
    analysis of scholarly papers: 2000-2015. *Journal of Management, Spirituality & Religion 14* (2),
    pp. 135-59. tinyurl.com/3ndtn5z2

3   E. Seppälä. (2015, December 14). How meditation benefits CEOs. *Harvard Business Review.*
    tinyurl.com/2s8m82ps

4   T. Ryan. (2012). Virtual spirituality: The negotiation and (re)-presentation of psychic-
    spiritual identity on the internet (PhD diss., University of York).
    tinyurl.com/3k8vkcev

5   K. Ibrahim, M. Komariah, and Y. K. Herliani. (2022). The effect of mindfulness breathing
    meditation on psychological well-being: A quasi-experimental study among nurses working
    for COVID-19 patients. *Holistic Nursing Practice 36* (1), pp. 46-51. tinyurl.com/3ue6njkp

6   V. Kinjerski and B. J. Skrypnek. (2008). Four paths to spirit at work: Journeys of personal
    meaning, fulfillment, well-being, and transcendence through work. *Career Development
    Quarterly 56* (4), pp. 319-29. tinyurl.com/ym36rtmj

7   M. Lips-Wiersma and A. J. Mills. (2014). Understanding the basic assumptions about
    human nature in workplace spirituality: Beyond the critical versus positive divide.
    Journal of Management Inquiry 23 (2), pp. 148-61. tinyurl.com/3bxxvhpe

8   L. Fry and M. Kriger. (2009). Towards a theory of being-centered leadership: Multiple
    levels of being as context for effective leadership. *Human Relations 62* (11), pp. 1667-96.
    tinyurl.com/52d6mujt

9   S. S. Nandram. (2019). *Integrative Spirituality in the Fourth Industrial Revolution: From How
    We Do Things to Why We Exist.* Inaugural lecture. Amsterdam: Vrije University Press.
    tinyurl.com/4ws7ceen

10 S. S. Nandram and P. K. Bindlish. (2023). Conceptualizing spirituality for management.
    International Journal of Indian Culture and Business Management 1 (1).
    tinyurl.com/mrnnmux8

11 S. S. Nandram. (2022). *Spirituality: The Discipline of Doing Business with the Unknown.*
    Inaugural lecture. Breukelen: Nyenrode Business Universiteit. Spiritualiteit, De discipline
    voor zakendoen met het onbekende.

12 A. Bożek, P. F. Nowak, and M. Blukacz. (2020). The relationship between spirituality,
    health-related behavior, and psychological well-being. *Frontiers in Psychology 11*, 1997.
    tinyurl.com/5bhv9v63

VALUES, BELIEFS, AND ATTITUDES

Written by Lisa Bevill

"Your beliefs become your thoughts, your thoughts become your words,
your words become your actions, your actions become your habits,
your habits become your values, and your values become your destiny."

—MAHATMA GANDHI

INTRODUCTION

Personal Story

Maya had always been passionate about the environment. She felt that each
one of us was responsible for protecting the planet, and she was determined to
have a positive impact on the world. When it came time to choose a career after
graduating from college, Maya faced a dilemma: a lucrative job offer from a large
corporation focused on maximizing profits with little regard for environmental
sustainability, or an opportunity with a smaller nonprofit dedicated to
conservation that offered a modest salary and espoused values perfectly aligned
with her own. Maya needed to make a choice after considering the trade-offs.

We all need to make choices, big and small, in our lives, yet how do we
understand and appreciate the core drivers of these decisions? What decisions
have you made in your own life? Can you identify the underlying values that
supported these decisions? What will Maya decide?

Figure 4.6: The nature of our values, beliefs, and attitudes

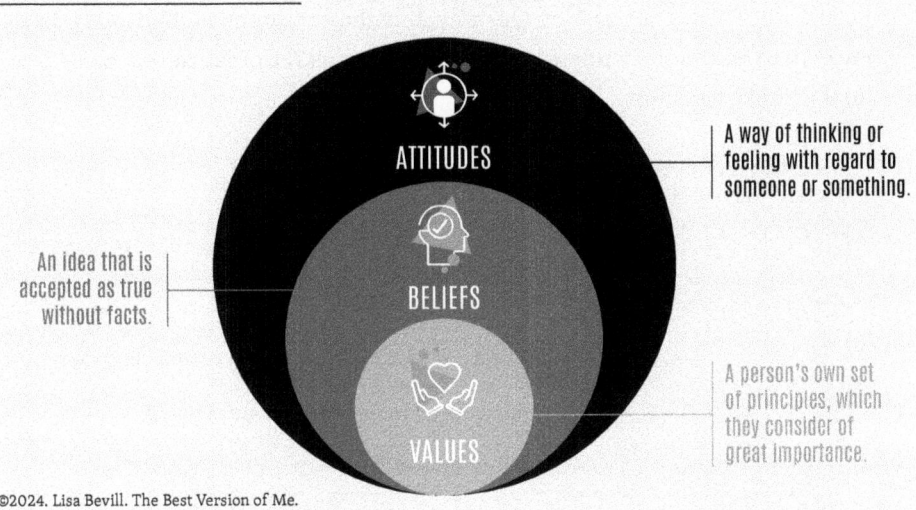

ATTITUDES

A way of thinking or feeling with regard to someone or something.

An idea that is accepted as true without facts.

BELIEFS

A person's own set of principles, which they consider of great importance.

VALUES

©2024. Lisa Bevill. The Best Version of Me.

At one point or another, we have all faced Maya's conundrum, which illustrates the nature of our **values, beliefs, and attitudes**—the concepts we will explore in this chapter. We will discuss how they shape our lives and how we can use them to live a more fulfilling and meaningful life. I will also suggest some ways to identify and examine your own values and beliefs.

1. Values.

Values are the things that we consider important in life, our general intentions and aspirations.[1] They are the guiding principles that shape our thoughts, feelings, and actions. Conscious, subconscious, or unconscious, values are often abstract, not always precisely articulated, often intangible, yet they are very powerful. As Maya reflected on her values and beliefs, she realized that she couldn't compromise her deeply held convictions for the sake of financial gain. Instead, she turned down the corporate job offer and boldly decided to join the nonprofit, despite the financial challenges and uncertainty.

Maya values environmental sustainability and personal responsibility, which is why she chose the nonprofit, even though it meant making less money and working harder. Her work would make a difference in the world, and that was more important to her than money. Her new role brought her a sense of fulfillment and purpose, and she found herself surrounded by like-minded people who shared her passion for protecting the environment. She took great joy in her work as she witnessed the positive impact the organization made on the local ecosystem.

Table 4.3: Examples of values

Honesty	Valuing truthfulness and integrity in all interactions.
Respect	Valuing the dignity and worth of every individual, regardless of differences.
Responsibility	Valuing taking ownership of one's actions and obligations.
Equality	Valuing fairness and equal opportunities for all.
Compassion	Valuing empathy and care toward others in need.
Collaboration	Valuing teamwork and cooperation to achieve shared goals.
Personal growth	Valuing continuous learning, self-improvement, and development.

2. Beliefs.

In time, Maya's dedication and commitment paid off. She gained recognition for her expertise and became an influential voice in the field of conservation. Her values and beliefs not only shaped her career but also inspired others to reevaluate their own actions and make conscious choices to protect the environment.

Beliefs are deeply held attitudes about oneself, other people, and the world.[2] They affect our understanding of the world and how it works, including higher, overarching truths about our world and society, as well as beliefs about ourselves as individuals. It is often difficult to recognize these underlying beliefs because they are so ingrained in how we interpret the world, but doing so can help us overcome invisible barriers to growth and development.

For centuries—even millennia—one commonly held belief was that the Earth was flat. This widespread belief created a collective, unfounded truth that was widely accepted and remained unchallenged until a movement to explore and discover more took shape. Considering an alternative truth required a grounded sense of self and confidence in one's values to consider an alternative truth, especially when faced with great resistance from so many.

Another belief that persisted into the twentieth century was that running a sub-four-minute mile was impossible. Faced with this belief, many never even attempted such a feat, whereas some tried but failed. However, in 1954, British medical student Roger Bannister challenged this common belief, and his values enabled him to overcome this unfounded truth when he ran a mile in 3:59:4. Within one year of Bannister's achievement—because a new truth (or belief) had been established—thirty-seven more people broke the record. As of June 2022. As of June 2022, at least 1,775 athletes have run a mile in under four minutes.[3]

When we accept beliefs as absolute truth, we yield our potential and growth to accepted, yet often unfounded, barriers of the status quo.

Table 4.4: Examples of beliefs

Belief in equality	Believing that everyone that everyone deserves equal rights and opportunities.
Religious belief	Personal belief in a higher power or spiritual practices.
Belief in personal agency	Believing that individuals have the power to make choices and shape their own lives.
Belief in justice	Believing that fairness and just outcomes should be upheld in society.
Belief in the power of education	Believing that education is essential for personal growth and societal progress.
Belief in the importance of family	Believing in the significance of family bonds and relationships.
Belief in cultural diversity	Recognizing and appreciating the value of different cultures and traditions.

3. Attitudes.

Maya's story illustrates the importance of aligning our values and beliefs with our choices and actions—with our attitudes. By staying true to her convictions, Maya found personal satisfaction, made a meaningful impact, and inspired others.

Attitudes refer to a person's disposition—their way of thinking and feeling about someone or something.[4] They are our emotional reactions to people, places, things, and events. Values, beliefs, and attitudes are all interrelated: just as our values shape our beliefs, our beliefs shape our attitudes. They play a pivotal role in shaping our perceptions and responses to the world around us.

Table 4.5: Examples of attitudes

Positive attitude	Approaching situations with optimism and a constructive mindset.
Open-mindedness	Being receptive to new ideas, perspectives, and experiences.
Tolerance	Demonstrating acceptance and respect toward individuals with different backgrounds, beliefs, and values.
Adaptability	Being flexible and able to adjust to changing circumstances.
Empathy	Understanding and sharing the feelings of others.
Curiosity	Having a desire to learn, explore, and seek knowledge.
Perseverance	Maintaining determination and resilience in the face of challenges.

HOW DO VALUES, BELIEFS, AND ATTITUDES SUPPORT YOUR WELL-BEING?

Values and beliefs are integral components of our identity and profoundly influence our well-being. Behaviors serve as the outward expression of internalized systems, encompassing attitudes, beliefs, and values.

> **"When our actions align with our values, it can lead to a sense of fulfillment and purpose, contributing positively to our overall well-being."**

These internalized systems serve as guiding principles that influence our behaviors, emotional responses, and decision-making processes. When our actions align with our values, it can lead to a sense of fulfillment and purpose, contributing positively to our overall well-being.[5] Conversely, dissonance between our behaviors and deeply held values can lead to internal disconnection and emotional burden.

Values are instilled through a combination of family, cultural context, and innate characteristics. For instance, consider someone raised in a family that values empathy and compassion. This person may prioritize helping others and engaging in charitable activities, leading to a sense of fulfillment and happiness with their actions. Values and beliefs are the foundation of our approach to life, shaping how we interpret events and make decisions. Our emotional responses are driven by the amygdala, the primitive emotional center of our brain, which reacts to the world based on these deeply ingrained values. Understanding this connection provides an opportunity to gain clarity on what truly matters, enabling us to respond with intention and a grounded connection to our values.

The Power of Aligned Values and Beliefs

Aligning our actions with our values fosters authenticity and a greater sense of purpose. Someone who values environmental sustainability, like Maya, may actively participate in local clean-up initiatives and reduce their carbon footprint, or even choose a career in the sustainability field, and as a result feel fulfilled by contributing to a cause they care deeply about. It is this alignment that allows us to navigate challenges and decisions with a sense of inner conviction.

On the contrary, living at odds with our values can lead to emotional and physical consequences. When our behaviors do not align with our inner compass, an internal conflict arises, causing emotional burden and stress. If Maya had accepted the job offer in a high-stress corporate environment, where profits were prioritized above all else—even though her personal values revolved around sustainability, personal responsibility, and the courage to do what is right— the constant conflict between her values and work demands could have led to general dissatisfaction and burnout, negatively impacting her well-being.

> **"Positive beliefs in the possibility of accomplishment and learning allow us to surpass limitations."**

Beliefs also play a crucial role in well-being, shaping our capacity to meet challenges and fostering personal growth. Positive beliefs in the possibility of accomplishment and learning allow us to surpass limitations, leading to greater growth and achievement. A positive belief or expectation of the future — defined by the VIA Institute on Character as the character strength hope[6] — is associated with greater personal satisfaction and well-being. Conversely, limiting beliefs can hinder personal progress, inhibiting us from reaching our full potential. For example, people who believe they are not smart enough to pursue higher education may forgo opportunities to improve their skills and career prospects, therefore limiting their growth. Values, beliefs, and attitudes play a fundamental role in shaping our perceptions, emotional responses, and behaviors. Alignment and authenticity with our values in turn shape a deeper meaning and purpose in life.

Making the Best Decisions for Your True Self

Understanding the meaning and importance of personal values is essential for personal growth and fulfillment. Identifying and living by our values can have a profound impact on various aspects of our lives, including our mental and emotional well-being. Engaging in activities that align with our values can combat depression and anxiety, improve our overall mental health, and increase our motivation and passion for our work.

Moreover, personal values enhance self-awareness, which is crucial for personal development and decision-making. Recognizing and articulating our values empowers us to better understand ourselves, set meaningful goals, and strengthen our relationships with others. As a result, we can better advocate for ourselves and make difficult but ultimately rewarding decisions that are in line with our true selves.

It is important to remember that personal values are not static. Our personal and professional lives are constantly changing, so it makes sense for our personal values to change, too. At any time, you could be offered a new job, decide to start a family, or move on from a toxic relationship. Our values need to adapt just as we need to learn to adapt to such changes. Regularly reassessing our values ensures that they remain in harmony with our aspirations.

BOOSTING YOUR WELL-BEING THROUGH VALUES, BELIEFS, AND ATTITUDES

Values, beliefs, and attitudes serve as the compass that guides us through life's journey, shaping our thoughts, actions, and the impact we have on the world around us. They are the pillars of our identity, defining what we hold dear and the principles we stand for. As we navigate through life's complexities, it becomes essential to continuously deepen our understanding of these core convictions and actively engage in practices that help us reinforce and advance them.

Practice self-reflection. Practicing self-reflection is a fundamental step in advancing our values, beliefs, and attitudes. Regularly taking time for introspection allows us to gain a deeper understanding of our core principles and assess whether our decisions and behaviors align with them. This practice of self-awareness enables us to identify areas where we may need to improve and make conscious efforts to live in harmony with our values, consider our beliefs, and challenge our attitudes.

Continue learning. Education and learning are pivotal to the advancement of our values. To create a meaningful impact in our lives and the world around us, we must stay well informed about the topics and issues relevant to our values. Reading and attending workshops or webinars broadens our knowledge and perspectives, helping us better articulate and advocate for our values while remaining open to the ideas and viewpoints of others.

Engage in conversations with others. By the same token, engaging in meaningful conversations with individuals who hold different perspectives allows us to gain insights into diverse viewpoints and challenges us to critically examine our own beliefs. Seeking common ground or areas of mutual understanding in these dialogues promotes empathy and tolerance and fosters constructive dialogue.

Practice what you believe is important. Leading by example is another powerful way to inspire others and advance our values, beliefs, and attitudes. Striving to embody our principles in daily life demonstrates authenticity and consistency between our words and actions. It requires a conscious effort to align our actions with our deeply held convictions, even when it may seem easier and safer to do the opposite.

One way to do this is by volunteering and contributing to causes that align with our values. By actively participating in organizations or initiatives that champion our beliefs, we can contribute our time, skills, and resources to make a positive impact in the world and create meaningful change in areas that matter to us. Such actions not only benefit the causes we support but also provide us with a sense of fulfillment and purpose in life.[7]

Seeking support. Seeking support and connection with like-minded individuals is vital for sustaining our commitment to our values and beliefs. Surrounding ourselves with a supportive community or group that shares similar values provides encouragement, validation, and a sense of belonging. Collaborating with others who are passionate about similar causes amplifies our impact and enables us to achieve collective goals.

Embrace growth and adaptability. Perhaps the most important thing we can do on our journey of advancing our values, beliefs, and attitudes is to embrace change, growth, and adaptability. As we gain new insights and experiences, we may find our perspectives evolving. Being open to learning and subsequent change allows us to adapt our values and beliefs based on new information and understanding, and empowers us to make more informed decisions and respond thoughtfully to evolving circumstances.

Observe your values in action. Bringing mindful awareness to the impact of our actions for assessing whether we are effectively advancing our values, beliefs, and attitudes. Observing whether we are living in accordance with our values and making the desired differences helps us stay focused and able to reassess our strategies if necessary. This ongoing process of observation, self-reflection, learning, and practice ensures that we remain aligned with our core principles and maintain a meaningful impact on our lives and the world around us.

QUESTIONS FOR SELF-REFLECTION

- *What brings me a sense of fulfillment and purpose in life?*
  Reflecting on the activities, experiences, and moments that bring you the most satisfaction can provide valuable insights into your core values. Identify the pursuits that leave you feeling fulfilled and aligned with your true self, as they often point to the principles that resonate most deeply with your heart and soul.

- *When have I felt most passionate and energized about a cause or belief?*
  Recall instances in your life when you felt strongly about a particular cause or belief. Consider the moments that ignited a fire within you, prompting you to take action or speak up. Such passionate feelings are often rooted in your core values, guiding you toward areas where you can make a meaningful impact.

- *What principles do I hold dear and strive to uphold in my actions?*
  Examine the guiding principles that consistently shape your decisions and behaviors. These steadfast principles are reflections of your values, which form the moral compass by which you navigate life. Identifying these enduring beliefs can help you recognize the values that define who you are and what you stand for.

RESOURCES FOR EXPLORATION AND LEARNING

TOP 3: ARTICLES
The following articles provide insights to support the self-discovery process and opportunities to consider the process of defining our values and strengths for greater authenticity and confidence in who we are and the impact on our actions.

Clothier, P. and R. Steinholz. (n.d.). **Ethical business practice.** Barrett Values Centre.
▶ tinyurl.com/yn8w9ef3

Gander, F., L. Wagner, L. Amann, and W. Ruch. **What are character strengths good for? A daily diary study on character strengths enactment.** *Journal of Positive Psychology 17 (5), pp. 718–28.*
▶ tinyurl.com/3raf69r8

Smernoff, E., I. Mitnik, K. Kolodner, and S. Lev-Ari. (2015). **The effects of "The Work" meditation (Byron Katie) on psychological symptoms and quality of life—A pilot clinical study.** Explore (NY) 11 (1), pp. 24–31.
▶ tinyurl.com/msyscaxv

TOP 3: BOOKS

Barrett, R. (2018). **Everything I Have Learned about Values. Morrisville,** NC: Lulu Publishing
Understanding how our values are shaped can seem daunting. Explore this book for greater understanding, nuance, and elements that shape the values that guide our actions.

Katie, B., and S. Mitchell. (2021). **Loving What Is: Four Questions that Can Change Your Life.** New York: Harmony Books.
This book provides a framework and process for discovery as to what actually causes our suffering to support greater clarity, appreciation, and action.

Niemiec, R. M., and R. E. McGrath. (2019). **The Power of Character Strengths: Appreciate and Ignite Your Positive Personality.** Cincinnati: VIA Institute on Character.
▶ tinyurl.com/2z9v36mn
This book builds on positive psychology to create a new appreciation of what makes us who we are and how, through this discovery, we can leverage strengths to support growth, meet challenges in new ways, and continue with confidence and learning in reaching our potential.

TOP 3: ASSESSMENTS AND TESTS

The following assessments provide insight into who we are as well as a more nuanced understanding of and language for supporting our foundation in the interconnection of values, strengths, and behaviors.

Judge-Your-Neighbor Worksheet.
The Work of Byron Katie.
▶ tinyurl.com/ffzemshm

Personal Values Assessment.
Barrett Values Centre.
▶ tinyurl.com/hfyvn2ed

VIA Character Strengths Survey.
Values in Action Institute on Character.
▶ tinyurl.com/52azb2f9

TOP 3: VIDEOS

Doing the Work to Be Free. Byron Katie.
▶ tinyurl.com/5n8w9yxx
Watch the Wisdom 2.0 video from Katie Byron on the power of doing work to be free.

The Importance of Values. Richard Barrett.
▶ tinyurl.com/43372m9z
Richard Barrett, Founder and Chair of Barrett Values Centre, speaks on the importance of values personally, organizationally and societally.

The Science of Character. VIA Institute.
▶ tinyurl.com/92hhn98r
Character strengths are described as the capacities humans have for thinking, feeling, and behaving. Specifically, they are the psychological ingredients for displaying virtues or human goodness. Watch the video to learn more.

TOP 3: FREE ONLINE COURSES

Introduction to Values-Based Leadership. University of Cape Town.
▶ tinyurl.com/mrxuxw3z
Unpack the need for values-based leadership and learn what this means both within and external to the business context.

Oriental Beliefs: Between Reason and Traditions.
Université Catholique de Louvain.
▶ tinyurl.com/yktcz6y5
Explore the spiritual and magical beliefs of cultures, from ancient Egypt to modern Japan, as we discuss gods, the universe, cosmos, dreams and so much more!

Soul Beliefs: Causes and Consequences—Unit 1: Historical Foundations.
Rutgers University.
▶ tinyurl.com/2b7zecvn
This course explores several facets of this relatively unexplored but profoundly important aspect of human thought and behavior.

ENDNOTES

1 M. S. Boone, J. A. Gregg, and L. W. Coyne. (2022, July 22). We are what we do. Psychology Today. tinyurl.com/395cawz5

2 G. O. Gabbard. (2014). Psychodynamic Psychiatry in Clinical Practice. (5th ed.). Washington, DC: American Psychiatric Publishing.

3 National Union of Track Statisticians. (2022, June 6). The sub-4 alphabetic register (1,755 athletes as of June 6, 2022). tinyurl.com/25bckp46

4 P. J. Luyten, E. Fonagy, M. Target, and S. J. Blatt. (Eds.) (2015). Attitude. In *Handbook of psychodynamic approaches to psychopathology* (pp. 57–69). New York: Guilford Press.

5 Bojanowska, A., Kaczmarek, Ł.D. *How Healthy and Unhealthy Values Predict Hedonic and Eudaimonic Well-Being: Dissecting Value-Related Beliefs and Behaviours.* J Happiness Stud 23, 211–231 (2022). tinyurl.com/5n97mzzu

6 VIA Institute on Character. (n.d.). Hope. tinyurl.com/66de8e2h

7 E. Perry. (2022, July 27). What does it mean to have personal values? BetterUp. tinyurl.com/2w8zkbfv

"Authentic happiness derives from raising the bar for yourself, not comparing yourself to others. Imagining the future best self can be a hugely powerful catalyst for change."

—Martin Seligman

05
ENVIRON-
MENT

NATURE ENVIRONMENT
SOCIAL ENVIRONMENT
WORK ENVIRONMENT
CLIMATE ENVIRONMENT

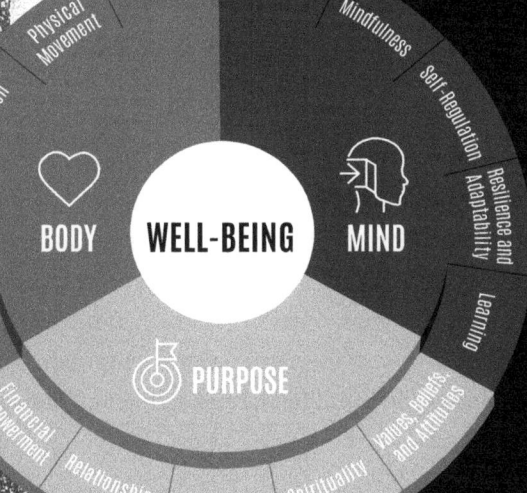

Nature
Environment

Social
Environment

Work
Environment

Climate
Environment

> "Look deep into nature,
> and then you will understand everything better."
>
> —ALBERT EINSTEIN

The fourth and final part of our book considers one's environments. Following the exploration of body, mind, and purpose, we emphasize the power we possess as individuals to influence and shape four environments for our betterment, underlining the idea that though we are products of our environments, we also have the agency to mold them in ways that support and enhance our journey toward becoming the best version of ourselves.

Nature Environment

This chapter explores how exposure to nature—from forests to oceans—positively affects our physical health, mental clarity, and emotional well-being through stress reduction and mood enhancement. We also discuss actionable steps for individuals and organizations to incorporate the natural environment into their well-being. By highlighting the importance of nature in our lives, this chapter encourages a deeper connection with the natural world, emphasizing its crucial role in achieving a balanced and fulfilling life and aiding our journey to become the best version of ourselves.

Social Environment

We explore the concept of social environment and its critical role in shaping our lives. This chapter defines social environment as the combination of relationships, culture, values, institutions, and physical spaces that influence an individual's experiences, social interactions, and opportunities.

We examine key characteristics, including the nature of our interactions and the influence of our community and culture, and how these factors collectively impact our well-being. The chapter also discusses strategies for cultivating a positive social environment. By understanding and actively shaping our social surroundings, we aim to create a more supportive and enriching atmosphere, which is essential for personal growth.

Work Environment

The work environment is defined here as a combination of physical space, social dynamics, and psychological conditions in the workplace. This chapter differentiates between positive and negative work environments, emphasizing their impact on job satisfaction, productivity, and overall well-being. Special focus is given to the expectations and needs of Generation Z, highlighting the importance of a supportive and fulfilling work environment for this group now entering the workforce. We also outline the key elements of a great workplace, including supportive leadership, positive culture, and opportunities for growth. Additionally, the chapter provides strategies to optimize your work environment, aiming to enhance both personal and professional well-being.

Climate Environment

This chapter outlines the main causes of climate change and discusses its direct impact on human well-being, including physical and psychological effects. We also present the importance of engaging in purposeful climate-related actions such as adopting sustainable practices and advocating for environmental protection policies. These actions not only help mitigate the global climate crisis but also enhance personal well-being by fostering a sense of responsibility. This chapter aims to empower readers to take actionable steps toward a more sustainable lifestyle, emphasizing the role individual actions play in both global environmental health and personal fulfillment.

Written by Patricia Garcia

INTRODUCTION

It is well known that human development is influenced by the environment. The term "nature environment" refers to the natural world or the natural surroundings in which living organisms, including humans, exist. It encompasses all elements of the physical environment that are not created or significantly altered by human beings.

In today's professional world and across numerous countries, most individuals spend their time indoors and online. However, recent studies suggest that nature can help our brains and bodies stay healthy, and that engaging with the nature environment can have positive impacts on individuals and their overall quality of life.

> ## "Trees are always a relief, after people."
> —DAVID MITCHELL

Personal Story

Once upon a time in a bustling city, there lived a woman named Julia. She was a hard-working professional, spending most of her days in a high-rise office building, surrounded by concrete and glass. Although she excelled in her career, Julia felt a growing sense of restlessness and fatigue, and the endless skyscrapers and honking cars made her uneasy. Her days were consumed by the fast-paced rhythm of urban life, leaving her feeling drained and disconnected.

One sunny weekend, Julia decided to embark on a spontaneous adventure. She packed a small backpack, put on her hiking boots, and set off for some fresh air in a nearby national park. As she entered the park's lush greenery, the noise of the city gradually faded away, replaced by the harmonious sounds of birds chirping and leaves rustling in the gentle breeze. As Julia observed the natural beauty around her, she felt an immediate sense of calm.

Julia took her time exploring the park's trails, marveling at the towering trees and vibrant wildflowers. She sat by a sparkling stream, feeling its cool waters trickle through her fingers. In that moment, she experienced an overwhelming sense of tranquility she hadn't felt in years. The worries and stresses of her urban life seemed to melt away, replaced by a profound connection to the natural world. The tranquility of the setting enveloped her, allowing her mind to quiet and her worries to fade into the background.

When Julia finally returned home that evening, she carried with her a renewed sense of well-being. Her visit to the park had rekindled her appreciation for the simplicity and beauty of nature that existed beyond the confines of urban life.

From that day forward, Julia made a conscious effort to incorporate nature into her daily routine. She planted flowers on her windowsill, took leisurely walks in local parks, and even organized outings with friends to explore the wonders of the great outdoors.

Julia's journey exemplifies the vital role that the natural environment plays in nurturing our well-being.

HOW DOES THE NATURE ENVIRONMENT SUPPORT YOUR WELL-BEING?

Biopsychology, also known as biological psychology or psychobiology, is the study of the interaction between biology and behavior, including how our biological processes influence our psychological experiences.

The nature environment can have a significant impact on well-being in key ways, including[1]:

1. **Stress reduction and relaxation.**
Spending time in nature has been shown to reduce stress levels. Biopsychological research suggests that exposure to natural environments can lower blood pressure, reduce heart rate, and decrease the production of stress hormones such as cortisol.

2. **Attention restoration.**
In our modern world, we are constantly bombarded with stimuli and information, which can lead to mental fatigue and decreased attention span. Nature environments provide a restorative effect on attention.

3. **Mood enhancement and emotional well-being.**
The presence of natural elements such as greenery, sunlight, and fresh air has a positive impact on brain activity and neurotransmitter levels, promoting feelings of calmness, happiness, and relaxation.

4. **Physical health benefits.**
Interacting with nature by walking or exercising outdoors has physical health benefits. Biopsychology indicates that outdoor activities in natural environments can improve cardiovascular health, boost the immune system, increase vitamin D levels, and enhance overall physical fitness.

5. **Biophilia and connection with nature.**
The concept of biophilia suggests that humans have an innate affinity and connection with nature. Being in nature or even viewing natural scenes can evoke positive emotions, reduce stress, and improve overall cognitive functioning.

6. **Restoration and recovery.**
Biopsychological studies show that exposure to nature promotes restoration and recovery from mental fatigue and stress. The attention required in natural environments is different from that of urban environments, allowing the brain to relax and replenish cognitive resources.

Figure 5.1: Cultivate your tree

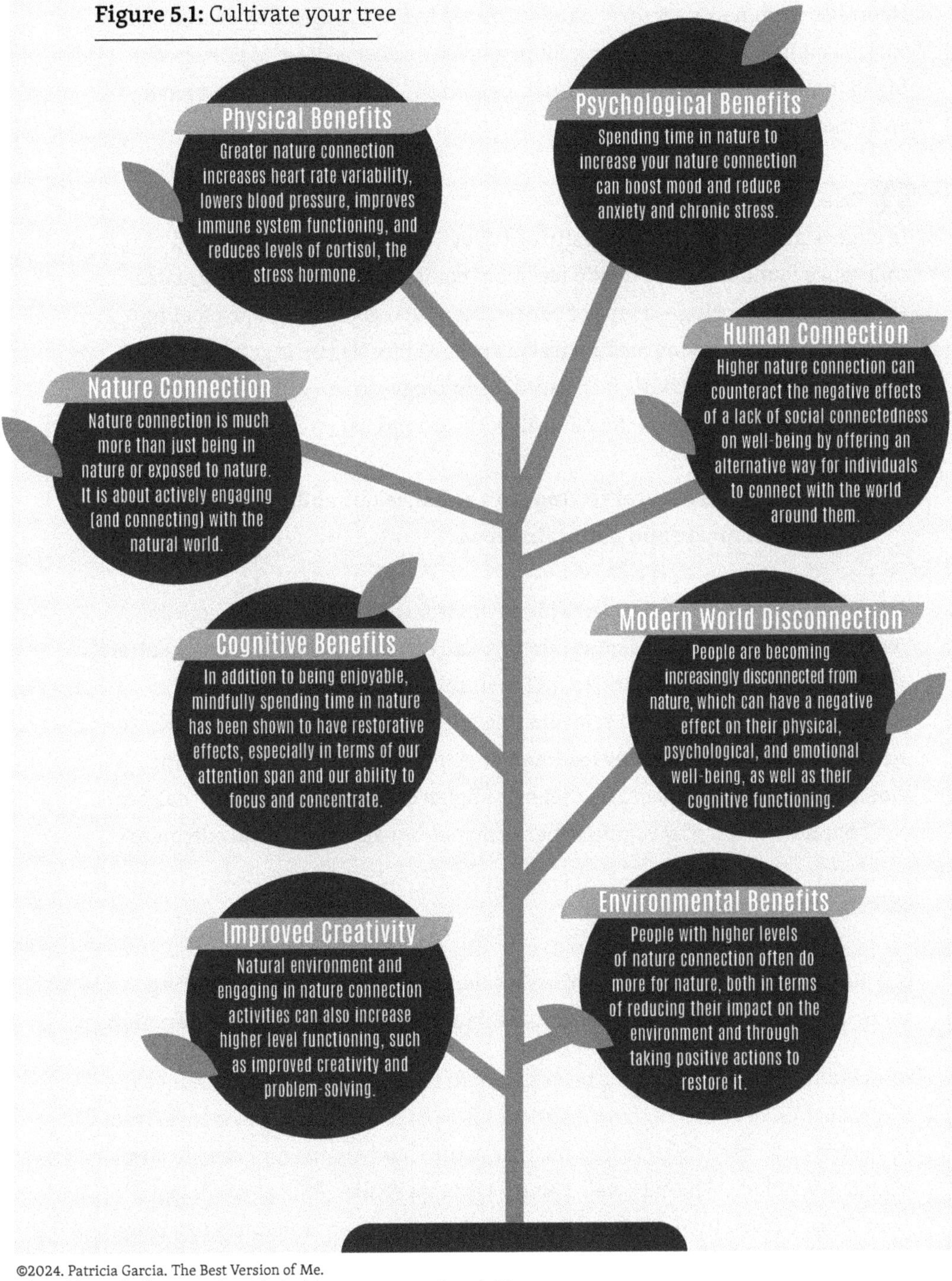

Physical Benefits
Greater nature connection increases heart rate variability, lowers blood pressure, improves immune system functioning, and reduces levels of cortisol, the stress hormone.

Psychological Benefits
Spending time in nature to increase your nature connection can boost mood and reduce anxiety and chronic stress.

Human Connection
Higher nature connection can counteract the negative effects of a lack of social connectedness on well-being by offering an alternative way for individuals to connect with the world around them.

Nature Connection
Nature connection is much more than just being in nature or exposed to nature. It is about actively engaging (and connecting) with the natural world.

Cognitive Benefits
In addition to being enjoyable, mindfully spending time in nature has been shown to have restorative effects, especially in terms of our attention span and our ability to focus and concentrate.

Modern World Disconnection
People are becoming increasingly disconnected from nature, which can have a negative effect on their physical, psychological, and emotional well-being, as well as their cognitive functioning.

Improved Creativity
Natural environment and engaging in nature connection activities can also increase higher level functioning, such as improved creativity and problem-solving.

Environmental Benefits
People with higher levels of nature connection often do more for nature, both in terms of reducing their impact on the environment and through taking positive actions to restore it.

7. Therapeutic benefits.

Nature environments are increasingly utilized in therapeutic interventions for various mental health conditions. Biopsychology informs these approaches, highlighting the positive effects of nature on brain function, stress reduction, and emotional well-being.

8. Environmental connection.

In a meta-analysis at the University of Darby (UK), Alison Pritchard and colleagues found that people who feel more connected to nature have greater eudaimonic well-being—a type of contentment that goes beyond just feeling good and includes having meaningful purpose in life. Nature is good for us. We know that. But in today's fast-paced, technology-driven world, it's easy to become disconnected from the natural world around us.

> **"Exposure to natural settings can enhance our ability to concentrate and maintain focus."**

Attention Restoration Theory (ART) is an environmental psychology concept suggesting that exposure to natural settings can enhance our ability to concentrate and maintain focus. According to ART, natural environments play a role in recuperating from stress and rejuvenating specific components of the executive attentional system, ultimately leading to heightened cognitive functioning. Pioneered by Rachel Kaplan and Stephen Kaplan during the 1980s, ART has been corroborated not only by cognitive performance but also by medical outcomes.

Effects of Exposure to Nature

A. Reduction of stress and cortisol levels, increase in mood-regulating neurotransmitters such as serotonin, and improvement in cognitive function.

- Spending time in nature has been shown to lower stress levels and reduce the production of the stress hormone cortisol. "There is mounting evidence, from dozens and dozens of researchers, that nature has benefits for both physical and psychological human well-being," says Lisa Nisbet, PhD, a psychologist at Trent University in Ontario, Canada, who studies connectedness to nature.

"You can boost your mood just by walking in nature, even in urban nature. And the sense of connection you have with the natural world seems to contribute to happiness even when you're not physically immersed in nature."[2]

- Exposure to nature has been linked to increased serotonin levels in the brain, which can contribute to improved mood and well-being. Cognitive psychologist Ruth Ann Atchley "notes that modern-day humans are beset by a host of mental distractions and threats," adding that "nature is a place where our mind can rest, relax and let down those threat responses. Therefore, we have resources left over—to be creative, to be imaginative, to problem solve— that allow us to be better, happier people who engage in a more productive way with others."[3]

- Natural environments provide "soft fascinations"[4] that can be reflected upon in "effortless attention," such as clouds moving across the sky or water bubbling over rocks in a stream. Conversely, mind wandering allows the mind to wander freely and relax the stringent focus of everyday life. Changes in mood have also been linked with inattention, with sadness found to be a significant precursor of mind wandering. Studies have evaluated the role of soft fascination and mental bandwidth in ART and mind wandering and have found that they can facilitate creative incubation and enhance attentional focus and brain network activation.[5]

- Research has shown that immersion in natural settings can improve creative reasoning and problem-solving skills. Exposure to natural settings seems to replenish some lower-level modules of the executive attentional system, which can lead to improved cognitive function. One study found that "four days of immersion in nature, and the corresponding disconnection from multi-media and technology, increase[d] performance on a creativ[e], problem-solving task by a full 50% in a group of naive hikers."[6] Other studies have found that viewing natural environments stimulates curiosity and fosters flexibility and imagination, leading to improved creativity.

B. Increase in social connections and sense of community.

Nature presents opportunities for social interactions and community engagement, which hold significant importance for enhancing psychological well-being. The captivating beauty and awe-inspiring elements of nature have the capacity to evoke positive emotions, ignite creative impulses, and instill a profound sense of purpose and significance within individuals.

In an extensive research analysis, Dr. Gregory Bratman and colleagues unveiled compelling evidence linking contact with nature to heightened levels of happiness, subjective well-being, positive emotional states, constructive social interactions, and a deepened sense of meaning and purpose in life. This connection to nature was also shown to correspond with reduced levels of mental distress.[7]

> **"Individuals who dedicated a minimum of two leisure hours to nature-related activities during the preceding week reported significantly greater levels of health and overall well-being."**

Given the manifold advantages associated with nature exposure, it is only natural for individuals to ponder: how much outdoor time is sufficient? An attempt to address this query was undertaken by Matthew White and his team, who investigated nearly 20,000 adults across the United Kingdom. Their findings indicated that individuals who dedicated a minimum of two leisure hours to nature-related activities during the preceding week reported significantly greater levels of health and overall well-being. This trend remained consistent across various demographic subsets, including older adults and individuals grappling with chronic health conditions. Remarkably, the positive effects were equally pronounced whether these individuals allocated their nature engagement to a single, continuous 120-minute session or distributed it over multiple intervals throughout the week.[8]

The Downside of Not Being Exposed to Nature

If you are not exposed to nature regularly, you may experience negative changes to your well-being, including increased stress and mental fatigue, reduced cognitive functioning, decreased physical health, impaired psychological well-being, weakened connection with the environment, reduced social interaction and community connection, and increased disconnection from natural rhythms.[9]

It is important to note that the specific downsides of not being exposed to nature can vary from person to person, and the extent of these impacts depends on various factors such as individual preferences, lifestyle, and access to natural environments. However, incorporating regular contact with nature, even in small ways, can help mitigate these potential downsides and promote overall well-being.

Nature and Mental Health

A growing body of research points to the benefits that exposure to the natural world has on improving health, reducing stress, and promoting healing. As a result, policymakers, employers, and health care providers are increasingly considering the human need for nature in how they plan and operate. For example, the United Nations has recognized the importance of mental health and well-being as a fundamental human right, and provided relevant recommendations[10]:

- **Sustainable Development Goals (SDGs).** The UN's 2030 Agenda for Sustainable Development includes a commitment to promoting well-being and ensuring healthy lives for all. SDG 3 focuses on good health and well-being, highlighting the importance of mental health as an integral part of overall well-being.

- **The Convention on the Rights of Persons with Disabilities** emphasizes the rights and dignity of persons with disabilities, including those with mental health conditions. It encourages governments to take measures to ensure the full inclusion and participation of individuals with disabilities, which can involve providing access to nature and outdoor spaces for their mental well-being.

- **World Health Organization (WHO) Mental Health Guidelines.**
  The WHO provides guidelines and resources on mental health promotion, treatment, and recovery. Though the WHO does not specifically address nature and mental health, it does highlight the importance of creating supportive environments and promoting positive mental well-being through various means, including engaging in physical activity and connecting with the natural environment.

- **Promotion of Green Spaces and Urban Planning.** The UN encourages the creation and preservation of green spaces in urban areas. Urban planning that incorporates access to nature, parks, and green infrastructure has been shown to positively impact mental health and well-being, providing opportunities for stress reduction, physical activity, and social interaction.

As we have seen, studies indicate that spending time in nature can reduce stress levels, alleviate symptoms of depression and anxiety, and improve overall mental well-being. By engaging with nature regularly through activities such as walking, gardening, or simply spending time outdoors, people can improve their mental and emotional health.

Even people who are incarcerated have the right to access the outdoors as an important aspect of their overall well-being and human rights. Though the specifics of outdoor access may vary across jurisdictions, there is a recognition that prisoners should have reasonable opportunities to spend time outside.

BOOSTING YOUR WELL-BEING THROUGH YOUR NATURE ENVIRONMENT

At a **personal level**, there are several actions you can take to positively impact your well-being:

1. **Spend time in nature.** Spending time outside by walking in a park, hiking in the mountains, or simply sitting in a garden can improve your overall well-being.

2. **Practice mindfulness in nature.** Use your time in nature to practice mindfulness and be fully present in the moment. Engage your senses; observe the sights, sounds, and smells of the environment; and cultivate a sense of gratitude and appreciation for the natural world around you.

3. **Engage in outdoor activities.** Participate in outdoor activities that promote physical movement and well-being. This can include activities such as jogging, cycling, gardening, or practicing yoga in natural surroundings.

4. **Disconnect from technology.** Take breaks from technology and screens by immersing yourself in nature. Reduce your dependence on electronic devices and embrace the tranquility and simplicity of the natural environment.

5. **Support environmental conservation.** Contribute to the preservation and protection of the natural environment by supporting local conservation initiatives. This can involve volunteering for environmental organizations, participating in community clean-up efforts, or supporting sustainable practices in your daily life.

At an **organizational level**, organizations can play a crucial role in promoting the well-being of individuals through the natural environment, through actions such as:

1. **Providing green spaces.** Creating or enhancing green spaces within an organization's premises, including gardens, rooftop spaces, or other outdoor seating areas, offers employees opportunities to connect with nature during work breaks and improve overall well-being.

2. **Encouraging outdoor breaks.** Encouraging employees to take regular breaks and spend time outdoors during the workday can improve well-being. This can include advocating for walking meetings, providing designated outdoor areas for breaks, or organizing team-building activities in natural settings.

3. **Implementing wellness programs.** Developing wellness programs that incorporate nature-based activities such as outdoor retreats or yoga or meditation classes in natural surroundings will help employees benefit from being in the natural environment. Some organizations may even wish to provide incentives for employees to engage in outdoor activities.

4. **Fostering environmental awareness.** Promoting environmental consciousness and sustainability within the organization will encourage employees to adopt eco-friendly practices such as recycling, reducing waste, and using energy-efficient measures.

5. **Supporting environmental initiatives.** Engaging in corporate social responsibility activities related to environmental conservation, such as partnering with environmental organizations, participating in tree-planting drives, or sponsoring conservation projects, will demonstrate to employees the organization's commitment to both the natural environment and employee well-being.

By acting at both personal and organizational levels, individuals and organizations can contribute to enhanced well-being through the natural environment. These actions not only benefit individuals' health and happiness but also contribute to the overall sustainability and preservation of the natural world.

TIPS

Here are some tips you can follow to include nature in your routines and work environment:

- Decorate with natural elements

- Take a daily walk

- Bring nature indoors

- Listen to natural sounds

- Take photos of nature

- Watch videos of nature

- Keep windows and curtains open

- Choose walking, biking, and driving routes with more natural surroundings

- Take deep breaths

CONCLUSION: CALL TO ACTION

Individuals should make a conscious effort to incorporate nature into their daily lives, whether through regular outdoor activities, nature walks, or simply spending time in green spaces. Organizations can prioritize nature-based initiatives such as incorporating nature into leadership programs and creating restorative environments for employees. Society can benefit from recognizing the importance of nature and implementing policies that protect and preserve natural spaces.

QUESTIONS FOR SELF-REFLECTION

1. **How often do I spend time in nature?**
2. **Do I choose walking, biking, and driving routes with more natural surroundings?**
3. **How do I feel when I am in nature?**

RESOURCES FOR EXPLORATION AND LEARNING

TOP 3: ARTICLES

 Fredericks, A. D. (2022, November 28). **How exposure to nature influences creativity.** Psychology Today.
▶ tinyurl.com/yck4hszy

 Suttie, J. (2016, March 2). **How nature can make you kinder, happier, and more creative.** *Greater Good Magazine.*
▶ tinyurl.com/4tdd9hzp

 Williams, K. J. H., K. E. Lee, T. Hartig, L. D. Sargent, N. S. G. Williams, and K. A. Johnson. (2018). **Conceptualizing creativity benefits of nature experience: Attention restoration and mind wandering as complementary processes.** *Journal of Environmental Psychology* 59, pp. 36–45.
▶ tinyurl.com/ynswbz6u

TOP 3: BOOKS

Li, Q. (2018). **Forest Bathing: How Trees Can Help You Find Health and Happiness.**
New York: Viking.
A guide to the Japanese practice of forest bathing, exploring its beliefs, culture, and traditions, as well as various studies on its health benefits. It also presents easy-to-follow steps for practicing forest bathing in any environment.

Williams, F. (2017). **The Nature Fix: Why Nature Makes Us Happier, Healthier, and More Creative.** New York: W. W. Norton.
Explores the scientific evidence behind the positive impact of nature on our well-being, providing insights into how spending time in nature can enhance our happiness, health, and creativity.

Wilson, E. O. (1986). **Biophilia.** Cambridge, MA: Harvard University Press.
Explores the idea that humans have an innate affinity for the natural world, and how this tendency might be a biologically based need integral to our development as individuals and as a species.

 TOP 3: ASSESSMENTS AND TESTS

 Connectedness to Nature Scale (CNS).
▶ tinyurl.com/yptjtmcz
The CNS measures to what degree people feel part of nature (see F. S. Mayer and C. McPherson Frantz. (2004). The connectedness to nature scale: A measure of individuals' feeling in community with nature. *Journal of Environmental Psychology* 24 (2), pp. 503–15. The study shows that this is a personality trait that is predictive of responsible environmental behavior and subjective well-being.

 The Nature Relatedness Scale (NR-6).
▶ tinyurl.com/2zyv2d5h
The NR-6 is a widely used self-report measure that assesses an individual's sense of connection and relatedness to nature.

 The Perceived Restorativeness Scale (PRS).
▶ tinyurl.com/w6957a54
The PRS is designed to assess the perceived restorative qualities of natural environments.

TOP 3: VIDEOS

 Forest Bathing. Qing Li.
▶ tinyurl.com/4cut5v8a
This interview with Dr. Qing Li offers valuable advice on how to benefit from the natural healing power of trees.

 The Surprising Science of Happiness. Dan Gilbert.
▶ tinyurl.com/4m7c9xxt
This TED talk with Dan Gilbert explores the factors that contribute to our happiness, including our relationship with nature and the natural world.

 Why Our Brains Need Nature. Richard Louv.
▶ tinyurl.com/3kzcrp54
This TEDx talk with Richard Louv explores the importance of nature to our mental and physical health and well-being.

 TOP 3: PODCASTS

 The Mindful Kind. Rachael Kable.
▶ tinyurl.com/mr3aedvv
Rachael Kable shares exciting insights into mindfulness journeys and provides listeners with simple and effective practices to incorporate mindfulness into their daily lives, focusing on stress management, self-love, and improving mental health and well-being.

 On Being. Krista Tippett.
▶ tinyurl.com/yc232p4s
Krista Tippett aims to provide listeners with insights into the human experience and to encourage reflection and contemplation on life's big questions.

 The Wild. Chris Morgan.
▶ tinyurl.com/4w33878b
Chris Morgan explores how nature survives and thrives alongside humans, taking listeners on a journey of discovery and appreciation across the Pacific Northwest.

REFERENCES

GoodTherapy.org. (2018, August 15). Ecotherapy/nature therapy. tinyurl.com/bdehj5wa

Herchet, M, S. Varadarajan, I. Kolassa, and M. Hofmann. (2022). How nature benefits mental health. *Zeitschrift für Klinische Psychologie und Psychotherapie 51* (3–4), pp. 223–33. tinyurl.com/47mkyvdm

Holland, I., N. V. DeVille, M. H. E. M. Browning, R. M. Buehler, J. E. Hart, J. A. Hipp, R. Mitchell, D. A. Rakow, J. E. Schiff, M. P. White, J. Yin, and P. James. (2021). Measuring nature contact: A narrative review. *International Journal of Environmental Research and Public Health 18* (8), 4092. tinyurl.com/yc2j32ft

Mental Health Foundation. (n.d.). Nature: How connecting with nature benefits our mental health. tinyurl.com/2her5s95

Mind. (n.d.). Nature and mental health. tinyurl.com/57bxsr79

NeuroscienceNews.com. (2022, April 20). Measuring nature's effects on physical and mental health. tinyurl.com/59ak6xea

Nisbet, E. K. and J. M. Zelenski. (2013). The NR-6: A new brief measure of nature relatedness. *Frontiers in Psychology 4.* tinyurl.com/yc4adbsb

Owens, M., and H. L. I. Bunce. (2022). The potential for outdoor nature-based interventions in the treatment and prevention of depression. *Frontiers in Psychology 13.* tinyurl.com/5n8c2rr2

Peterson, T. J. (2021, May 7). Ecotherapy (nature therapy): How it works, activities, and what to expect. ChoosingTherapy.com. tinyurl.com/53rdh28u

Sahlin, E., J. V. Matuszczyk, G. Ahlborg, and P. Grahn. (2012). How do participants in nature-based therapy experience and evaluate their rehabilitation? *Journal of Therapeutic Horticulture 22* (1), pp. 8–23. tinyurl.com/mr3sjdsv

ENDNOTES

1 A. Pritchard, M. Richardson, D. Sheffield, and K. McEwan. (2019). The relationship between nature connectedness and eudaimonic well-being: A meta-analysis. *Journal of Happiness Studies 21*, pp. 1145–67. tinyurl.com/26jju3vv

2 Trent University. (n.d.). Psychological and other benefits from nature. tinyurl.com/5dcwdwmj

3 A. D. Fredericks. (2022, November 28). How exposure to nature influences creativity. Psychology Today. tinyurl.com/mrnxc8vt

4 A. Basu, J. Duvall, and R. Kaplan. (2019). Attention restoration theory: Exploring the role of soft fascination and mental bandwidth. *Environment and Behavior 51* (9–10), pp. 1055–81. tinyurl.com/yftdccnc

5 J. H. Williams, K. E. Lee, T. Hartig, L. D. Sargent, N. S. G. Williams, and K. A. Johnson. (2018). Conceptualising creativity benefits of nature experience: Attention restoration and mind wandering as complementary processes. *Journal of Environmental Psychology 59*, pp. 36–45. tinyurl.com/397fjrud

6 R. A. Atchley, D. L. Strayer, and P. Atchley. (2012). Creativity in the wild: Improving creative reasoning through immersion in natural settings. *PLoS ONE 7* (12): e51474. tinyurl.com/3cy8yp8c

7 G. N. Bratman, C. B. Anderson, M. G. Berman, B. Cochran, S. de Vries, J. Flanders, C. Folke, H. Frumkin, J. J. Gross, T. Hartig, P. H. Kahn Jr, M. Kuo, J. J. Lawler, P. S. Levin, T. Lindahl, A. Meyer-Lindberg, R. Mitchell, Z. Ouyang, J. Roe, L. Scarlett, J. R. Smith, M. van der Bosch, B. W. Wheeler, M. P. White, H. Zheng, and G. C. Daily. (2019). Nature and mental health: An ecosystem service perspective. *Science Advances 5* (7). tinyurl.com/yeywzkan

8 M. P. White, I. Alcock, J. Grellier, B. W. Wheeler, T. Hartig, S. L. Warber, A. Bone, M. H. Depledge, and L. E. Fleming. (2019). Spending at least 120 minutes a week in nature is associated with good health and wellbeing. *Scientific Reports 9*, 7730. tinyurl.com/4ads9nj9

9 M. P. Jimenez, N. V. DeVille, E. G. Elliott, J. E. Schiff, G. E. Wilt, J. E. Hart, and P. James. (2021). Associations between nature exposure and health: A review of the evidence. *International Journal of Environmental Research and Public Health 18* (9):4790. tinyurl.com/6t2m7v57

10 World Health Organization. (2022, June 17). Mental health. tinyurl.com/2b7rcvp2

SOCIAL ENVIRONMENT

Written by Dr. Katie Coates

> "We humans are social beings. We come into the world as the result of others' actions. We survive here in dependence on others. Whether we like it or not, there is hardly a moment in our lives when we do not benefit from others' activities. For this reason, it is hardly surprising that most of our happiness arises in the context of our relationships with others."
>
> —THE DALAI LAMA XIV

Personal Story

Linda was in her forties and had just dropped her youngest child off at college. Linda had been a homemaker for the past twenty years, and her priority was taking care of her children and her home. Her mother had stayed home to raise her family, and Linda felt strongly that she should do the same. Now, she found herself in a very uncomfortable situation. She became overwhelmingly sad and depressed. She was anxious and angry, and her relationship with her husband was suffering. She had a few close friends but didn't see them regularly. She didn't work or engage in community, spiritual, or religious activities. She felt alone. Her life had become unidimensional, and now that her children had moved on, she didn't know how to deal with it or the world around her. She sought expert help from a therapist and realized she had been so focused on caring for her family that she had neglected caring for herself and her relationships. She reflected on her social environment and her goals for the future. She and her husband rekindled their relationship and started doing more together. She spent more time with her friends. She had a secret passion for becoming a writer and joined a community writing club. She even created a family Slack channel so that she, her husband, and her children could use technology to communicate and stay connected. Linda evaluated and expanded her social environment and is now living her best life. She doesn't regret one minute of the time she invested in supporting her family. She is also grateful for now understanding the importance of taking care of her social life and relationships and the impact that has on her overall happiness and well-being.

INTRODUCTION

Humans are fundamentally wired to socially connect. Your environment and mental and physical health are intrinsically linked. The places you spend your time—home, work, school, community—and the people you spend your time with significantly impact your well-being, identity, and quality of life. The people and experiences in our lives shape us. As in Linda's case, her identity was solely connected to being a mother, and when things changed, that caused mental stress and anxiety. She needed to assess her social situation and make some adjustments in her life to be happy again.

Our social environment is a complex web of relationships, cultures, values, institutions, and physical spaces that influence an individual's experiences, social interactions, and opportunities. The following section explores the key characteristics and factors of our social environment.

Key Characteristics of Our Social Environment

Our social environment is influenced by a diverse range of factors that shape how we interact with others and our society at large, including:

1. Relationships. Connections and interactions with family, work colleagues, friendships, romantic partnerships, social groups, and communities are critical elements of an individual's social environment. The family is often the most influential part of social health. Family dynamics and values shape a person's development, social behavior, and worldview. Peers and friendships can affect attitudes and social behaviors and also heavily influence a person's social environment.

2. **Culture.** Culture plays a significant role in shaping social norms, values, and beliefs. It includes the traditions, rituals, language, religion, and shared knowledge that are handed down from one generation to the next. Cultural norms significantly impact how individuals communicate and interact within their communities.

3. **Social institutions.** Schools, workplaces, government organizations, political affiliations, religious institutions, and community influence the social environment. Their systems, beliefs, and regulations provide frameworks for social interaction and community involvement and shape social practices.

4. **Socioeconomics.** Education level, occupation, economic status, and access to resources play an essential role in shaping an individual's social life. These factors affect where people live, the education they receive, and the opportunities available to them.

5. **Technology and media.** Access to modern technology and social platforms has ushered in new ways of communicating and engaging with others. Smartphones, tablets, the Internet, social media, and movies provide connections and information that can help or hinder the social environment.

Figure 5.2: Factors that influence your social environment

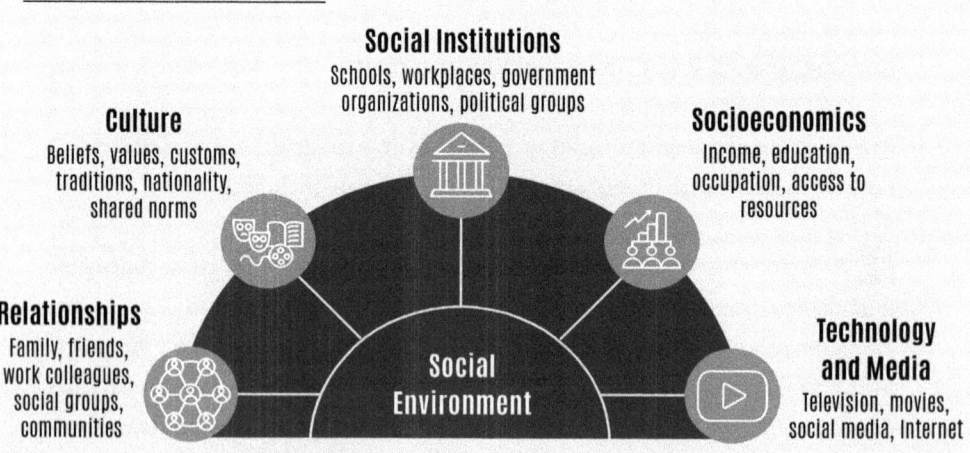

©2024. Katie Coates, PhD. The Best Version of Me.

Relationships, culture, social institutions, socioeconomic status, and technology and media all shape our social environment. Let's now take a closer look at how your social environment supports your overall well-being.

HOW DOES YOUR SOCIAL ENVIRONMENT SUPPORT YOUR WELL-BEING?

A positive social environment tells our bodies we are safe, reducing physical arousal and increasing mental and physical well-being. For example, individuals who experience social isolation have more than twice the risk of dying from heart disease as compared to those who have strong social connections. Solid social relationships improve immune function, reduce stress levels, and support less cardiovascular strain.[1]

Here's how your social environment supports your well-being.

Creates a sense of belonging. A sense of belonging can support self-esteem and contribute to a more positive outlook on life. Strong relationships, especially with family, foster feelings of love, stability, and security. Healthy, positive family relationships are enduring and consequential across the lifespan. The family also shapes identity and feelings of belonging through shared experiences and cultural heritage, values, and beliefs. Additionally, feeling connected to a social group or community can provide a sense of belonging, identity, and purpose.

> **"People who have robust support systems tend to have healthier coping mechanisms, experience lower levels of anxiety and depression, and have higher overall life satisfaction."**

Provides support with life changes and stress. A solid social support network, including family, friends, and colleagues, can provide emotional encouragement, practical advice, and motivation. People who have robust support systems tend to have healthier coping mechanisms, experience lower levels of anxiety and depression, and have higher overall life satisfaction than those who do not.[2]

The quality of your social interactions influences how you deal with challenges and stress. Having fun with friends and family can provide a needed distraction. Engaging with others can help you see an issue from a different perspective. These types of positive social interactions with others create solid emotional support for dealing with life's challenges. Organizations have recognized the importance of well-being and social support in the workplace. As a result, many organizations have implemented well-being programs that encourage social connection.

Conversely, feeling isolated and lonely can have detrimental effects on well-being. A lack of relationships and social support can increase stress, anxiety, and depression. If you don't have people to help you manage the stress of everyday life, your body steps into fight or flight mode, which produces higher levels of stress hormones that can increase levels of inflammation and lead to the deterioration of many body systems.[3]

Developing social support, friendships, and secure relationships is essential for establishing coping mechanisms and building resilience. Spending time with family and friends and forging strong, positive relationships with others reduces depression, anxiety, and other mental illnesses.

Enhances learning and growth. Relationships are at the core of your social life and are crucial to your growth and development. Other people can challenge us, push us to think differently, support us, and hold us accountable for making changes in our lives. Positive relationships promote adaptability and resilience. The assurances received in relationships provide the motivation to push forward, grow, and succeed. Engaging with others helps train your brain to develop circuits for managing reactions, responses, and emotions.[4] In work relationships, coaching and mentoring help individuals improve skills and plan their future careers. These attributes can enhance job satisfaction and retention, help individuals feel a sense of purpose, and identify workplace growth opportunities.

Additionally, the behaviors and attitudes of those around you can influence your choices and lifestyle habits. If your social environment includes individuals who engage in healthy behaviors, you may be more likely to adopt similar practices.

These individuals may also serve as accountability partners to help motivate you to stay on track.

Supports social connection through technology and media. Smartphones and social media now play a significant role in shaping our lives. We are increasingly communicating via devices, and an incredible amount of our lives flows through technology. Social media can help people stay connected, share experiences, and sustain relationships with friends. There are also multiple communities online for sharing information and resources, learning new things, buying and selling items, and so on. Social media also helps us be aware of issues and provides a forum to voice and share opinions, which are all positive aspects of social media.

However, social media also comes with significant challenges. A study by Cigna reported that excessive social media usage is one of the most critical risk factors for loneliness.[5] We cannot assume that online spaces are the same as physical spaces. People crave human touch, and digital connection does not provide the sensory and emotional experiences we need. There is also a tendency for people to compare themselves to others online. Unrealistic comparisons can lead to negative self-perceptions and feelings of inadequacy, leading to a decline in well-being. Social media also provides a space for online bullying and hate and an overload of information and misinformation, which can also impact an individual's mental health and well-being.

Technology and social media are here to stay and will continue to advance. Though there are benefits to our social environment as a result of social media, it is essential to be aware that these media can also significantly inhibit our ability to meaningfully interact with each other and negatively impact our well-being.

Increases lifespan. There is some evidence to suggest that healthy relationships can actually increase your lifespan. Spending time with family, friends, and communities has been linked to a healthier, happier, and longer life. In some cases, those with unhealthy physical habits but a strong social environment lived longer than those without strong relationships.[6]

BOOSTING YOUR WELL-BEING THROUGH YOUR SOCIAL ENVIRONMENT

Having a healthy social environment helps you feel a sense of belonging, provides support when you need it, encourages you to grow and develop, and increases positive connections with others—it may even help you live longer! Having close, trusted, and intimate relationships positively impacts mental and physical health. There are many strategies that can help you create a positive social environment and therefore boost your well-being.

Spend time with family and friends. Connecting with others to have informal conversations, share mutual interests, or see the world from another perspective is a powerful tool for managing stress.. Laughing and venting with good friends results in a rush of endorphins that uplift your immune system. For the sake of your well-being, you need close friends—at least one you see in person regularly.[7]

Consider the diversity of relationships. Having multiple healthy social connections in your broader life context can support your overall well-being. Beginning in childhood, we are encouraged to participate in a variety of activities, including school, sports, family, friends, religious and community events, and so on. Engaging in various social activities and connecting with people from different backgrounds and interests enriches your social environment and creates a multidimensional life.[8] Having a multifaceted life means our identities are not overly tied to one activity, such as work or parenting, which can lead to burnout. One longitudinal study of 9,000 randomly selected Swedes corroborated the positive impact of multiple social roles on well-being. The study found that participants with an increased number of social roles had decreased risk of insomnia and lingering illnesses.[9]

> "People in good social health can form meaningful connections with others to both provide and receive social support."

Develop skills. The impact of stressors on an individual's well-being depends on their social health and coping skills. Social health is one of the dimensions of modern health and represents an individual's ability to build healthy, nurturing, genuine, and supportive relationships. People in good social health can form meaningful connections with others to both provide and receive social support.[10]

Building social health requires the development of skills and coping strategies to manage healthy relationships and navigate stress, setbacks, and adversity. The essential skills to develop include problem-solving, communication, and conflict resolution.

Understand yourself and others. Human development theory can play a role in helping individuals foster a healthy social environment by providing valuable insights into understanding oneself and others. These theories focus on how humans grow and mature over time. Key themes include how you develop self-awareness, communication skills, socialization, and friendships throughout your life. Robert Kegan's constructive developmental theory focuses on the distinct ways of perceiving and making sense of the world throughout different stages of development. Kegan considers the socialized mind and the development of a self-authoring mind. At the socialized mind stage of development, individuals tend to define their identity and sense of self primarily through the social roles, values, beliefs, expectations, and norms of their communities. Self-authoring is a higher stage of cognitive development that follows the socialized mind. At this stage, individuals become more self-reflective and capable of examining their beliefs and values independently of external influences. They begin to take responsibility for their own identity and life choices and make decisions based on their internal compass rather than conforming to societal expectations. Those who reach the self-authored stage establish better boundaries and have better-developed skills to manage healthy social relationships.[11] Exploring these theories can help you gain insights into your and others' perspectives, foster empathy and mutual understanding in social interactions, and develop the mindsets and skills you need to improve your social health.

Manage microstress. Microstresses are small moments of stress or tiny aggravations in your life that typically go unnoticed or are dismissed but can add up to cause significant anxiety. As part of their study on microstress, Rob Cross and Karen Dillon interviewed hundreds of people that claimed to be hanging on by a thread. Their concern and feelings of being overwhelmed were rarely due to a macrostressor. Instead, it was the accumulation of tiny microstressors that they didn't even think about, most of which were caused by people closest to them. Strategies for reducing microstress include being aware that you are experiencing microstress, identifying where the microstress is coming from, and learning how to address it by strategically saying no, managing technology and social collaborative overload, and setting relationship boundaries.[12]

Take a technology and social media break. Periodically assess your social media and technology usage and behavior. It may be time for a digital detox if it is consuming too much of your time or not bringing you positive energy and joy. Putting the device down or choosing to spend more in-person time with others can help you recharge and regain clarity on the things that truly matter.

Seek expert help. Experience varies significantly by individual, and not all social environments are positive and supportive. Negative relationships or toxic social dynamics can harm well-being and may require assistance from expert mental health professionals. Never hesitate to seek help if you need it.

Your social environment has a significant impact on your overall health and well-being. Finding the right balance of social interactions that work for you is important. It is also critical to nurture and manage positive relationships, seek support when needed, and set boundaries in toxic relationships and media influences to maintain a healthier, more fulfilling—and potentially longer—life.

QUESTIONS FOR SELF-REFLECTION

Just as you take care of your body with exercise and your mind with meditation, taking care of your social environment is vital. "Social fitness" should also be part of your life routine.[13] The following questions can help you assess your social environment and identify areas where you need to make adjustments.

- What is my current social environment? What are the sources of support in my life? For safety and security, learning and growth, confiding and venting, fun and relaxation, intimacy?

- What are my values, interests, and personal goals, and how does my social environment support me?

- What is the quality of my relationships?
  - Which ones give me energy?
  - Do any cause tension or anxiety?
  - Am I spending quality time with the people I care most about?
  - Which of my relationships enhance the best version of me?
  - Do I need to set different boundaries with any of my relationships?

- What are the educational, community, and political influences in my life and relationships?

- What role do digital communications and social media play in my life and relationships?

RESOURCES FOR EXPLORATION AND LEARNING

TOP 3: ARTICLES

Cross, R., and K. Dillon. (2023, February 7). **The hidden toll of microstress.** *Harvard Business Review.*
▶ tinyurl.com/5n7ectu6
Microstresses are small moments of stress that seem manageable on their own. Fresh research will teach you how to recognize and manage microstress's most common forms.

Ramirez-Duran, D. (2021, May 2). **What is social well-being? 12+ activities for social wellness.**
▶ tinyurl.com/mszsxkpv
This article will discuss social wellbeing at the levels of positive relationships (e.g., friends, family, romantic partner) and larger systems (e.g., school, workplace, culture).

Waldinger, R. (2023, February 16). **Author talks: The world's longest study of adult development finds the key to happy living.** McKinsey & Company.
▶ tinyurl.com/23be8wsm
Harvard study director Robert Waldinger provides the data-backed answer to what makes people live happier and longer lives and shares the choices anyone can make to start feeling more fulfilled right now.

TOP 3: BOOKS

Brassey, J., A. De Smet, and M. Kruyt. (2022). **Deliberate Calm: How to Learn and Lead in a Volatile World.** New York: Harper Collins.
This book provides tools and techniques that can help you build skills to respond in conflict situations and manage stress in a healthier, more productive manner.

Goleman, D. (2007). **Social Intelligence: The New Science of Human Relationships. New York: Bantam.**
This book delves into principles of neuroscience and emotional intelligence that can help foster positive social connections.

Parker, P. (2018). **The Art of Gathering: How We Meet and Why It Matters.**
New York: Riverhead.
This book explores how we spend our time together and approaches to gathering that will help create meaningful social experiences.

TOP 3: ASSESSMENTS

 Conflict Styles Assessment. United States Institute of Peace.
▶ tinyurl.com/44ft2wes
This 30-question assessment gives you insights into your approach to dealing with conflict.

 Microstress Diagnostic. Harvard Business Review.
▶ tinyurl.com/5n7ectu6
In the middle of the article, you can download a diagnostic to help you identify your sources of microstress.

 Social Awareness Assessment. Social Awareness Month.
▶ tinyurl.com/p3wf6tc3
This questionnaire helps you explore your social well-being.

 TOP 3: VIDEOS

 The Art of Happiness. The Dalai Lama and Howard C. Cutler.
▶ tinyurl.com/yc439zyu
Through conversations, stories, and meditations, the Dalai Lama shows us how to defeat day-to-day anxiety, insecurity, anger, and discouragement.

 The Power and Science of Social Connection. TEDx. Emma Seppälä.
▶ tinyurl.com/6fntucjm
Emma Seppälä's areas of expertise are health psychology, well-being, and resilience. The TEDx Talk will feature her research on "The Power and Science of Social Connnection."

 Social Well-Being—Importance of Social Connections—Social Life— Social Interactions. Whats Up Dude.
▶ tinyurl.com/28mmd6pe
This video discusses the importance of social well being, social connections, social relationships and social interactions with other people. It also address social relationships and health, and how social media is bad, and good for people.

TOP 3: PODCASTS

The Link between Social Media and Mental Health. Lisa Coyne.
▶ tinyurl.com/47cbve49
Jenn talks to Dr. Lisa Coyne about the impact of social media on our mental health. Lisa explains how to set ground rules for digital consumption for you and your loved ones and answers questions about loosening the grasp social media has on so many of us.

The School of Greatness Podcast Series. Lewis Howes.
▶ tinyurl.com/545rcpz7
This podcast series features many experts on a wide range of topics including entrepreneurship, health, mindset, and relationships.

Verywell Mind Podcast Series.
▶ tinyurl.com/4t6jxphw
This podcast series shares guidance and tips for improving psychological well-being and cultivating mental strength. The School of Greatness podcast has grown rapidly to be one of the top-ranked Business and Self-Development podcasts, and has over 150 million downloads. Episodes range from interviews with incredible world-class game changers in entrepreneurship, health, mindset, and relationships.

TOP 3: FREE ONLINE COURSES

Coursera: Conflict Management Specialization. University of California, Irvine.
▶ tinyurl.com/yckpdky9
In this course, you'll learn to strengthen your personal and professional relationships by constructively addressing conflicts between individuals and within organizations.

EdX: Digital Well-Being and Productivity. Jesus College, University of Cambridge.
▶ tinyurl.com/ytwsbek8
This course draws on insights from business, psychology, philosophy, and the tech industry to help you develop digital habits and routines that work for your lifestyle. It will also help teachers and leaders to think about how to build good habits in others in their organizations and teams.

TED-Ed: How Friendship Affects Your Brain. Shannon Odell.
▶ tinyurl.com/3kr2yh9b
If it seems like friendships formed in adolescence are particularly special, that's because they are. Childhood, adolescent, and adult friendships all manifest differently in part because the brain works in different ways at those stages of life. During adolescence, there are changes in the way you value, understand, and connect to friends. Shannon Odell explores the neuroscience of friendship.

ENDNOTES

1   M. Heid. (2015, March 18). You asked: How many friends do I need? *Time.* tinyurl.com/4dfwatj4

2   J. Pfeffer. (2018, September 11). The overlooked essentials of employee well-being. *McKinsey Quarterly.* tinyurl.com/2p9sjm5f

3   G. M. Slavich. (2020). Social safety theory: A biologically based evolutionary perspective on life stress, health, and behavior. *Annual Review of Clinical Psychology* 16, pp. 265–95. tinyurl.com/fbcjhe7a

4   R. Cross and K. Dillon. (2023). *The Microstress Effect: How Little Things Pile Up and Create Big Problems—And What To Do about It.* Boston: Harvard Business Review Press.

5   D. Walsh. (2022, September 14). Study: Social media linked to decline in mental health. MIT Sloan: Ideas made to matter. tinyurl.com/ehc3a54v

6   R. Waldinger and M. Schulz. (2023). *The Good Life: Lessons from the World's Longest Scientific Study of Happiness.* New York: Simon & Schuster.

7   Heid 2015.

8   Cross and Dillon 2023.

9   M. Nordenmark. (2004). Multiple social roles and well-being: A longitudinal test of the role stress theory and the role expansion theory. *Acta Sociologica* 47 (2), pp. 115–26. tinyurl.com/59b9bhmc

10 E. Coe., M. Dewhurst, L. Hartenstein, A. Hextall, and T. Latkovic. (2022). Adding years to life and life to years: At least six years of higher quality for everyone is within reach. McKinsey Health Institute. tinyurl.com/24fkvujz

11 R. Kegan. (1994). *In Over Our Heads: The Mental Demands of Modern Life.* Cambridge, MA: Harvard University Press.

12 Cross and Dillon 2023.

13 Waldinger and Schulz 2023.

WORK ENVIRONMENT

Written by Bahia El Oddi

"Free yoga lessons and sushi are nice. However, culture is much more than that;
it's the environment that helps people do their best work."

—GUSTAVO RAZZETTI

INTRODUCTION

In today's world, a substantial portion of our lives is dedicated to work:
we spend on average 30% of our weekly life at work.[1] From the integration of
personal and professional lives to the relationships with colleagues and
managers, the organization of work, the physical and virtual environment, and
the purpose of the organization have an impact on how we experience the
work environment. This chapter aims to explore and delve into the multifaceted
nature of the work environment, shedding light on its impact on the overall
well-being of individuals. Let me start with a story ...

Personal Story

Nine minutes into a budget review meeting, you turn your camera and mic off so
you can scold your dog and then tenderly soothe your toddler, who is crying in
the other room. Then—lights, camera, action—you're back on screen, brushing
off the top half of a suit and amplifying a professional smile. Your kids are
watching you pretend that "it is your best day ever and every day from now until
forever," just as they do on social media.[2]

We now continually shift back and forth between identities: code-switching between personal and professional selves; toggling not just between screens but between personalities and worlds, just as everyone else does, too—even in our own household and our dreams, as work invades our minds during meals and at night.

The work environment refers to the physical, social, and psychological conditions in which work takes place. It encompasses the surroundings, atmosphere, culture, and interactions with others, including leaders, within a workplace setting. The work environment can vary significantly depending on the industry, organization, specific roles, and leadership. Dimensions of the work environment may include:

- Nature of work (complex, meaningful, interesting);
- Work location (physical location, virtual, hybrid);
- Work schedule (regular hours, shifts, full time/part time);
- Work relationships (colleagues, leaders, customers, vendors, partners);
- Work experience (positive/negative, engaging, challenging, stressful);
- Work-life balance (no emails after 6:00 p.m., working from home, flexible working hours);
- Leave policy (maternity/paternity leave, sick leave, compensatory leave).

HOW DOES YOUR WORK ENVIRONMENT SUPPORT YOUR WELL-BEING?

Positive and Negative Work Environments

A work environment can be perceived along a spectrum from extremely positive to extremely negative. A positive work environment is characterized by factors such as open communication, mutual respect, collaboration, opportunities for growth and development, fair policies and procedures, supportive relations, and a healthy work-life balance. It promotes employee well-being, job satisfaction,

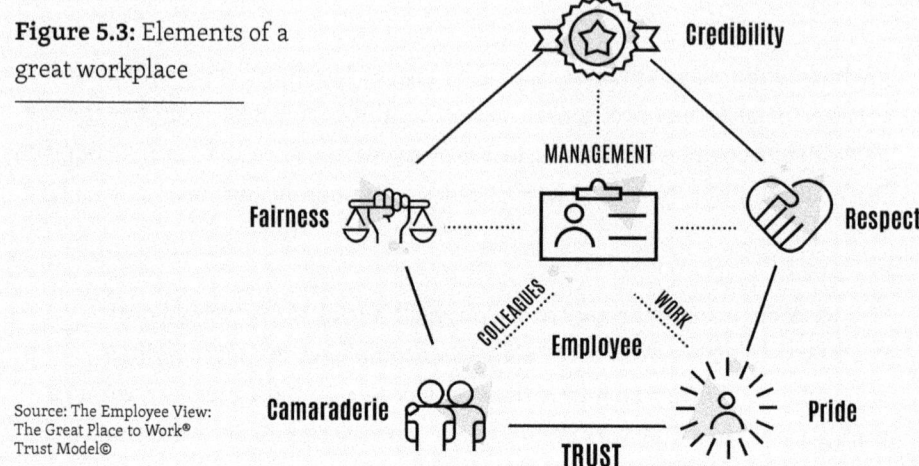

Figure 5.3: Elements of a great workplace

Source: The Employee View: The Great Place to Work® Trust Model©

engagement, and productivity. Conversely, a negative work environment can be marked by factors such as high stress levels, lack of support, poor communication, gossip, conflicts, unrealistic workloads, and limited opportunities for growth, which can negatively impact employee well-being, job satisfaction, and overall performance.

> **"Your boss is more important for your health than
> your medical doctor."** —Mayo Clinic

According to Great Place to Work,[3] a global consulting authority on workplace culture, the definition of what constitutes a "great place to work" is about the level of trust that employees have in their leaders, the level of pride they have in their jobs, and the extent to which they enjoy their colleagues more than a company with lavish perks, fancy parties, and amazing benefits. With over thirty years of conducting annual research among more than twelve million employees from thousands of organizations across ninety countries, Great Place to Work has shown that people experience a great workplace when they consistently:

- Trust the people they work for (based on perceptions of credibility, respect, and fairness);

- Have pride in what they do;

- Experience camaraderie with their colleagues.[4]

What Do People Expect from a Modern Work Environment?

In a modern and caring workplace, employees have certain expectations that contribute to their overall well-being and job satisfaction. First, they place great value on working for organizations that have a clear purpose that aligns with their personal values and goals. Second, they expect a supportive and inclusive environment that values diversity and promotes equal opportunities for all. Employees desire clear communication channels, transparency in decision-making, and opportunities to provide feedback and be heard. They expect healthy work-life balance, with flexible working arrangements and policies that prioritize their physical and mental health. Continuous learning and development opportunities are highly valued, as employees seek opportunities to enhance their skills and careers within the organization. Additionally, a caring work environment fosters a culture of recognition and appreciation. Finally, employees expect fair compensation and benefits that align with industry standards, in equity with other employees in the same roles, as well as a commitment from the organization to prioritize a positive work environment where people can be their best whole selves with a mindset of authenticity.

The Future of the Workplace:
Well-Being as a Nonnegotiable for a Positive Work Environment

Well-being is becoming a top priority for both employees and leaders: 75% of employees and 89% of C-suite leaders say that improving their well-being has become a top priority for them, with 68% and 81%, respectively, mentioning that improving their well-being has become even more important than advancing their career.[5] As a result, expectations for organizational support of workplace well-being are also shifting, with more workers willing to quit their job to focus on their health. For example, research has shown that though 57% of employees are seriously considering quitting for a more supportive job, nearly 70% of executive leaders are thinking about doing so.[6]

The Inconvenient Truth about Work: Well-Being as a Red Flag

COVID-19 has transformed the very nature of the workplace, accelerating trends that were already in play and calling into question many things we took for granted before the pandemic. For many organizations, hybrid work is here to stay: some organizations encourage employees to use the office as a place for collaboration, learning, and innovation rather than individual work. At the same time, companies are becoming more intentional about their cultures, with a particular emphasis on diversity, equity, and inclusion.

But beyond these positive trends, employees are also facing an inconvenient truth about their work environment: workplace well-being has become more challenging than ever. Though work has been a key factor of our health and well-being since the dawn of time, and the lines between work and nonwork in our lives have blurred over the years, the pandemic accelerated this trend by remote and hybrid work becoming the new norm. Virtual tools and digital platforms such as e-mail, Slack, and Zoom have infiltrated our most intimate spaces; constant connectivity is expected in the virtual economy. Our homes are our offices, but also our schools, restaurants, and theaters. And this blending of personal and professional lives doesn't come without consequences: research has highlighted the negative effects of the increased erosion of boundaries between work and nonwork on employees' mental health, including stress, exhaustion, and loneliness, which increased exponentially during the pandemic.[7]

> **"To win in the marketplace,**
> **you must first win in the workplace."**
> —Doug Conant

Good Workplace Well-Being Is Good Business

Issues related to workplace well-being are costly, too. Prioritizing well-being can therefore be a source of sustainable competitive advantage over time. The World Health Organization estimates that twelve billion working days are lost annually worldwide to depression and anxiety, at a cost of $1 trillion per year in lost productivity.[8] Well-being at work is also having an increasing impact in terms of employees' experience, attrition, and engagement.[9]

Figure 5.4: Impact of poor workplace well-being

Employees facing mental health or well-being challenges report more negative experiences at work.
Likelihood of reporting negative work experiences for those with at least one mental health or well-being challenge relative to other employees.

4X	3X	3X	3X
more likely to say they intend to leave	more likely to report low job satisfaction	more likely to experience toxic workplace behavior	more likely to report low engagement at work

Source: J. Brassey, E. Coe, R. Giarola, B. Herbig, B. Jeffery, and R. Merkand. (2022, October 10). Present company included: Prioritizing mental health and well-being for all. McKinsey Health Institute. mckinsey.com/mhi/our-insights/present-company-included-prioritizing-mental-health-and-well-being-for-all

Look Out and Care for the Next Working Generations

Many researchers and experts posit that Gen Z is facing more mental health challenges at work than any previous generation. Jumping into their careers in the past few years—with some only just entering the workforce during the pandemic—has put them in particularly difficult situations. According to Cigna International Health, 91% of 18-to-24-year-olds report being stressed, compared to 84% on average, and almost all (98%) are dealing with symptoms of burnout.[10]

As more members of Gen Z enter the workforce, employers will need to make employee well-being and mental health a priority to effectively support this upcoming generation of workers, which will ultimately have a ripple effect and sustain overall workplace well-being. This situation gives leaders the opportunity to move the needle on workplace well-being, to explore ways to help workers struggling with mental health and well-being challenges, and to consider ways to create healthier environments for employees. As employers broaden their horizons beyond reactive management of poor mental health to proactive mitigation of its drivers, they can both benefit and differentiate themselves by strengthening policies that reinforce a culture of care and purpose.

BOOSTING YOUR WELL-BEING THROUGH YOUR WORK ENVIRONMENT

Professionals and leaders have various strategies at their disposal to enhance their own and their employees' well-being by optimizing their work environment. Figure 4.3 shows the different strategies, which are captured as two sides of the same coin.

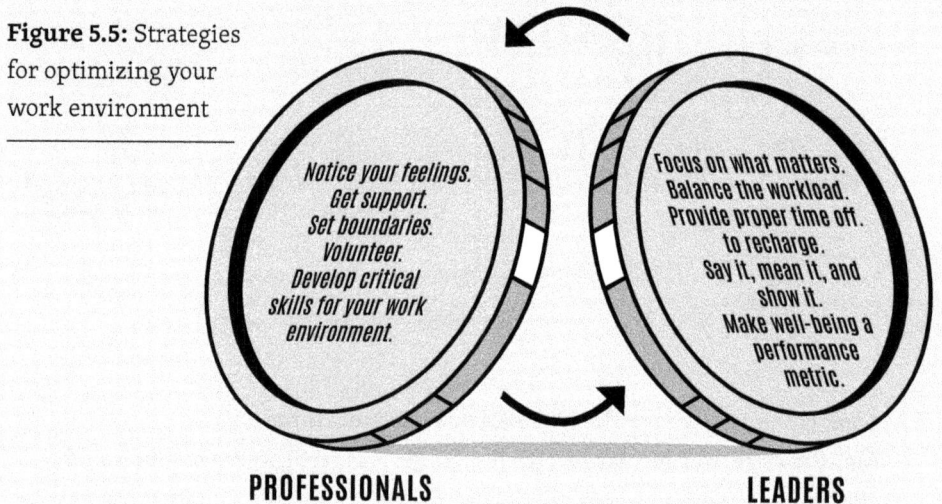

Figure 5.5: Strategies for optimizing your work environment

Notice your feelings.
Get support.
Set boundaries.
Volunteer.
Develop critical skills for your work environment.

Focus on what matters.
Balance the workload.
Provide proper time off.
to recharge.
Say it, mean it, and show it.
Make well-being a performance metric.

PROFESSIONALS   LEADERS

Source: "Burning up and burning out: Human sustainability in a time of emotional climate change," by B. El Oddi and C.-I. Knoop, 2022, *Academicus International Scientific Journal* 25, pp. 56–74. Copyright 2022 by Academicus International Scientific Journal.

Strategies for Professionals

Notice your feelings. Everyone has some awareness of their baseline functioning at work. If you start to notice you're getting exhausted by your job or your productivity drops, it might be an indication that something is not going well. You might notice that you start work each day already drained, or you feel so anxious that you can't focus on what you are supposed to do. Or perhaps you are feeling so ineffective in your job that you find yourself engaged in more negative self-talk: "I'm no good at my job anyway. I'm useless ..."

If distress at work begins to damage your personal relationships (e.g., you are becoming more irritated at home or avoiding social activities you normally wouldn't), then take it as a warning sign that work is affecting your mental health. At this point, think about what might be causing these feelings. Is there one aspect of your job responsibilities that is causing most of your distress? Do you have an underlying personal problem that has not been resolved? Is it some combination of the two?

Get support. Once you realize you need help, seek out a trusted friend, mentor, coworker, peer group, coach, or therapist—someone with whom you can feel seen, heard, and validated, and with whom you can be your fully authentic self without fear of judgment or negative repercussions. It's worth exploring if your company offers some kind of assistance or services related to mental health and well-being. Some organizations have indeed begun to offer counseling, assist with referrals to outside experts, or partner with other organizations that provide support.

Set boundaries. Once you feel supported by someone, you can start to work together on a plan to improve your well-being. Professionals face the constant challenge that their work is never truly finished. Regardless of the hours put in, there are always unanswered emails, pending tasks, presentations to finalize, and readings to catch up on. Set boundaries by incorporating a "personal well-being policy" (e.g., a hard stop after 6:00 p.m. on weekdays, weekends of tech detox). Then think about what you might need besides your daily workday: Is it a short- or long-term need (e.g., having an honest conversation with your manager about work-life balance versus asking for more flexibility in your work schedule)? Is it an incremental or a radical change (e.g., asking for a short-term leave or quitting your job entirely)?

Volunteer. Taking time to slow down, reflect on your well-being, and provide care for others is key. Activities such as volunteering have been proven to have a significant impact on a person's health and well-being, reducing stress levels and improving mood.[11] About 80% of people who volunteer say that volunteering lowers their stress levels.[12] Psychologists even call it a "helper's high"; just like a runner's high after a workout, giving back releases "happy hormones" in the giver's body that leads to a feeling of exhilaration followed by a sense of calm.[13]

Develop critical skills for your work environment. Nurturing lifelong learning can be key in supporting your well-being at work. A number of skills can be helpful in dealing with workplace challenges such as time management, conflict resolution, self-regulation, handling difficult conversations, and so on. Lifelong learning can also provide you the opportunity to reflect upon your professional aspirations or upon which type of work culture would fulfill you the most.[14] The reasons to continue learning are many, and evidence indicates that lifelong learning isn't simply an economic imperative but a social, emotional, and physical one as well. We live in an age of abundant opportunity for learning and development. Capturing it can be one of life's most rewarding pursuits.

Strategies for Leaders. Are you a leader or manager with the capacity to actively change the way that your company affects employees' well-being? These are few extra tips to think about.

Focus on what matters. The major workplace stressors have been known for decades: inadequate staffing, poor workplace culture, lack of support, and poor management.[15] The adage is that people don't leave companies; they leave ineffective and unsupportive managers. Cultivating empathy can be key for avoiding these situations. Research has repeatedly proven that the ability to have and display empathy is fundamental to effective leadership.[16] Asking simple questions such as, "How are you feeling? What are your main sources of stress at work?" is one of the most effective ways to support your employees to be at their best at work.

Provide proper time off to recharge. The allocation of paid vacation days that allow employees to rejuvenate varies considerably from one country to another. For instance, in Europe, the typical range of vacation days spans from twenty to thirty-two, whereas in the US, it is usual for employees to receive just ten days of vacation annually.[17] Additionally, many people opt not to utilize their vacation days due to overwhelming work commitments or concerns about the perception created when taking time off. As a leader, how can you ensure that your employees take proper time to recharge in order to flourish at work?

Balance the workload. If employees are struggling with well-being issues that prevent them from being fully engaged and productive, adjust expectations and redesign workload, even more so for future generations, whose attention span is dramatically decreasing. How can you address work design upstream? What expectations need to be revised downward?

Say it, mean it, and show it. It's important for leaders to share their struggles, but it's more important to share their solutions. If you want well-being in the workplace, you need to pay for it. If you do not, you will pay for it anyway through presenteeism (i.e., "keep going" at work without being productive), absenteeism, and health expenses. How can you signal concretely to your employees that they matter?

Make well-being a performance metric. Organizations gather data on how well employees feel supported by their managers, and how well managers perform on this dimension is increasingly part of review conversations. Managers must strive to be mentors, coaches, and supporters of their employees— yet still drive business performance. Leading organizations in the service industry have instituted "weekly team pulse checks." As leader or manager at your company, how would you go about including metrics related to well-being in your performance reviews?

CONCLUSION

As retirement is delayed across the world, and boundaries between personal and professional lives continue to blur, ensuring that our work environment supports our well-being will be increasingly paramount. Our hope is that the facts, data, and tips made throughout this chapter will be helpful to that end, with one key purpose in mind: be the best version of you.

QUESTIONS FOR SELF-REFLECTION

- **Meaning and boundaries:** What does work mean to and for you? How do you balance your professional, academic, and personal lives? How difficult is it for you to set boundaries between them?

- **Remote work:** How do you manage workload (your own and the team's), especially when working remotely? Have you been blending personal and professional lives or setting clear boundaries between them?

- **Support network:** Which support network do you want for yourself and for others?

- **Emotional "footprint":** How do emotions affect your work, performance, and behaviors toward your team and your colleagues?

- **Measuring well-being:** How do you measure well-being at work? What are key definitions and goals? Which metrics do you use to know if you are supporting your team(s)? What are the trade-offs from the choices you are making?

RESOURCES FOR EXPLORATION AND LEARNING

TOP 3: ARTICLES

Brassey, J., E. Coe, M. Dewhurst, K. Enomoto, R. Giarola, B. Herbig, and B. Jeffery. (2022, May 27). **Addressing employee burnout: Are you solving the right problem?** McKinsey Health Institute.
▶ tinyurl.com/58ypnzz7
Employers today have invested unprecedented resources in employee mental health and well-being. With burnout at all-time highs, leaders wonder if they can make a difference. This research suggests they can.

Harkonen, S. (2023, February 16). **The wisdom of our nervous system.** IE Insights.
▶ tinyurl.com/3mtjr5vs
It's not all in the mind. This article introduces us to how nervous system safety impacts stress, resilience, and individual performance at work.

Young, A. M. (2023, March 23). **What lies underneath the secrets and silence at work?** Psychology Today.
▶ tinyurl.com/y6kbwrcy
This article helps us realize the downside of keeping our "game faces" on when silently suffering at work and gives some advice about how to support yourself and others around you.

TOP 3: BOOKS

Clifton, J., and J. Harter. (2021). **Well-Being at Work.** Washington, DC: Gallup Press.
From Amazon's description: "Coauthored by Gallup's CEO and its Chief Workplace Scientist, Well-being at Work explores the five key elements of well-being—career, social, financial, physical and community—and how organizations can help employees and teams thrive in those elements. Well-being at Work introduces a metric to report a person's best possible life: Gallup Net Thriving, which will become the 'other stock price' for organizations."

Knoop, C.-I., and J. Quelch. (2018). **Compassionate Management of Mental Health in the Modern Workplace.** Cham: Springer.
From Amazon's description: "This proactive guide brings the relationship between work life and mental well-being into sharp focus, surveying common challenges and outlining real-life solutions. The authors' approach posits managers as the chief mental health officers of their teams, offering both a science-based framework for taking stock of their own impact on the workplace and strategies for improvement."

Razzetti, G. (2022). **Remote not Distant: Design a Company Culture that Will Help You Thrive in a Hybrid Workplace.** Chicago: Liberationist.
Wellness can be extra challenging in a virtual workplace. Workers may lack a sense of connection with their team and their leaders. In Remote not Distant, author Gustavo Razzetti discusses how culture drives workplace wellness within a hybrid company.

TOP 3: ASSESSMENTS AND TESTS

Well-Being Measures. Harvard Lee Kum Sheung Center for Health and Happiness.
▶ tinyurl.com/yc4tfmwu
This website provides a repository of validated well-being and resilience scales and indices including objective, subjective, and workplace well-being measures.

Worker Well-Being Questionnaire. National Institute for Occupational Safety and Health (NIOSH).
▶ tinyurl.com/5n7u9z96
This test is "designed to provide an integrated, holistic assessment of a worker's social environment, workplace conditions, and well-being. It is comprised of five domains: (1) work evaluation and experience; (2) workplace policies and culture; (3) workplace physical environment and safety climate; (4) health status; and (5) home, community, and society."

Your 21-day Challenge: Work Stressors. Human Sustainability Inside Out.
▶ tinyurl.com/bp923ufk
This 21-day challenge invites you to be an active observer and influencer of stressors at work—those that you experience, those you might be imposing, and those that you might be able to alleviate.

TOP 3: VIDEOS

Film: *The Good Boss*. (2021). Dir. Fernando León de Aranoa, 120 mins.
Trailer: ▶ tinyurl.com/8unujx4j
The movie is a 2021 Spanish corporate satire, and the plot tracks a charismatic and manipulative factory owner who meddles in the lives of his employees in an attempt to win an award for business excellence.

Series: *Severance*. (2022). Dir. Ben Stiller and Aoife McArdle.
Trailer: ▶ tinyurl.com/4kfy2pm8
Severance is an American science fiction-psychological thriller television series that follows Mark (Adam Scott), an employee of Lumon Industries who agrees to a "severance" program in which his nonwork memories are separated from his work memories.

Webinar: Applying the US Surgeon General's Framework for Workplace Mental Health and Well-Being in Healthcare and Beyond. HERO.
▶ tinyurl.com/yydwb25w
In this webinar, speakers "discuss the state of Workplace Mental Health and Well-Being and share the latest findings from the U.S. Surgeon General's report," focusing on "the five essentials for workplace mental health and well-being with a special emphasis on healthcare settings."

TOP 3: PODCASTS

The Anxious Achiever. *Harvard Business Review.*
▶ tinyurl.com/deuhzsd8
"Rethink mental health and work, with candid stories from leaders who've been there."

Help, I'm in a Toxic Workplace. FT Working It.
▶ tinyurl.com/ycr3vz45
"Organizational change consultants explain how to fix a dysfunctional working environment."

Making Wellbeing Work. Susanna Harkonen and Natalie Wood.
▶ tinyurl.com/2z8euj2f
This podcast helps us get right all types of topics around workplace well-being, including what is (and isn't) well-being in the workplace; the role of the organization, the individual, and the manager; obstacles and best practices; truths and untruths about workplace well-being and mental health; and how to build or fund a sustainable healthy work environment.

TOP 3: FREE ONLINE COURSES

Empathy and Emotional Intelligence at Work. University of California, Berkeley.
▶ tinyurl.com/msvu76wx
From the website: "Learn research-based skills to strengthen empathy and trust, improve collaboration, and create more innovative, productive, and satisfying experiences at work."

Open Minds E-Learning. Mental Health Foundation.
▶ tinyurl.com/ykthrrtn
From the website: "For workplaces and people managers, it's important to be inclusive and supportive of people experiencing mental distress, but it's not always easy to know how to get started. This e-learning course, which includes videos, factsheets and templates, can show you how. It provides people managers with the skills and resources to open up the conversation about mental health challenges and support employees through the tough times."

Personal Growth & Well-being. Coursera.
▶ tinyurl.com/d7zvv9fw
This course examines healthy work environments. You will learn ways to deal with stress and discuss balancing work with life. "By the end of the course, you will be able to describe how you grow and stay well, both at work and in your own time."

ENDNOTES

1   International Labour Organization. (2022). Working time and work-life balance around the world. tinyurl.com/2ra2a3f6

2   *Barbie*. (2023). Dir. Greta Gerwig, 113 mins.

3   Great Place to Work. (n.d.).greatplacetowork.me

4   Great Place to Work. (n.d.). Trust Model. greatplacetowork.me/our-methodology

5   J. Fisher, S. Hatfield, and P. H. Silvergate. (2022, June 22). The C-suite's role in well-being. Deloitte Insights. tinyurl.com/55cjxvtp

6   Fisher, Hatfield, and Silvergate 2022.

7   S. Torkington. (2023, June 23). These 4 charts show workplace well-being is getting worse. This is what companies can do about it. World Economic Forum. tinyurl.com/4efpdmv5

8   World Health Organization. (2022, September 28). Mental health at work. tinyurl.com/nhes47sz

9   T. Mawhinney and K. Betts. (n.d.). Understanding Generation Z in the workplace. Deloitte Perspectives. tinyurl.com/3t6bbyee

10 Cigna. (2022). Exhausted at work—The employer opportunity. Cigna 360 Global Well-Being Survey 2022. tinyurl.com/2h8f5p4z

11 E. Dunn and A. Whillans. (2016, October 21). The psychology of giving: 5 ways giving makes your life better. University of British Columbia. tinyurl.com/yc4sy8tz

12 Project Helping. (n.d.). Volunteering and mental wellness. tinyurl.com/4mb5wpbm

13 S. McDonalds. (n.d.). How gratitude improves your mental health at work. Hi5. tinyurl.com/38pztctd

14 J. Coleman. (2017, February 7). Lifelong learning is good for your health, your wallet, and your social life. *Harvard Business Review*. tinyurl.com/dpacd2eu

15 World Health Organization 2022.

16 T. Brower. (2021, September 19). Empathy is the most important leadership skill according to research. *Forbes*. tinyurl.com/46zj8t7c

17 European Commission. (2016, October 19). Which country in the EU has the most annual holidays? tinyurl.com/4v2ce3vr;
World Economic Forum. (2018, August 22). People in these countries get the most paid vacations days. tinyurl.com/25tarpf7

"There is no question that workplace wellness is worth it. The only question is whether you're going to do it today or tomorrow."

—Warren Buffett

CLIMATE ENVIRONMENT

Written by Dr. Maria Kottari

> "Solving the climate crisis is within our grasp,
> but we need people like you to stand up and act."
>
> —AL GORE

INTRODUCTION

Throughout the latest decade, year after year, heat records have been broken globally. In addition, sea surface temperatures have also hit new highs; the Antarctic ice cover has reached its lowest levels; and many countries have experienced flooding, extreme heat waves, and wildfires that have disrupted everyday life. One after the other, extreme weather events have been headline news worldwide. In July 2023, United Nations Secretary-General António Guterres made a dramatic call to combat climate change, stating that "record-shattering ... temperatures show Earth has passed from a warming phase into an era of global boiling."

Personal Story

I was lucky enough to grow up in Greece by the Ionian Sea and experience the Mediterranean climate. The Mediterranean climate is (or perhaps more accurately, was) an enjoyable climate—if not the most pleasant climate in the world—with dry, sunny summers that are mild to hot, and winters that are mild to cool with moderate to high rainfall. The Mediterranean climate is also characterized by four distinctive seasons. I usually say, jokingly, that Vivaldi's "Four Seasons" made absolute sense when I was a kid. In this baroque music piece, each season has three movements that follow a fast-slow-fast pattern that expertly demonstrates the seasons' cyclical nature. This predictable alteration of the seasons felt like an embrace during my childhood. I anticipated the joys that came with each season—the clothes, fruits, and so on—all linked to unique traditions and terminology dating from antiquity.

But with the increase of climate change, the Mediterranean climate is becoming less and less pleasant as a result of unbearable temperatures, extreme droughts, and wildfires. Moreover, the Mediterranean region has become a climate change hotspot, where all related vulnerabilities are exacerbated. I've lived in the Netherlands since 2016, but I hear about the drastic changes to my home climate from friends and family members, especially the older ones, who find it particularly difficult to cope with high temperatures. Harmony and stability are long gone; Vivaldi's "Four Seasons" doesn't make sense anymore.

Climate is frequently confused with weather. However, climate is the weather of a specific region averaged over several decades, whereas weather refers to short-term atmospheric conditions. Climate change refers to long-term shifts in temperatures and weather patterns, which can occur naturally due to changes in the sun's activity, for example, or large volcanic eruptions. But since the 1800s, climate change—and its rapid acceleration, in particular—is the result of human activity. With the Industrial Revolution, humans began burning fossil fuels such as coal and oil. Over the past two hundred years, the atmospheric concentration of greenhouse gases such as carbon dioxide and methane has trapped the sun's radiation and raised the temperature of the planet. In addition, humans' destruction of forests and use of agriculture have further increased emissions of greenhouse gases. Still, climate change is more complex than just rising temperatures; for example, it also disrupts the balance of ecosystems that maintain life and biodiversity, thereby impacting the health of all living things. Climate change also causes more extreme weather events, including more intense and frequent hurricanes, floods, heat waves, and droughts, and leads to sea level rise and coastal erosion due to warming oceans, melting glaciers, and loss of ice sheets.

One potentially relevant factor that has yet to be widely researched is the role of population dynamics and population growth in the acceleration of climate change.[1] Simply put, the existence of every additional person on the planet will increase greenhouse gas emissions. According to recent official statistics, the global population reached approximately eight billion in 2023 and is expected to reach ten billion in 2050.[2] As a result, the increased population, combined with industrialization and urbanization trends in low-income countries and heavy-consumption lifestyles and production practices in high-income countries, will dramatically increase greenhouse gas emissions and further advance climate change. Decoupling economic growth from rising emissions will be essential for effectively combating climate change. However, both politicians and scholars are reluctant to include population planning in discussions about climate change given that such a discussion may be ethically and socially controversial.

Figure 5.6:
Key drivers of climate change

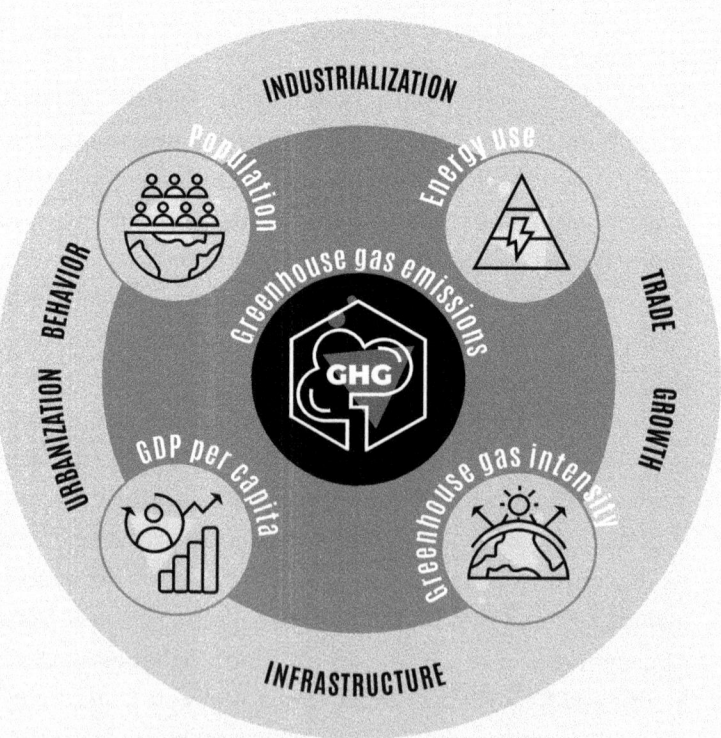

©2024. Dr. Maria Kottari. The Best Version of Me. Based on IPCC Synthesis report, 2021.

The scientific community has a strong consensus about the current and future state of climate change. For example, Figure 5.6, which was included in the Intergovernmental Panel on Climate Change (IPCC) Synthesis Report for the Sixth Assessment Report, shows global warming over multiple generations and went viral across social media worldwide. IPCC visual storyteller Arlene Birt, who designed the image, said she wanted to convey the severity and speed of current climate change to the general public. The image conveys another critical message, too: though past generations have had different experiences with climate change, future generations are set to experience global warming, extreme weather events, and consequences to human health and ecosystems beyond anything we have seen.

The extent to which current and future generations will experience a different world depends on choices made now and in the near term, as depicted in Figure 5.6. Scan the QR code to learn more.
▶ tinyurl.com/4beyck66

HOW DOES CLIMATE CHANGE IMPACT YOUR WELL-BEING?

Overall, the impact of climate change on human well-being is complex and multifaceted, with both direct and indirect effects in the present and the future. The consequences of climate change can manifest in various ways, including physical, psychological, and social impacts with far-reaching and long-lasting effects. The following are some examples of how climate change affects human well-being.

Physical health. Climate change can affect physical health as a result the of increased frequency and severity of extreme weather events such as heat waves, droughts, and floods. According to the World Meteorological Organization, man-made global warming has caused over two million deaths and $4.3 trillion in economic losses over the last fifty years.[3] In particular, the global death toll caused by extreme weather events has reached one million people.

Climate change also exacerbates air pollution, which can lead to respiratory and cardiovascular illnesses. At the same time, extreme temperatures can induce heat stroke, dehydration, malnutrition, disrupted sleep patterns, and other health problems. Moreover, climate change can increase the spread of vector-borne infectious diseases such as malaria and dengue fever and affect the nutritional value of crops.

Certain population groups are more vulnerable to the impact of climate change on physical health. For example, research has shown that rising temperatures and poor air quality can negatively affect children who have asthma or allergies, negatively influence outcomes of pregnancy, and lead to food insecurity. In addition, the trauma and anxiety people experience from both extreme weather events and the predictions for a further deteriorating climate can heighten mental health problems and lead to developmental delays and even changes in people's genetic makeup.[4]

Climate change affects women's well-being disproportionally, especially in the Global South. Scientific evidence has shown that climate change has profound and unequal impacts on women and girls, particularly those who are vulnerable or dependent on natural resources.[5] Changes in aridity and rainfall can affect access to clean drinking water and increase the burden of water collection on women. Pregnant women are particularly affected by climate change, and preterm births, poor maternal health, and stillborn rates are all expected to climb as global temperatures continue to rise.[6]

Last but not least, climate change also takes a heavy toll on older people, and subsequently on their caregivers, thereby overextending health systems' capacity for care and widening existing economic and health disparities.[7]

Livelihood and social and economic well-being. Climate change can cause species and habitat loss, which can have cascading effects on ecosystems. Such changes negatively impact livelihoods via agricultural productivity, water availability, access to natural resources, and damage to infrastructure, property, and businesses. This can, in turn, lead to job loss in the fishing, forestry, and tourism industries. A decrease in biodiversity can also negatively impact cultural and spiritual practices and aesthetic and recreational values. For instance, Indigenous peoples such as the Aborigines and Torres Straits Islanders of Australia, and the Māori of New Zealand, depend on terrestrial, coastal, and marine ecosystems for use as traditional sources of food and materials and for their cultural and spiritual significance—both likely to be adversely affected by climate change.

Climate change is responsible for the displacement of communities due to onset hazards such as floods, storms, wildfires, extreme temperatures, rising sea levels, and desertification. According to the United Nations High Commissioner for Refugees, an annual average of 21.5 million people were forcibly displaced each year between 2008 and 2016 by weather-related events.[8] Such climate migration is expected to surge further in the coming decades, with a forecast of 200 million people requiring humanitarian assistance annually due to the effects of climate change.[9]

Mental health. Despite the nexus between overall well-being and climate change, research thus far has focused predominantly on the physical toll as opposed to the mental burden. Climate change can cause anxiety, depression, and other mental health issues in individuals who experience the impacts firsthand or who are concerned about the planet's future. Climate change can also lead to feelings of helplessness, hopelessness, and despair, especially regarding climate change inaction or denial, defined as the dismissal or unwarranted doubt that contradicts the scientific consensus on climate change by the general population and political leaders alike. In addition, climate change can also lead to social and political unrest, and the effects of which can further impact mental health.

The effects of climate change on mental health are disproportionate among certain groups depending on socioeconomic status, gender, and age. For instance, Indigenous people may be more likely to define their well-being in terms of harmony with the natural environment, which is significantly disrupted by climate change. Young children and adolescents are also uniquely affected compared to older generations. They can experience strong reactions in response to the scale of the climate crisis and the lack of climate action. In addition, climate change affects several environmental, social, and economic determinants, which leads to significant mental health burdens globally.[10] For instance, in regions heavily dependent on agriculture, forced population migration due to unfavorable environmental conditions may aggravate social dynamics, negatively impacting the well-being of the populations concerned. Moreover, migration itself is a significant risk factor for mental health issues.

Climate anxiety. Also known as eco-anxiety, climate anxiety is rooted in uncertainty about the future and distress about the dangers of a changing climate. Climate anxiety is often accompanied by feelings of grief, anger, guilt, and shame, which in turn can affect mood, behavior, and thinking. However, climate anxiety should be not considered an individual problem. According to Dr. Gareth Morgan, a clinical psychologist and co-chair of the UK Association of Clinical Psychologists, "When we regard climate anxiety as an individual problem, it positions not being concerned about the climate crisis as the healthy norm. And this supports the continued societal silence on discussing the emotional impact of climate breakdown."[11]

BOOSTING YOUR WELL-BEING THROUGH CLIMATE-RELATED ACTIONS

Though climate advocacy and activism have become increasingly prominent in recent years, their roots lie in the environmental movements in the US in the 1960s and 1970s, which focused on pollution. Pressure from these movements led Congress to pass legislative measures to promote cleaner air and water and culminated in the organization of the first Earth Day.[12] Today, the most prominent example of climate activism is that of Swedish activist Greta Thunberg, who has raised awareness on climate change issues, advocated for immediate climate action to alleviate consequences for future generations, and inspired the youth-led, global climate movement Fridays for Future.[13]

Climate litigation has become an increasingly powerful instrument to enforce or enhance climate commitments by governments and other responsible bodies. Indeed, communities and groups of individuals worldwide have taken their governments to court over their climate (in)action.[14] For example, a group of Swiss women pensioners brought a ground-breaking climate change case at the European Court of Human Rights, claiming that their country's inaction in the face of rising temperatures has put them at risk of dying during heatwaves and violated their human rights.[15] In September 2023, six young people from Portugal took thirty-two countries to trial at a hearing before the European Court of Human Rights for failing to do their part to avert climate catastrophe. In both cases, the verdict is still due, but they are telling examples of raising public awareness of how climate change violates fundamental human rights.[16]

You can take many actions to address climate change at an individual and community level, and doing so can also have a positive impact on your well-being. Here are some examples:

- **Reduce your carbon footprint.** One of the most significant ways to address climate change is by reducing your carbon footprint, including using energy-efficient appliances; decreasing your consumption of meat and dairy products; choosing sustainable transportation options such as biking, walking, or public transit; and limiting long-haul flights.

- **Connect with nature.** Spending time in nature can positively impact mental health and well-being. Connecting with nature can also increase awareness and understanding of environmental issues, including climate change. For instance, try going for a walk in the park, gardening, planting trees, hiking, or camping.

- **Support renewable energy and energy efficiency.** Renewable energy sources are cleaner and can reduce the air pollution and health risks associated with fossil fuels. Support local and national decision-makers who advocate for renewable energy policies and clean energy investment plans. Within your own household, invest in energy-efficiency measures such as replacing ordinary light bulbs with LED bulbs or replacing old appliances with energy-efficient ones. If you can afford it, install solar panels on your rooftop to produce your own clean electricity.

- **Educate yourself and others about the causes and effects of climate change.** You can find plenty of material online, including articles, videos, and courses at various levels, that easily explain scientific facts. However, be sure to rely on credible sources of information such as well-known media and official public portals. Be vigilant of media that take a radically optimistic or pessimistic point of view regarding climate change action. Raise awareness among your family members, friends, and community and support those who make changes to their lifestyle. Challenge those whose are unconvinced about the truth of climate change, but be diplomatic and find common ground by asking questions and helping others deconstruct their beliefs.

- **Reduce waste.** By reducing the amount of waste you generate, you can likewise reduce greenhouse gas emissions, conserve resources, and save money. For example, try to minimize food waste, learn about composting (e.g., fruit and vegetable scraps, egg shells, coffee grounds, grass clippings, leaves), and utilize reusable products such as grocery bags and bottles for beverages on the go. Avoid single-use food containers and utensils, purchase second-hand items when possible, and recycle or donate as much as you can.

- **Propose climate-friendly projects in your workplace.** Suggest planting trees as part of your team-building days or suggest that the management board invest in carbon off-setting projects that compensate for corporate CO_2 emissions such as CO_2 emissions avoidance or removal as well as development of renewable energy technologies. To the extent possible, support and partner with organizations who advocate for action on climate change and avoid those who do not.

- **Engage in advocacy and activism.** Volunteer with nongovernmental organizations and start-ups, attend rallies and protests, sign petitions, and contact your elected officials to demand change. Doing so can not only improve your sense of purpose and social connection but also help you feel more empowered and hopeful about the future and therefore ease climate anxiety.

"**Some people say that I should study to become a climate scientist so that I can 'solve the climate crisis.' But the climate crisis has already been solved. We already have all the facts and solutions. All we have to do is to wake up and change.**"
—Greta Thunberg, *No One Is Too Small to Make a Difference*

Figure 5.7:
Overview of
climate actions
that impact
your well-being

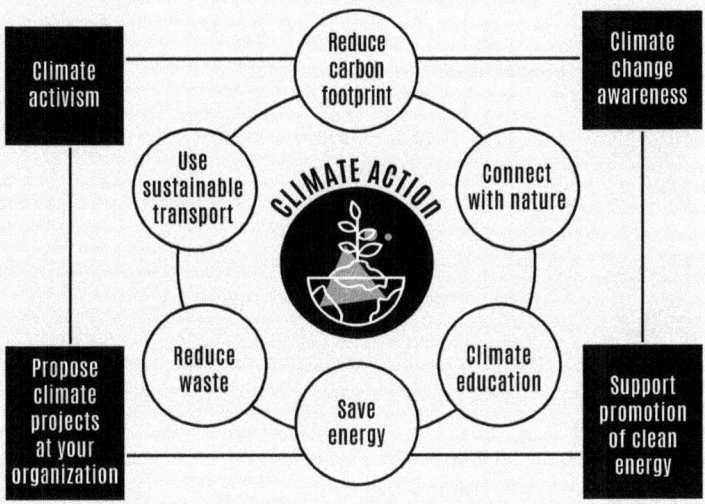

As we have seen, taking action on climate change can positively impact your
well-being, including your physical and mental health, social connection, and
purpose. By changing our daily lives and advocating for change to policies and
systems, we can create a more sustainable and equitable future for ourselves
and for future generations. In addition, effective communication with others
can spark further sustainable behavior and climate-friendly choices. All in all,
compassion is vital: compassion for the climate deniers, whose opinions may be
difficult to change; compassion for yourself; and compassion for everyone who
understands the urgent need for climate change action.

QUESTIONS FOR SELF-REFLECTION

- Do I understand what climate change is and how it affects my life and
  the lives of future generations?

- Do my lifestyle and habits contribute to global warming?
  Am I willing to change them?

- What prevents me from taking climate action?

RESOURCES FOR EXPLORATION AND LEARNING

TOP 3: ARTICLES

Bonnisseau, N. (2022, March 4). **The FAQs of climate change.** Plan A.
▶ tinyurl.com/ajeeekfm
An objective, cold, sometimes unpleasant, never unverified climate action facts.

UNDP Climate Promise. (2023, February 2). **The climate dictionary: An everyday guide to climate change.**
▶ tinyurl.com/45s2j4s7
A great resource of climate change terms and concepts. If you're struggling to keep up with the climate conversation, the Climate Dictionary is for you.

United Nations. (n.d.). **Causes and Effects of Climate Change.**
▶ tinyurl.com/mwhp7dr6
Fossil fuels—coal, oil and gas—are by far the largest contributor to global climate change, accounting for over 75 per cent of global greenhouse gas emissions and nearly 90 per cent of all carbon dioxide emissions. Learn more about causes and effects of climate change.

TOP 3: BOOKS

Hayhoe, K. (2021). **Saving Us: A Climate Scientist's Case for Hope and Healing in a Divided World.** New York: One Signal Publishers.
In *Saving Us*, Hayhoe argues that when it comes to changing hearts and minds, facts are only one part of the equation. We need to find shared values in order to connect our unique identities to collective action.

Johnson, A. E., and K. K. Wilkonson. Eds. (2020). **All We Can Save: Truth, Courage, and Solutions for the Climate Crisis.** New York: One World.
All We Can Save illuminates the expertise and insights of dozens of diverse women leading on climate in the United States, and aims to advance a more representative, nuanced, and solution-oriented public conversation on the climate crisis.

Thunberg, G. (2019). **No One Is Too Small to Make a Difference.** London: Penguin.
This book collects Greta Thunberg's history-making speeches, from addresses at climate rallies around the world audiences at the UN, the World Economic Forum, and the British Parliament.

TOP 3: ASSESSMENTS AND TOOLS

Earth Day Climate Change Quiz.
▶ tinyurl.com/vz5a2trw
This quiz will help you assess your knowledge of the basic facts of climate change.

Earth Hero Application.
▶ tinyurl.com/mwcvxb3k
Earth Hero provides tools and ideas to empower all who want to reduce emissions, improve lives, and care for our shared planet.

United Nations Carbon Footprint Calculator.
▶ tinyurl.com/54d694b7
This calculator will assist you in keeping track of your carbon footprint through your household, transportation, and lifestyle choices.

TOP 3: VIDEOS

How Climate Change Affects Your Mental Health. TED Residency. Britt Way.
▶ tinyurl.com/bdf4r4p7
In this TED talk, Britt Wray explores how climate change is threatening our well-being—mental, social, and spiritual—and offers solutions for what we can do about it.

It's Impossible to Have Healthy People on a Sick Planet. TED Countdown Summit. Shweta Narayan.
▶ tinyurl.com/3x9w2bs4
In this TED talk, climate and health campaigner Shweta Narayan highlights the interdependence between environmental and human health and emphasizes the necessity of placing health at the heart of all climate solutions.

The Link between Climate Change, Health, and Poverty. TEDMED. Cheryl Holder.
▶ tinyurl.com/2rtxkhp5
In this TED talk, physician Cheryl Holder explains the climate change-health and poverty nexus and proposes impactful ways clinicians can protect their patients from climate-related health challenges in accordance with economic and social justice.

TOP 3: PODCASTS

Climate Change and Health. BBC.
▶ tinyurl.com/tduknkhm

In this podcast, Adam Rutherford talks to world-renowned researchers and scientists about a major global study that aimed to quantify how climate change has already damaged the health of millions of people worldwide.

How to Speak to a Climate Denier. The Climate Question.
▶ tinyurl.com/463hjwy3

In this podcast, the presenter Neal Razzel is joined by Sara Ott, a teacher and former climate change skeptic. This is the story of what changed her mind.

Understanding Climate Change. Mike Berners-Lee.
▶ tinyurl.com/2p9vajbd

This podcast hosts Mike Berners-Lee, professor and fellow of the Institute for Social Futures at Lancaster University. Berners-Lee is considered one of the leading experts studying carbon footprint and has written and published extensively on the subject. In this podcast, he discusses the big questions and criticism climate science is facing.

TOP 3: FREE ONLINE COURSES

Causes of Climate Change. University of Bergen.
▶ tinyurl.com/3p4hny9k

Through this introductory-level course, you will learn the physical processes behind climate variation around the world to better understand the causes of climate change.

Climate Change: Solutions. University of Exeter.
▶ tinyurl.com/44kxae3e

Through this intermediate-level course, you can explore the potential solutions for climate change and how they relate to the United Nations Sustainable Development Goals.

The Health Effects of Climate Change. Harvard Business School.
▶ tinyurl.com/bddeaew4

Through this free, self-paced, introductory-level online course, you can learn how global warming impacts human health and the ways we can minimize those impacts.

ENDNOTES

1   Population Connection. (n.d.). The connections between population and climate change info brief. tinyurl.com/3btcx23s

2   United Nations Department of Economic and Social Affairs, Population Division. (2022). World population prospects 2022: Summary of results. UN DESA/POP/2022/TR/No. 3. tinyurl.com/46k3h6rm

3   United Nations. (2023, May 22). Extreme weather caused two million deaths, cost $4 trillion over last 50 years. UN News. tinyurl.com/35d72fey

4   Harvard T. H. Chan School of Public Health. (n.d.). Climate change and children's health. tinyurl.com/yk39hf6d

5   S. Duerto Valero and K. Sheha. (2023, April 21). Why climate change matters for women. UN Women. tinyurl.com/4dbcwhxx

6   The Climate Reality Project. (2022, March 11). How climate change puts mothers at risk. tinyurl.com/3f2xmjhz

7   M. Walling. (2021, April 12). For the elderly, climate change poses more risks to wellness. Forbes. tinyurl.com/59x7p7c6

8   UNHCR. (2016, November 6). Frequently asked questions on climate change and disaster displacement. tinyurl.com/bp5mtrkd

9   USA for UNHCR. (2021, September 21). How climate change impacts refugees and displaced communities. tinyurl.com/3kwstuj7

10 World Health Organization. (2022, June 3). Why mental health is a priority for action on climate change. tinyurl.com/34t3n9f5

11 C. Skopeliti and S. Gecsoyler. (2023, March 30). "Terrified for my future": Climate crisis takes heavy toll on young people's mental health. Guardian. tinyurl.com/yub52cdd

12 "The first Earth Day in 1970 mobilized millions of Americans from all walks of life to birth the modern environmental movement. Since then, Earth Day has evolved into the largest civic event on Earth, activating billions across 192 countries to safeguard our planet and fight for a brighter future." EARTHDAY.ORG. (n.d.). earthday.org

13 Fridays for Future. (n.d.). fridaysforfuture.org

14 Urgenda. (n.d.) Global climate litigation. tinyurl.com/52f7w6r7

15 E. Farge. (2023, March 30). Elderly Swiss women bring European court's first climate case. Reuters. tinyurl.com/ytdzdac6

16 For more information on the case brought by the Portuguese youths, visit the Global Legal Action Network (GLAN) website, which is supporting the claimants: youth4climatejustice.org

06
CLOSING
THOUGHTS

"We delight in the beauty of the butterfly,
but rarely admit the changes it has gone through to achieve that beauty."

—MAYA ANGELOU

CATERPILLARS ARE COOL

We've come a long way in this journey to understanding how to become the best version of ourselves. We explored the importance of nurturing body, mind, and purpose. We dove into physical well-being, mental health, nutrition, sleep, relationships, financial empowerment, and many more aspects of a balanced and meaningful life. You have picked up this book, likely to become a better version of who you are today. This kind of self-leadership shows humility and humbleness. You realize that all human beings can strive to become an even better version of themselves. There are a couple of things to keep in mind while you continue on your journey, however, that I would like to touch on in this closing chapter.

To visualize the transformation we humans go through, this book is sprinkled with illustrative images of darting butterflies. In the journey to become the best version of ourselves, we may well resemble caterpillars morphing into butterflies. The cinematographically appealing metamorphosis from a crawling caterpillar mucking around in the dirt to a glorious, lightweight butterfly is awe-inspiring. The butterfly is a fairy-tale-like phenomenon, and its drastic metamorphosis leaves us humans desiring an end state of similar agility and perfection. But, before you see yourself flapping around with butterfly wings, allow me to take us one step back. Let's take a look at the caterpillar, which has a perfectly exceptional state of being in its own right.

Photo by Mihály Köles on Unsplash

This little buddy in the picture is a Malacosoma neustria or—more commonly—a lackey moth caterpillar. These caterpillars live in Europe and, like any caterpillar, they gorge on anything they can find. Any caterpillar's main goal is to eat as much as possible. In fact, a single caterpillar can increase its body weight 100 times or more between moldings.[1] Exponential growth is the name of their game.[2] To overwinter during the colder months, the lackey moth caterpillar spins intricate silken canopies. With its bright colors and bristles, this caterpillar is quite a sight, and it may even be considered more beautiful than its adult version, which is a plain beige moth. However, its beauty is not the quality that makes this creature especially interesting. Instead, a beautiful fact about all caterpillars is that they have the unique ability to regenerate.

If a caterpillar loses a limb or a portion of its body due to injury or predation, it can regrow the missing parts through a process called regeneration. The process of regeneration in caterpillars is a remarkable example of how biological systems can repair and replace damaged tissue. Caterpillars have specialized cells called imaginal discs, which contain all the genetic information needed to develop into the adult butterfly or moth. When the caterpillar reaches maturity and its brain releases a hormone called ecdysone, the process of metamorphosis will begin. The imaginal discs grow and develop into the various parts of the adult insect— yes, the butterfly—including wings, antennae, and legs.[3] But the ability to regenerate was available all along, tucked away in the caterpillar's plump little body. Just like you! (I'm not calling you plump.) I'm encouraging you to trust the process—you have the unique ability to regenerate already inside you. You just have to tap into it.

REGENERATION IS KEY

The process of regeneration is fascinating and beautiful, as demonstrated by the incredible resilience and adaptability of caterpillars. It is also a powerful reminder that when we humans experience setbacks or challenges, we have the potential to heal, grow, and transform. We all go through various forms of regeneration throughout our lives. Sometimes these changes are subtle, like a caterpillar molting and growing larger. Other times, these changes are more dramatic, like the transformation of a caterpillar into a butterfly. But regardless of the magnitude of the change, regeneration is an essential part of growth and development.

Although natural, regeneration is not always easy. In fact, it can be quite painful and uncomfortable at times. When a caterpillar morphs into a butterfly, it essentially dissolves into a gooey mess inside its cocoon before reassembling itself into a new form. So, if you're feeling stuck right now, you might just need to give yourself some time before you change from a pupae into a butterfly. Sometimes people find solace in understanding the cadence of change, which is beautifully depicted in William Bridges's book *Transitions: Making Sense of Life's Changes*. In the book, the greatest lesson is that such changes and transitions are natural, and we do ourselves a service to lean into these processes by embracing, recognizing, and even celebrating all the curveballs life throws our way.

Just like the caterpillar, we too go through periods of discomfort and struggle in order to grow and transform. It's through these difficult times that we learn the most about ourselves and what we're capable of. And it's these transformations that often lead to the greatest moments of joy and fulfillment in our lives. Humans have an incredible capacity for regeneration and growth, both in response to challenging experiences and as part of our ongoing development as individuals. By cultivating resilience, embracing opportunities for growth, and committing to lifelong learning and development, we can tap into this potential and become the best version of ourselves.

It almost sounds like a heroic effort to become the best version of ourselves. In a society that idolizes heroes, we often overlook the beauty of everyday life. If we are receptive to it, we will be able to see regeneration everywhere in our surroundings. Without too much effort, I can list some amazing examples of regeneration within my own close circle of friends and family. For example, my mom started a new job at sixty-two. Though others may dream of early retirement, my mom actively went out to look for a job that would fulfill her. She doubted whether people would hire her, but she also recognized that she was ready for a change. There is also my dad, who pursued his lifelong dream to run the New York City marathon. Though it had been thirty years since my dad set foot in an aircraft, that did not hold him back; he traveled to New York City by himself to run the marathon (which he completed in an enviable time, by the way). Or my husband, who adjusted to a vegan diet to increase his chances of seeing our children grow older, given that his father passed away at the incredibly young age of fifty-two. Or my sister, who shared the news that she is expecting a baby again after losing her daughter. My godfather, who survived a car crash in which he lost his daughter, and afterward supported his son's rehabilitation for years. My godfather enjoying all that life has to offer, with his son, daughter, and beautiful wife, while also holding space for grief and longing, is the epitome of regeneration. And my greatest teacher in gratitude, my mother-in-law, surprised us all—and probably herself the most.. On the day of her seventieth birthday, my mother-in-law dared to take her first-ever rollercoaster ride, to the delight of her two grandchildren. Although we recognize the power of people rising from the ashes like a phoenix after a significant challenge, there is also so much to recognize and honor on a much smaller scale. These are ordinary lives, lived by extraordinary people, who show incredible resilience, a growth mindset, and grit. Each demonstrates remarkable regeneration and—for me—serves as an endless source of inspiration.

IT STARTS WITH YOU

The reason why some people are interested in reinventing and regenerating themselves whereas others are not is a puzzle in modern psychology. In *YOU! The Positive Force in Change: Leveraging Insights from Neuroscience and Positive Psychology,* authors Eileen Rogers and Nick van Dam explore a range of topics related to positive psychology such as resilience, empathy, mindfulness, and a growth mindset that may impact a person's ability to become the best version of themselves. There is great value in the power of positive thinking and the importance of taking proactive steps to create positive change.

Humans have the ability to bounce back from difficult experiences and to recover from adversity. This resilience is rooted in our innate capacity for adaptation and change, as well as in our ability to draw on social support, positive emotions, and coping strategies to help us navigate challenging situations. Though challenging experiences can be incredibly difficult to go through, they can also be opportunities for personal growth and transformation. Positive psychologists have found that many people who have experienced trauma later report a range of positive changes, including greater appreciation for life, increased resilience, and a greater sense of personal strength and purpose.

So, how do we embrace the process of regeneration in our own lives?

- **Practice gratitude and self-acceptance.** A butterfly doesn't exist without a caterpillar. Self-acceptance is a necessary foundation for personal growth. Being content with who you are in this moment means acknowledging and embracing your strengths, weaknesses, and limitations, while also recognizing your potential for growth and improvement. It means approaching yourself with kindness and compassion, and without judgment, and allowing yourself the space to make mistakes and learn from them.

- **Aim for incremental and sustainable changes.** Overhauling your entire life and implementing all the recommendations in this book at once may be overwhelming. However, incremental changes have a significant impact over time, and research shows that people have an easier time sticking with them because they are more sustainable.

- **Create a vision of what you want to become.** Just like a caterpillar needs a blueprint for its transformation into a butterfly, we humans also need to have a clear vision of what we want to become. This vision can serve as a guidepost to help us navigate the ups and downs of the transformation process.

Metamorphosis isn't a solo journey. The caterpillar has the support of other insects and animals in its ecosystem; we too need the support of others as we navigate our own transformations. Whether it's family, friends, or an online community, having a support system in place can make all the difference.

THE BUTTERFLY EFFECT

The caterpillar's journey to becoming a butterfly is not just a tale of personal metamorphosis; it's also a testament to the profound impacts of seemingly small actions. When you strive to be your best self, the ripples of that effort extend far beyond what you can see.

Though initially applied to weather patterns, MIT professor Edward Lorenz's "butterfly effect" suggests that the flap of a butterfly's wings in one part of the world could set off a chain of events that leads to significant changes elsewhere. Similarly, your individual efforts toward growth, however small, can influence others and create change on a grander scale.

In essence, personal growth isn't just about the individual; it's about your community, society, and the world at large. Every positive change you make contributes to a collective transformation. By prioritizing your own growth, you also play a part in the greater metamorphosis of our world.

As you close this book and reflect on your journey, remember that every step, every challenge, and every triumph not only brings you closer to your best self but also contributes to a more connected and resilient world.

Embrace your journey, trust in the process, and always remember: your wings have the power to create whirlwinds of change.

RESOURCES FOR EXPLORATION AND LEARNING

 TOP 3: BOOKS

Bridges, W. (2019 [1980]). **Transitions: Making Sense of Life's Changes.**
Boston: Da Capo Lifelong Books.
From the Hachette Book Group's description of the book: "First published in 1980, Transitions was the first book to explore the underlying and universal pattern of transition. Named one of the fifty most important self-help books of all time, Transitions remains an essential guide for coping with the inevitable changes in life. Transitions takes readers step-by-step through the three perilous stages of any transition, explaining how each stage can be understood and embraced. The book offers an elegant, simple, yet profoundly insightful roadmap to navigate change and move into a hopeful future."

Brown, B. (2015). **Daring Greatly: How the Courage to Be Vulnerable Transforms the Way We Live, Love, Parent, and Lead.** New York: Avery.
From Amazon's description of the book: "Every day we experience the uncertainty, risks, and emotional exposure that define what it means to be vulnerable or to dare greatly. Based on twelve years of pioneering research, Brené Brown PhD, MSW, dispels the cultural myth that vulnerability is weakness and argues that it is, in truth, our most accurate measure of courage. Brown explains how vulnerability is both the core of difficult emotions like fear, grief, and disappointment, and the birthplace of love, belonging, joy, empathy, innovation, and creativity."

Cain, S. (2022). **Bittersweet: How Sorrow and Longing Make Us Whole.** New York: Crown.
From Amazon's description of the book: Bittersweet "explores the power of the bittersweet personality, revealing a misunderstood side of mental health and creativity while offering a roadmap to facing heartbreak in order to live life to the fullest. Bittersweetness is a tendency to states of longing, poignancy, and sorrow; an acute awareness of passing time; and a curiously piercing joy at the beauty of the world. It recognizes that light and dark, birth and death—bitter and sweet—are forever paired."

 TOP 3: VIDEOS

 Butterfly: A Life. National Geographic.
▶ tinyurl.com/cw8ettua
Prepare to be spellbound as you observe a modest caterpillar embark on a truly miraculous metamorphosis in this mesmerizing video. Behold the astonishing journey of this diligent caterpillar as it emerges as a resplendent butterfly. This video beautifully illustrates the potent message woven into the fabric of our book— that you already possess the innate ability to transform yourself.

Nature. Beauty. Gratitude. TED Talk. Louie Schwartzberg.
▶ tinyurl.com/38akudum
True happiness is born from the wellspring of gratitude. In our fast-paced, forward-leaning society, we often find ourselves in relentless pursuit of the novel, the extravagant, and the unattainable. Yet, when we simply pause, open our hearts, and savor the present moment, we unearth the extraordinary gifts that life and civilization have already bestowed upon us. This remarkable time-lapse photography, complemented by the profound wisdom of Benedictine monk Brother David Steindl-Rast, serves as a profound meditation on the art of cherishing each day with a heart full of gratitude.

The Person You Really Need to Marry. TED Talk. Tracy McMillan.
▶ tinyurl.com/72vwuhtp
The profound concept in this story is wholeheartedly embracing a relationship with yourself, a commitment that signifies self-love and acceptance. It's about recognizing your inherent completeness just as you are. Tracy McMillan, a distinguished television writer and renowned author in the realm of relationships, also penned the thought-provoking book *Why You're Not Married ... Yet: The Straight Talk You Need to Get the Relationship You Deserve*, originally inspired by her widely circulated 2011 Huffington Post blog.

TOP 3: PODCASTS

The Happiness Lab. Laurie Santos.
▶ tinyurl.com/yn29mycj
From the podcast website: "Laurie has studied the science of happiness and found that many of us do the exact opposite of what will truly make our lives better. Based on the psychology course she teaches at Yale—the most popular class in the university's 300-year history—*The Happiness Lab* with Dr. Laurie Santos will take you through the latest scientific research and share some surprising and inspiring stories that will change the way you think about happiness."

Re: Thinking. Adam Grant.
▶ tinyurl.com/4cxec3a4
From the TED website: "As an organizational psychologist, Adam Grant believes that great minds don't think alike; they challenge each other to think differently. In his new show, he has lively discussions and debates with some of the world's most interesting thinkers, creators, achievers, and leaders. ... By diving inside their minds, Adam is on a mission to uncover bold insights and share surprising science that can make us all a little bit smarter."

Tribe of Mentors. Tim Ferriss.
▶ tinyurl.com/4nuct6ts
Becoming the best version of yourself is not a solo journey. Throughout history, individuals have sought the guidance of mentors to enhance various facets of their lives. It's crucial to recognize the supportive ecosystems that surround us because they play an essential role in our journey toward self-improvement. Enter "Tribe of Mentors," a compelling podcast series curated by Tim Ferriss. It beckons to those who seek mentorship on their path to becoming the best version of themselves, reminding us that the wisdom and experiences of others remain indispensable on our journey of personal growth.

ENDNOTES

1   L. I. van Griethuijsen and B. A. Trimmer. (2014). Locomotion in caterpillars. *Biological Reviews of the Cambridge Philosophical Society 89* (3), pp. 656–70. tinyurl.com/5356xaur

2   K. Gotthard. (2008). Adaptive growth decisions in butterflies. *BioScience 58* (3), pp. 222–30. tinyurl.com/3wpetp35

3   H. F. Nijhout. (1994). *Insect Hormones.* Princeton, Princeton University Press. tinyurl.com/5n7phcxe

"There are no regrets in life,
just lessons."

—Jennifer Aniston

ABOUT THE AUTHORS

Dr. Nick van Dam
Book Editor, Author of Chapter "The Best Version of Me," Section Introductions,
and Well-Being Model

Dr. Nick van Dam is a humanist at heart, firmly placing his faith in the inherent goodness and boundless potential of individuals. His unwavering belief in the innate qualities and talents that people possess inspires his work and interactions, fostering a positive and empowering environment for those around him. His guiding mantra, which aligns with his personal purpose, is: "Elevating YOU! Measure success by the ways you touch the lives of people!"

He is an internationally recognized thought leader, advisor, executive coach, researcher, facilitator, and best-selling (co-)author of more than 27 books on corporate learning, talent management, organizational behavior, and leadership development. Nick has written numerous articles for various publications and has been quoted by *Bloomberg Businessweek, Financial Times, Fortune, Harvard Business Review, Times of India, Information Week, Chief Learning Officer Magazine,* and the *Wall Street Journal.*

Nick has over 25 years of business experience as a former partner, global chief learning officer, human resources executive, and client advisor at McKinsey & Company and Deloitte. He has provided services to more than 100 clients globally. Since 2019, he has held the position of senior advisor and faculty member at McKinsey & Company.

Dr. van Dam (PhD, MA, EMC) serves as a full professor at Nyenrode Business University, IE Business School, and the University of Pennsylvania, where he works with candidates in the executive doctoral program for human capital leaders/chief learning officers. Nick is a visiting professor and thought leader at Harvard Business Publishing, Corporate Learning. He is also a core faculty member of *Le Centre Européen d'Education Permanente* (CEDEP) and director of the IE Center for Corporate Learning and Talent Management. In addition, he serves as the academic director of the Nyenrode University/IE Business School/Global L&D Leadership Program and Global HR Leadership Program. Nick has served as a dissertation committee member and/or dissertation chair for more than 15 candidates.

Nick is the co-founder of the e-Learning for Kids Foundation, which has provided free digital lessons for more than 30 million underprivileged elementary school children (▶ e-learningforkids.org).

His lifelong learning journey has included studies in economics and business economics (BEd, Vrije Universiteit, Amsterdam), organizational sociology (MA), Universiteit van Amsterdam), human capital development (PhD, Nyenrode Business University), and psychodynamic psychology (EMC, INSEAD). Moreover, he has successfully completed executive education programs at Harvard Business School (Boston), the Wharton School at the University of Pennsylvania (Philadelphia), and IMD (Lausanne).

[in] linkedin.com/in/nickvandam

BODY

Dr. Els van der Helm
Chapter: Sleep

Dr. Els van der Helm is a neuroscientist and adjunct professor at IE Business School. She has been named one of the top five sleep experts in the world and now advises corporations about sleep, performance, and well-being. She supports CEOs and decision-makers worldwide to help them get the best out of themselves, their team members, and their organization.

Els hosts keynotes, workshops, webinars, and sleep and well-being months, in combination with science-based assessments.

Els began her career in sleep during her master's program in neurosciences at Vrije Universiteit Amsterdam, studying the effect of sleep on cognitive performance at the Netherlands Institute of Neurosciences and Harvard Medical School. She also holds a summa cum laude master's degree in clinical neuropsychology from the University of Amsterdam.

Els has also studied the effect of sleep on the brain and performance as a Fulbright scholar during her PhD in psychology at University of California, Berkeley, before working at McKinsey & Company as a management consultant.

Her work has been featured in *Harvard Business Review*, *McKinsey Quarterly*, *Wall Street Journal*, *Time*, *Atlantic*, *Forbes*, and on the BBC. She regularly appears in the media, having hosted a Max Masterclass on primetime TV and online videos for Huffington Post, which reached millions of viewers.

[in] linkedin.com/in/elsvanderhelm

Hebe Boonzaaijer
Chapter: Energy

Hebe Boonzaaijer is an organizational psychologist and well-being advocate on a mission to create human-centered organizational cultures where people can be their best, both professionally and personally. She currently serves as a global well-being director at Equinix, a digital infrastructure company located in more than 30 countries, where she drives strategies that empower people to prioritize their well-being. Hebe brings 20 years of experience in the realm of well-being and human performance. Before joining Equinix, she served a wide range of international organizations, including Deloitte, on their well-being and human capital strategies. As a firm believer in the power of community and science, she was a founder of the well-being community in 2019 with Deloitte, Zilveren Kruis, and TNO, in which 20 organizations have united to research and innovate workplace practices to eliminate burnout and help workers thrive. Hebe holds a master's degree in organizational psychology (University of Amsterdam and University of New South Wales, Sydney). She has also completed postdoctoral research in mindfulness (Medical Department of Radboud University) and is an accredited mindfulness-based stress reduction teacher of mindfulness and breath work. She lives in nature, close to Amsterdam, with her husband, Marc, and two daughters.

in linkedin.com/in/hebeboonzaaijer

Marcella Sarno
Chapter: Nutrition

Marcella Sarno is a renowned professional with a diverse background, a passion for holistic well-being, and a commitment to helping others live healthier lives through better lifestyle and nutrition choices. As *dottoressa in lingue e letterature straniere* (doctor of foreign languages and literatures) and a certified integrative nutrition specialist, Marcella has established herself as a leading authority in the field of holistic health and wellness. She is the founder and CEO of the Marcella Method, a platform dedicated to transforming the lives of busy professionals by empowering them with the knowledge and tools to achieve optimal health.

Marcella's journey to becoming a trusted health coach and nutrition expert is a testament to her unwavering dedication and wealth of experience. She hails from a distinguished corporate background, where she excelled as a leadership and management development lead for more than eight years. With over 12 years of expertise in the health and wellness sector, she transitioned seamlessly into the world of integrative nutrition, recognizing the profound impact it can have on individuals' and professionals' overall well-being.

At the Marcella Method, Marcella leverages her extensive knowledge and experience to guide individuals on a holistic path toward improved health, performance, and life balance. Because she understands the unique challenges faced by busy professionals, she customizes her coaching to fit their lifestyles and goals and supports them with empathy and personalization. In addition to her role as a health coach, Marcella is a respected nutrition lecturer and public speaker. She shares her insights and expertise with audiences far and wide, inspiring others to take charge of their health and embrace a holistic approach to wellness. Her engaging and informative presentations are a testament to her passion for empowering individuals with the knowledge they need to lead healthier, more fulfilling lives.

Marcella knows that well-being is not only a personal goal but also a key factor for achieving high performance and career success. That's why she is dedicated to helping everyone, especially busy professionals, to embrace holistic health and nutrition. Through the Marcella Method, she continues to touch lives, helping individuals unlock their full potential and achieve optimal well-being through the power of lifestyle and nutrition choices. With Marcella as their guide, many people have discovered that they can indeed lead healthier, happier lives, no matter how busy their schedules may be.

[in] linkedin.com/in/marcella-sarno

Dr. Sanae Tabnaoui
Chapter: Physical Movement

Dr. Sanae Tabnaoui is an innovator, advisor, and dedicated *passeur de savoir* (knowledge broker) at the forefront of pioneering leadership chemistry—an optimal range of human functioning that promotes healthy performance and well-being in leaders and their teams, with a genuine interest in health promotion and integrative medicine.

She founded the Flourishing Incubator and created the VITAL model, the health innovators community, and the healthy performance zone framework to develop conscious and compassionate leaders in the life sciences. Her expertise extends to her role as an affiliate of Limitless Leadership, a human capital management award-winning leadership development consultancy. Sanae co-founded the Flourishing Lab Community with Natasha Salles-Bitter at Novartis, exploring practical methods to cultivate mental, physical, and social well-being.

With a PhD in physical chemistry from the Institut Curie, specializing in micro total analysis systems for which she holds a patent, Sanae's pivotal role in contributing to the development of therapies such as Cosentyx and Kymriah, as well as COVID-19 vaccine efforts, merges scientific rigor with impactful results. An executive master's degree has further enriched Sanae's lifelong learning journey in positive leadership and transformation, applied positive psychology (CAPP, CPPC) certifications, and a polyvagal-informed performance coach certification. In her chapter, "Physical Movement," Sanae shares her personal story and unique dance of life concept beyond providing scientific insights.

[in] linkedin.com/in/sanaetabnaouigassmann

Dr. Wouter van den Berg
Chapter: DNA

Dr. Wouter van den Berg is the first neuro-economist in the Netherlands. He holds master's degrees in business economics and neuroscience (both cum laude). During his PhD and postdoctoral research, he actively bridged the fields of behavioral economics, marketing, sales, neuroscience, endocrinology, and (molecular) psychiatry. Wouter's work is a combination of fundamental and translational research. He has studied the development of social status hierarchies in mice, discovering a key difference between male and female social strategies. In the field, he has used functional magnetic resonance imaging of the brain and genetic screening to determine the biology of sales and leadership behaviors. His work has been awarded the Sheth Foundation Best Paper Award.

Following his academic career, Wouter founded BrainCompass. BrainCompass builds assessment tooling by leveraging the latest neuroscientific insights on how nature and nurture influence professional development. BrainCompass assessments are used for talent and leadership development by a growing number of clients around the globe. Wouter is an adjunct professor at IE University and a TEDx speaker, and is regularly invited to give keynotes at universities and governmental and for-profit organizations.

[in] linkedin.com/in/wevandenberg

MIND

Judith Grimbergen
Chapter: The Arts

Judith Grimbergen has a passion for making life more beautiful. She is a trendwatcher, forecaster, designer, highly rated lecturer, writer, and coach. She teaches classes and conducts workshops for business professionals and students on visual drawing, visual thinking, design thinking, trend watching, and photography. Judith serves as an adjunct professor at IE University, Madrid. She studied the arts (completed three bachelor studies in painting and drawing, textile design, and interior design), has a master's degree in art history, and has taken classes in positive psychology and design thinking. She was born in the Netherlands, lived and worked in the United States for 12 years, and currently resides in Madrid. She is co-author of the Dutch book *Ga doen wat je écht belangrijk vindt!* (*Ask: What Matters in Life!*) and co-founder of the e-Learning for Kids Foundation (e-learningforkids.org), which has provided over 30 million children worldwide with free digital learning. In 2022, Judith published her latest book, *De Kunst Van Jezelf Presenteren* (*The Art of Presenting Yourself*).

[in] linkedin.com/in/judithgrimbergen

Barbara Doeleman-van Veldhoven
Chapter: Mindfulness

Barbara is founder and director of BFC Compassionate Care & Mindful Medicine. Her educational background, professional experience, and dedicated contemplative practice make her an expert in the integration of leadership, teamwork, science, mindfulness, compassion, and spirituality in day-to-day life. She coaches executives and professionals, facilitates teams, stewards mindfulness and compassionate leadership training, and guides retreats. She does this with lighthearted humor, kindness, groundedness, and sharp clarity. Though the roots of her practice and daily life are Dutch, her work includes international collaborations with other experts and contemporaries in the field—integrating compassion in teamwork and leadership to foster compassionate working cultures. She lives in the Netherlands with her husband, Wytze, and their sons, Eef and Ramses.

[in] linkedin.com/in/barbaradoelemanvanveldhoven

Dr. Lucrecia Grandolini
Chapter: Self-Regulation

Dr. Lucrecia Grandolini is an organizational psychologist passionate about fostering healthy and regenerative cultures. She thrives in combining academic rigor with practical insights from more than 15 years of experience across leadership, learning, management consulting, and clinical psychology. Currently, Lucrecia is the global head of learning at Investec. Her prior roles include management consultant within the human capital practice at Deloitte in London. Lucrecia holds a PhD in learning and leadership from the University of Pennsylvania, an MSc in social psychology from the London School of Economics, and an MA and BA in clinical psychology from Universidad Católica Argentina. Lucrecia lives in London with her loving husband and daughter.

[in] linkedin.com/in/lucregrandolini

Dr. Jacqueline Brassey
Chapter: Resilience and Adaptability

Dr. Jacqueline Brassey (PhD, MA, MAfN) is a co-leader at the McKinsey Health Institute, as well as a research fellow at Vrije Universiteit Amsterdam, an adjunct professor at IE University in Spain, and serves as an advisory council member of the World Wellbeing Movement, an advisory board member of Wellbeing at Work, and as a steering committee member at the WEF Healthy Workforces Initiative.

Jacqueline has more than 20 years of experience in business and academia and spent most of her career at Unilever before joining McKinsey & Company. Jacqui holds degrees in both organization and business sciences, as well as in medical sciences. She has a bachelor's in international business and languages from Avans University of Applied Sciences, a cum laude bachelor's and master's in policy and organization sciences from Tilburg University, a PhD in economics and business from Groningen University, and a joint master's in affective neuroscience from Maastricht University and the University of Florence. She has (co-)authored and presented more than 100 articles, books, book chapters, podcasts, and scientific papers.

She has lived in five different countries, loves running, hiking, and a good glass of wine, and currently lives with her South African/Dutch family in Luxembourg.

in linkedin.com/in/jacquibrassey

Jan Rijken
Chapter: Learning

Jan Rijken is an adjunct professor at IE University and Nyenrode Business School, and an internationally recognized thought leader, consultant, author, and speaker on corporate learning, leadership development, and personal growth and well-being. Jan is co-founder of the Nyenrode University/IE Business School Global Learning & Development Leadership Program, which he facilitates in parallel with the Global HR Leadership Program. Jan is a former chief learning officer at five corporate organizations: KPMG, Daimler, ABN-AMRO, SHV, and Wiley. He supports the learning profession via supervisory board roles and mentoring young talents. In addition, Jan is an inspiring and certified city guide in Arnhem (Netherlands).

Jan has shared his great failures and best practices in articles, books, podcasts on LinkedIn, and at multiple international conferences.

in linkedin.com/in/jan-rijken-b11a5a

PURPOSE

Ursula Fear
Chapter: Financial Empowerment

Ursula Fear is a dedicated South African skills development activist with over 24 years of experience. She has played a pivotal role in establishing qualifications on the South African Qualifications Framework, including the world's first enterprise resource planning qualifications. Ursula's expertise extends to her time as a partner at Deloitte, where she led the design, development, and deployment of mission-critical skills across more than 40 specializations. Notably, she was the first woman to serve on the Deloitte Consulting Executive Committee, focusing on talent and culture development. Her impact also spans the nonprofit sector, particularly with Teach South Africa, where she collaborated on strategy design. As an executive at Adcorp, Ursula served as managing director of the group's training businesses, which included artisan colleges, private universities, information and communications technology companies, and disability training providers. She is currently dedicated to growing skills in the South African Salesforce ecosystem. She is also part of a national initiative in South Africa called the Collective X, which aims at fostering sustainable, demand-led digital skills nationally.

[in] linkedin.com/in/ursula-fear-8499686

Carla Szemzo
Chapter: Relationships

Carla Szemzo is a global citizen with five nationalities who boasts an impressive educational background that has equipped her with a diverse skill set. She has more than 15 years of international professional experience, mainly in the education sector, having worked in United States, Europe, and Latin America. Today she is vice dean and an honorary professor at IE Business School. She is also a columnist for *Forbes*, where she launched a new section that integrates the latest trends in education with those in entrepreneurship and business.

She holds a bachelor's degree in communication with a major in strategic marketing from Universidad Católica in Venezuela. Her thirst for knowledge and commitment to professional growth led her to pursue a master's in international management from IE Business School in Madrid, enhancing her global perspective and management acumen. Furthermore, Carla's dedication to staying at the forefront of her industry is evident in her completion of various executive education programs. These include the Nyenrode/IE University Global Diploma Program in L&D Leadership, the Yale School of Management's program on Women on Boards, and the Harvard Graduate School of Education's course on Developing Strategies for Online Teaching and Learning.

[in] linkedin.com/in/carlaszemzo

Emily Ricci

Chapter: Contribution

Emily Ricci has been a people and talent leader for more than 18 years and is currently an adjunct professor of learning and development at IE University. Previously, Emily led learning and development for Americas Operations at Apple and learning, leadership, and organizational effectiveness at Robinhood. In the organizations she serves, Emily is responsible for setting and driving learning and leadership strategy, building foundational learning and leadership programs and systems, and creating critical knowledge and development architecture.

Emily has been a resident of Austin, Texas, since 2015, where she is chair of the Austin Public Broadcasting Service (PBS) community advisory board and chapter lead for Ignite ATX, a community public speaking forum. In her free time, Emily enjoys spending time with her son, traveling widely, staying active, and consuming as much music (and as many tacos) as possible.

in linkedin.com/in/emilyaricci

Dr. Sharda Nandram

Chapter: Spirituality

Dr. Sharda Nandram is a full professor in business and spirituality at Nyenrode Business University. She is also a full professor in the faculty of religion and theology at Vrije Universiteit Amsterdam, working on Hindu spirituality and society. In addition to these roles, Sharda is co-founder and consultant at Praan Group, member of the steering committee of European Spirituality in Economics and Society (SPES), and an executive member of the management, spirituality, and religion division of the Academy of Management. She also serves as adjunct professor at Banasthali University in Jaipur, India.

With 35 years of experience in the field of management, particularly in work and organizational psychology, entrepreneurship, and organizational innovation, she has developed a keen interest in the intersection of management, spirituality, entrepreneurship, and organizational innovation.

Sharda's research has focused on new forms of organizational architectures such as self-management, entrepreneurial behavior, and various research methodologies. She has published several papers in prominent academic and professional journals.

Sharda holds bachelor's and master's degrees in psychology and economics, and she received her PhD in social psychology. She has studied different spiritual traditions and embodied several spiritual practices by learning them in authentic ways.

in linkedin.com/in/ShardaNandram

Lisa Bevill
Chapter: Values, Beliefs, and Attitudes

Lisa Bevill is the academic director of the Center for Health & Well-Being at IE University. The Center was founded in 2019 with the mission to develop the human skills for flourishing and to support the core IE values in creating a community dedicated to making a positive impact. She is a champion of positive leadership, personal development, and a holistic approach to well-being and has extensive experience supporting each area throughout her career.

Lisa has been a professor of skills development, leadership, and well-being at IE Business School since 2008. She studied at the Gabelli School of Business at Fordham University, with minors in international business and Spanish, before moving to Europe in 2002, where she completed her international MBA at IE Business School. In 2019, Lisa completed her executive master's degree in positive leadership, strategy, and transformation and is certified as a professional certified coach by the International Coach Federation.

She is a native of California, positive by nature, and deeply curious. Lisa has spent the whole of her 25-year career in human development in Europe, working in global environments and developing individuals from over 140 nationalities. Lisa has a great appreciation for diversity and connection and utilizes both in her work to allow for personal and collective flourishing.

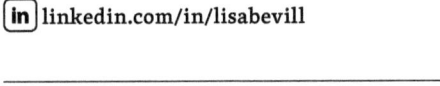 linkedin.com/in/lisabevill

---

ENVIRONMENT

Patricia Garcia, Esq.
Chapter: Nature Environment

Patricia Garcia, Esq., has practiced international law in Spain and with the United Nations in New York, where she served as a legal policy analyst. She has advised and negotiated with governments and international groups of companies in complying with all aspects of the Business and Human Rights Agenda, and in implementing international labor and environmental standards in the workplace. Patricia has also worked in development issues, with a focus on social justice and gender equality in Latin America.

In her role at A Better Balance, an association dedicated to fighting for the advancement of worker's rights with a focus on discrimination, Patricia represented clients before the New York City Commission on Human Rights. In addition, she held the role of manager of pro bono partnerships, running the Latina Justice Program and working closely with Goldman Sachs, Jones Day LLC, Outten and Golden LLC, and others.

Patricia has participated in international summits and conferences worldwide, including the third Global Sustainability Summit in Madrid and the Colloquium on Policy, Law, Contracts, and Sustainable Investments by the Institute for Human Rights and Business in New York.

She is head of the legal department at WeTravel Hub, a disruptive technology company. She also teaches at IE Business and Law Schools and Northwestern University Law School. Patricia is an executive coach with clients across Europe and the United States, and serves as lead facilitator on executive education programs. As a lifelong learner, she is currently pursuing a degree in psychology.

in linkedin.com/in/patricia-garc%C3%ADa-10b7a7234

Dr. Katie Coates
Chapter: Social Environment

Dr. Katie Coates has over 30 years of experience in learning and development, primarily in financial and professional services. She is currently director of learning at McKinsey & Company, where she is responsible for the leadership and technical skills development of over 20,000 support professionals.

Prior to joining McKinsey, Katie spent 20 years at Deloitte, where she held several leadership positions, including Deloitte audit deputy chief learning officer; learning and development operations leader, based in Hyderabad, India; learning design center of excellence leader; and Deloitte Consulting strategy and operations learning leader. She was also the director of learning design at Standard Chartered Bank in Hong Kong. Katie holds a master's degree in instructional systems design from Penn State University and a master's degree and PhD in human development from Fielding Graduate University.

Katie lives in Cochranville, Pennsylvania, with her husband, Marshall, and her daughter, Lilly.

in linkedin.com/in/coateskatie

Bahia El Oddi
Chapter: Work Environment

Bahia El Oddi is the founder of Human Sustainability Inside Out, a nonprofit organization that provides resources, programs, and activities to support communities' well-being and foster human connections. During the COVID-19 crisis, she created CoCaSha (Connect, Care, and Share), a social start-up empowering minority food entrepreneurs with digital skills to help them move their businesses online and weather the impact of the pandemic.

Bahia is also the co-founder of Dar El Oddi, a cultural center aiming to promote awareness about the richness and complexity of Morocco's history and its interconnectedness with foreign cultures, populations, and traditions.

Originally from Morocco, where she lived the first 17 years of her life, Bahia moved to Boston to pursue an MBA at Harvard Business School, where she graduated with honors. She then joined MIT Open Learning to found TRUE Africa University, an online university aiming to empower African talent to accelerate the continent's development.

Prior to receiving her MBA, Bahia worked at Bain & Company, then at Google, where she focused on enabling technologies to preserve arts and culture. She is currently executive director at IE University in Spain, working on executive programs for business leaders and companies across the world.

[in] linkedin.com/in/bahia-el-oddi

Dr. Maria Kottari
Chapter: Climate Environment

Dr. Maria Kottari is a principal consultant in green economy and innovation at Technopolis Group in the Netherlands (Amsterdam). She is an experienced expert in energy transition, climate change, and sustainability, with a solid network in subjects related to the EU and international politics and governance, energy and climate policies, sustainability, social and technological innovation, and socioeconomic challenges. Throughout her career in the public sector (European Commission's Joint Research Centre, European Union Agency for Cybersecurity), academia (European University Institute, University of Amsterdam), and consultancy (founder of the Energy Matrix), she has managed and been involved in various initiatives related to the policy and socioeconomic aspects of the energy transition and climate change mitigation and adaptation, in particular the just transition principles, sustainable finance, circular economy, gender equality, and citizen-driven innovation.

She is a native speaker of Greek, has a fluent command of English and French, and has an intermediate level of Dutch. She can also communicate in German and Arabic at different levels. She holds a PhD in international, European, and regional studies, focusing on energy and climate politics, from Panteion University in Athens.

[in] linkedin.com/in/mariakottari

CLOSING THOUGHTS: FROM CATERPILLAR TO BUTTERFLY

Bo Vialle-Derksen
Chapter: From Caterpillar to Butterfly

Bo Vialle-Derksen is an entrepreneur, author, and business advisor. She is co-founder of Cape People and Cognitive Technologies and senior advisor and lead for Europe, Middle East, and Africa at the Josh Bersin Company. She is an all-around human capital professional with extensive experience in optimizing and enhancing the human resources function to achieve people-driven business performance.

What energizes Bo is providing insights to allow for bold moves. As a human capital management consultant at Deloitte Consulting, Bo worked with board-level leaders of Fortune 500 companies. She supported large-scale talent transformations to achieve desired business results. As part of the human resources leadership team of a top-tier European financial technology firm, she was the product owner for Agile Ways of Working and headed their future skills initiative. She is a frequent keynote speaker and advisor.

Originally from the Netherlands, Bo has lived and worked in Amsterdam, New York, Cape Town, and Copenhagen, and currently resides in The Hague, the Netherlands. Bo holds a master's degree in educational sciences from the University of Leiden and is a certified SAFe® Agilist. She teaches in the Global HR Leadership Diploma Program in collaboration with IE Business University and Nyenrode University.

in linkedin.com/in/bo-vialle-derksen-484b741a

www.ingramcontent.com/pod-product-compliance
Ingram Content Group UK Ltd.
Pitfield, Milton Keynes, MK11 3LW, UK
UKHW022005270225
4796UKWH00009B/260

THE BEST VERSION OF ME

"This book has expanded the concept of self-improvement. The integration of body, mind, purpose, and environment in *The Best Version of Me* provides a valuable framework for anyone looking to elevate their lives. It's a compelling invitation to explore the limitless potential within each of us."

—*Diana Han, MD, Chief Health and Wellbeing Officer, Unilever*

"*The Best Version of Me* is one of the most complete and comprehensive books on professional well-being I've read. Filled with resources and inspirational ideas, the book is a timely and important guide for every business professional."

—*Josh Bersin, Global Industry Analyst and CEO, The Josh Bersin Company*

"A pivotal read for our times, *The Best Version of Me* equips you with the knowledge and tools to thrive in all areas of life."

—*Brian Murphy, Senior Director, Employee Skilling, Microsoft*

"[*The Best Version of Me*] is a must-read book for anyone interested in getting better at getting better. It is a multidimensional book aimed at urging us to look at all the right places for what can make us happier [and] feel more successful and confident. Simple and easy to assimilate. Written by the best. Strongly recommended."

—*S.V. Nathan, Partner and Chief Talent Officer, Deloitte India*

"From exploring the science of sleep to the art of mindfulness, *The Best Version of Me* is an invaluable resource for anyone seeking a healthier, happier life."

—*Marta Machicot, Chief People Officer, Telefónica*

THEBESTVERSIONOFMEBOOK.COM

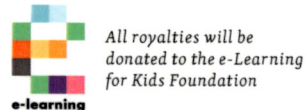

All royalties will be donated to the e-Learning for Kids Foundation

9 789464 912753